VMware Horizon View 6 Desktop Virtualization Cookbook

Over 100 hands-on recipes demonstrating the core
as well as latest features of your VMware Horizon
View infrastructure

Jason Ventresco

[PACKT] enterprise

PUBLISHING

professional expertise distilled

BIRMINGHAM - MUMBAI

VMware Horizon View 6 Desktop Virtualization Cookbook

First published: October 2014

Production reference: 1251014

Published by Packt Publishing Ltd.
Livery Place
35 Livery Street
Birmingham B3 2PB, UK.

ISBN 978-1-78217-164-5

www.packtpub.com

Credits

Author

Jason Ventresco

Reviewers

Dee Abson

Andrew Alloway

Joe Jessen

Sean Massey

Acquisition Editor

Subho Gupta

Content Development Editor

Shaon Basu

Technical Editors

Indrajit A. Das

Akash Rajiv Sharma

Copy Editors

Dipti Kapadia

Stuti Srivastava

Project Coordinator

Shipra Chawhan

Proofreaders

Simran Bhogal

Stephen Copestake

Samantha Lyon

Indexers

Hemangini Bari

Monica Ajmera Mehta

Rekha Nair

Graphics

Ronak Dhruv

Abhinash Sahu

Production Coordinator

Shantanu N. Zagade

Cover Work

Shantanu N. Zagade

About the Author

Jason Ventresco has been a veteran of the IT field for 15 years and is currently working for EMC^2 as a principal solutions engineer. In this role, he designs, builds, and tests the latest end user computing solutions in order to validate their performance and provide guidance to EMC^2 customers and partners. He previously worked as a member of the global infrastructure team for FHI 360 and as an IT consultant for WorkSmart and Xerox Global Services. Jason has authored *Implementing VMware Horizon View 5.2* and *VMware Horizon View 5.3 Design Patterns and Best Practices*, both by Packt Publishing.

Jason lives in Raleigh, North Carolina, with his wife and daughter. He holds two degrees: a Master of Science in Information Security & Assurance from Norwich University and a Bachelor of Science in Information Technology from the University of Phoenix. In his free time, he likes to travel, ride his WaveRunner, and attend Carolina Hurricanes games.

I would like to thank my wife, Christine, and my daughter, Amanda, for supporting me through all phases of my career, including the many hours I spent writing this book. I love you both very much!

I would also like to thank my parents, Richard and Linda Ventresco, for raising me and showing me that you can have anything you want if you are willing to put in the effort required. I love you, mom and dad!

I would also like to thank my fellow members of the EMC Solutions engineering team—both here in the US and in China. Working with them has helped provide me with the experience and knowledge required to write books such as this.

About the Reviewers

Dee Abson is a technical architect for a financial services company in Alberta, Canada. He has been working in the field of technology for over 20 years and specializes in server and virtualization infrastructure. Working with VMware products since ESX 2, he holds several VMware certifications, including VCP5-DCV. He has contributed to *vSphere Design Pocketbook 2.0 Blog Edition*, *PernixData Press* alongside other illustrious virtualization authors. Dee blogs at http://teebeedee.org, and you can connect with him through his Twitter handle, which is @deeabson.

> I would like to thank my lovely wife, Aimée, for her patience and understanding during my oft-protracted review sessions.

Andrew Alloway was born and raised in Edmonton, Canada. He graduated from the University of Alberta with a degree in Computer Science.

Working in the unique and challenging IT environment of Nuna Logistics Limited, he supported northern mining sites. In 2012, some of his projects and works were featured in the Winter 2012 edition of Aptitude Magazine in an article titled *Building the road to streamlined license agreements*.

He is a supporter of open source technology and products, including Ubuntu, ICTFax, Apache, Drupal, and Piler.

He has designed and implemented projects including Exchange migrations, Lync deployments, System Center Configuration Manager, and various VMware products.

In 2013, Andrew attained his VMware Certified Professional 5 Data Center Virtualization certification.

Previously, he has worked on *VMware Horizon Workspace Essentials*, *Packt Publishing*.

> I would like to thank my family for all the support I have received over the years and my employers for investing in the development of my skills and career.

Joe Jessen is a veteran of the IT Industry and has held roles in private corporations, vendors, and consulting organizations. He has been involved with application and desktop delivery since 1996, setting the strategic direction for global organizations with their end user computing initiatives.

Joe recently spent 5 years as an industry analyst with a heavy focus on virtualization and is currently engaged with a large hardware and software vendor, focusing on desktop virtualization solutions. He was also the technical reviewer for *VMware Horizon View 5.3 Design Patterns and Best Practices*, *Packt Publishing*. You can follow him on his Twitter handle, which is `@JoeJessen`. You can view his LinkedIn profile at `http://www.linkedin.com/pub/joe-jessen/0/666/336/` and his website at `www.solutions101.us`.

Sean Massey has been working in the field of IT for 7 years. He is a systems administrator with a large electrical contractor in Appleton, WI, focusing on the servers, storage, and applications that run in the data center. He blogs at `http://seanmassey.net` and is a VMware vExpert and Pernix Pro. He currently lives in Kimberly, WI, with his wife, Laura, and their two children.

www.PacktPub.com

Support files, eBooks, discount offers, and more

You might want to visit www.PacktPub.com for support files and downloads related to your book.

Did you know that Packt offers eBook versions of every book published, with PDF and ePub files available? You can upgrade to the eBook version at www.PacktPub.com and as a print book customer, you are entitled to a discount on the eBook copy. Get in touch with us at service@packtpub.com for more details.

At www.PacktPub.com, you can also read a collection of free technical articles, sign up for a range of free newsletters and receive exclusive discounts and offers on Packt books and eBooks.

http://PacktLib.PacktPub.com

Do you need instant solutions to your IT questions? PacktLib is Packt's online digital book library. Here, you can access, read and search across Packt's entire library of books.

Why subscribe?

- ▶ Fully searchable across every book published by Packt
- ▶ Copy and paste, print and bookmark content
- ▶ On demand and accessible via web browser

Free access for Packt account holders

If you have an account with Packt at www.PacktPub.com, you can use this to access PacktLib today and view nine entirely free books. Simply use your login credentials for immediate access.

Instant updates on new Packt books

Get notified! Find out when new books are published by following @PacktEnterprise on Twitter, or the *Packt Enterprise* Facebook page.

Table of Contents

Preface

VMware Horizon View 6 Desktop Virtualization Cookbook is meant to be a hands-on guide on how to deploy and configure various key features of the VMware Horizon with View platform, including some new features first introduced in Version 6. The examples provided in this book focus on 11 different Horizon View topics and instruct you on their purpose, configuration, and administration. Using the examples provided in this book, you will be able to implement and manage these features in your own VMware Horizon with View environment.

There are many places in this book that refer you to the official VMware Horizon with View documentation. You are encouraged to review this documentation as it complements the material in this book and contains additional information that can provide a deeper understanding of the technical details and capabilities of the entire VMware Horizon with View platform.

The ever-evolving VMware Horizon family of products

Over the last 4 years, VMware has poured a great deal of development effort into VMware Horizon View. This includes the acquisition of multiple companies whose products would help create what we now call VMware Horizon with View. VMware Horizon with View currently includes the following components:

- **VMware Horizon View** (`http://www.vmware.com/products/horizon-view`): This is the desktop virtualization platform, that is, the focus of most of the recipes of this book.

- **VMware Horizon Mirage** (`http://www.vmware.com/products/horizon-mirage`): This provides a number of different capabilities including desktop, laptop, and full-clone virtual machine management and data protection. Mirage is particularly helpful as an OS migration tool, and will be demonstrated in *Chapter 9, Using VMware Mirage with Horizon View*.

- **VMware vRealize Operations for Horizon** (`https://www.vmware.com/products/vrealize-operations-horizon/`): Formerly known as vCenter Operations Manager for VMware Horizon View, this platform provides comprehensive monitoring of the performance of the Horizon View and vSphere platforms. *Chapter 8, vRealize Operations for Horizon* provides examples on how to deploy and use vRealize Operations for Horizon.

- **VMware ThinApp** (`http://www.vmware.com/products/thinapp`): This enables agentless Windows application virtualization, which requires no changes to the environment in which they are used. Applications packaged using ThinApp are isolated from the guest OS and can be streamed from a remote file share or executed from local or portable storage. *Chapter 6, Delivering Applications Using VMware ThinApp* provides examples on how to use ThinApp to package applications and deliver them using Horizon View.

- **VMware Virtual SAN** (`http://www.vmware.com/products/virtual-san`): This is a hyper-converged software-defined storage platform that is part of VMware vSphere. Using Virtual SAN, we can create clustered, high-performing, and highly available vSphere datastores using hard disks and solid state drives installed directly in our vSphere servers. *Chapter 10, Implementing VMware Virtual SAN for Horizon View* provides examples on how to use VMware Virtual SAN to provide storage for our Horizon View desktops.

- **VMware Horizon Workspace Portal** (`http://www.vmware.com/products/workspace-portal`): This provides a scalable, policy-based workspace management platform for access to Horizon View desktops, streamed applications, a SaaS application catalog, and data stored in the VMware AirWatch Mobile Content Management platform.

- **VMware AirWatch Mobile Content Management** (`http://www.air-watch.com/solutions/mobile-content-management`): This provides a secure file storage and collaboration platform that integrates with VMware Horizon Workspace and enables access to data from a variety of different mobile and desktop platforms.

The following are just some of the other additions that VMware has made, or will soon add, to their end user computing solutions. They provide an insight into where the Horizon product line is going:

- **VMware CloudVolumes** (`http://cloudvolumes.com/products/for-horizon/`): This provides rapid, seamless application delivery using virtual machine disks that are directly attached to virtual desktops even when they are powered on. CloudVolumes will be integrated into a future version of VMware Horizon with View.

- **VMware Horizon Air** (`http://www.vmware.com/products/horizon-air-desktops`): Formerly known as Desktone, this separate platform is designed for organizations or service providers who want to deliver **desktops as a service** (**DaaS**).

▸ **VMware projects Fargo** (`http://blogs.vmware.com/cto/vmware-docker-better-together/`) and **Meteor** (`http://blogs.vmware.com/tribalknowledge/2014/08/vmware-continues-set-innovation-agenda-end-user-computing.html`): These will enable very rapid, on-demand delivery of streamed applications and virtual desktops. These technologies will likely be integrated into future versions of VMware Horizon with View and VMware Horizon Air.

The topics covered in this book will help us develop a deeper understanding of how to deploy and administer some of the newest, most popular features of VMware Horizon with View while also covering some core features that have existed for some time. The more we understand about what the platform can do, and how to do it, the more useful it will be in our environment.

If we learn anything from these first few pages, it is that VMware Horizon is an evolving product, continually adding new capabilities and features.

What this book covers

Chapter 1, VMware Horizon View Architecture Fundamentals, covers a number of key considerations that will influence the design, implementation, and assessment of a VMware Horizon with View infrastructure.

Chapter 2, Implementing a VMware Horizon View Cloud Pod, covers how to enable, configure, and administer a Horizon View cloud pod, which enables the deployment of multisite, multipod Horizon View environments that support global user Horizon View desktop entitlements.

Chapter 3, Horizon View Installation, Backup, and Recovery Using the CLI, covers how to use the command line to perform several key tasks involving the installation, backup, and recovery of different Horizon View components.

Chapter 4, Managing VMware Horizon View with PowerCLI, covers the different PowerCLI commands that can be used to manage nearly all aspects of the Horizon View platform and provides examples on how they are used.

Chapter 5, Implementation of Horizon View Persona Management, covers the implementation and management of Horizon View Persona Management and examines some important considerations that must be made when working with the tool.

Chapter 6, Delivering Applications Using VMware ThinApp, covers how to use ThinApp to virtualize applications, discusses different reasons why organizations might wish to do so, and shows how to deliver ThinApp-packaged applications using Horizon View.

Chapter 7, Deploying Horizon View Clients in Kiosk Mode, covers the configuration of Kiosk Mode Horizon View Clients and provides examples on how they are deployed and used with Horizon View.

Chapter 8, vRealize Operations for Horizon, covers how to install and configure vRealize Operations for Horizon as well as examples of how it can be used to monitor a Horizon View infrastructure.

Chapter 9, Using VMware Mirage with Horizon View, covers how to use VMware Mirage to manage Horizon View desktops, protect user data, and perform operating system migrations.

Chapter 10, Implementing VMware Virtual SAN for Horizon View, covers how to size, implement, and use Virtual SAN for our Horizon View environment.

Chapter 11, Implementing Application Streaming Using Windows Remote Desktop Services, covers how to configure Windows Remote Desktop Services for use with Horizon View, configure and manage a Horizon View Application Pool, stream applications using the Horizon View client, and monitor the status of Windows Remote Desktop Services hosts and Horizon View application-streaming client sessions.

What you need for this book

The following software is required to perform the tasks outlined in this book:

- ▶ VMware vSphere 5.5 update 1.0 or newer (included as part of VMware Horizon with View)
- ▶ The VMware Horizon with View 6 Connection Server, Composer, agent, and client software
- ▶ VMware ThinApp 5.1
- ▶ VMware vRealize operations for Horizon 1.6
- ▶ VMware Horizon Mirage 5.1 software
- ▶ Windows Server 2008 R2 (or newer; x64 edition)
- ▶ Microsoft SQL Server 2008 R2 (or newer)
- ▶ Windows 7 (or newer, x32 or x64)

Who this book is for

This book is for anyone who wants a more detailed explanation concerning the deployment and configuration of several different core VMware Horizon View features. The information covered concerns topics such as Horizon View Cloud Pods, application streaming using Microsoft Windows Remote Desktop Services, using VMware VSAN for Horizon View desktop storage, and VMware Mirage integration. This is to ensure that you are up-to-date with the latest features of Horizon View. The chapters provide a detailed review of other core features of VMware Horizon View, providing examples and instructions that can assist with new View deployments or existing implementations.

Conventions

In this book, you will find a number of styles of text that distinguish between different kinds of information. Here are some examples of these styles, and an explanation of their meaning.

Code words in text are shown as follows: "The primary command-line switch that must be used to update the global entitlement is `--editSite`, to which you add any additional switches that you might need."

A block of code is set as follows:

```
nic1.network01.maxvm=250
nic1.network02.maxvm=250
```

Any command-line input or output is written as follows:

```
 Send-SessionLogoff -Session_id (Get-RemoteSession -Username "vjason.
local\elensherr").session_id
```

New terms and **important words** are shown in bold. Words that you see on the screen, in menus or dialog boxes for example, appear in the text like this: "This counter is displayed as **Memory\Committed Bytes** in Windows Performance Monitor."

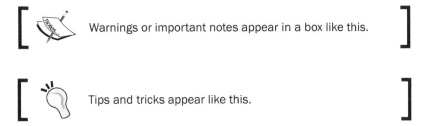

Warnings or important notes appear in a box like this.

Tips and tricks appear like this.

Reader feedback

Feedback from our readers is always welcome. Let us know what you think about this book—what you liked or may have disliked. Reader feedback is important for us to develop titles that you really get the most out of.

To send us general feedback, simply send an e-mail to `feedback@packtpub.com`, and mention the book title through the subject of your message.

If there is a topic that you have expertise in and you are interested in either writing or contributing to a book, see our author guide on `www.packtpub.com/authors`.

Customer support

Now that you are the proud owner of a Packt book, we have a number of things to help you to get the most from your purchase.

Errata

Although we have taken every care to ensure the accuracy of our content, mistakes do happen. If you find a mistake in one of our books—maybe a mistake in the text or the code—we would be grateful if you would report this to us. By doing so, you can save other readers from frustration and help us improve subsequent versions of this book. If you find any errata, please report them by visiting `http://www.packtpub.com/support`, selecting your book, clicking on the **errata submission form** link, and entering the details of your errata. Once your errata are verified, your submission will be accepted and the errata will be uploaded to our website, or added to any list of existing errata, under the Errata section of that title.

Piracy

Piracy of copyright material on the Internet is an ongoing problem across all media. At Packt, we take the protection of our copyright and licenses very seriously. If you come across any illegal copies of our works, in any form, on the Internet, please provide us with the location address or website name immediately so that we can pursue a remedy.

Please contact us at `copyright@packtpub.com` with a link to the suspected pirated material.

We appreciate your help in protecting our authors, and our ability to bring you valuable content.

Questions

You can contact us at `questions@packtpub.com` if you are having a problem with any aspect of the book, and we will do our best to address it.

1

VMware Horizon View Architecture Fundamentals

In this chapter, we will cover the following recipes:

- ▸ Identifying why we need VMware Horizon with View
- ▸ Understanding the risks of end user computing
- ▸ Understanding how our desktop configuration impacts our design
- ▸ Determining our Horizon View desktop infrastructure requirements
- ▸ Analyzing our Horizon with View environment

Introduction

The foundation of any VMware Horizon with View implementation lies in a solid understanding of the goals that the project seeks to achieve. These goals are important, as they provide with us a metric for determining whether or not the project is delivering the capabilities we require. Additionally, many of these goals can influence the project design process as well as the resources required, which is why it is important to identify them early on in the project when it is easier to make changes.

This chapter discusses a number of key considerations that will influence the design, implementation, and assessment of a VMware Horizon with View infrastructure.

The current name of the suite of products that includes VMware Horizon View is **VMware Horizon with View**. This chapter and others will use both terms, as some chapters will refer to just View while others will refer to other Horizon components.

Identifying why we need VMware Horizon with View

This recipe will outline a number of different reasons why organizations might opt to implement a virtual desktop solution using VMware Horizon with View.

How it works...

VMware Horizon with View can provide us with a number of different capabilities that can complement, extend, or replace our existing **end user computing** (**EUC**) platforms. Identifying which of these apply in our organization is important, as they can influence all phases of our project, starting with the design and ending with the rollout itself.

Migrating our legacy desktops

Migrating to a newer version of Microsoft Windows is a difficult project for reasons that include:

- ▸ Hardware compatibility or capability issues that might require hardware upgrade or replacement
- ▸ Application compatibility testing
- ▸ Application support for a newer operating system (OS)
- ▸ User training for the new OS
- ▸ User downtime
- ▸ User data and desktop configuration migration
- ▸ Labor costs

What makes things even more difficult is if we are running an unsupported OS such as Windows XP and require official support from Microsoft. In some cases, we are paying at least $200 per desktop for this service (`http://software.dell.com/products/changebase/calculate.aspx`).

While VMware Horizon with View and its **VMware ThinApp** (`http://www.vmware.com/products/thinapp/`) application virtualization platform cannot by themselves solve issues related to the support of legacy applications or operating systems, they can provide organizations with a way to improve their end user computing environment with little or no changes to their existing legacy desktops. Horizon View provides users with a more relaxed desktop migration than is typically possible with a traditional reimage or replacement of an existing physical computer, where rolling back the migration is difficult or, sometimes, impossible. When migrating the users to Horizon View virtual desktops, any existing physical desktops need not be immediately removed or changed, usually enabling a less disruptive upgrade with the potential to move back to the physical desktop, if required.

Providing a more relaxed OS migration to the end users is not the only benefit of using Horizon View; the information technology (IT) staff will also benefit. While tools such as **VMware Horizon Mirage** (`http://www.vmware.com/products/horizon-mirage`) and Microsoft System Center Configuration Manager (`http://www.microsoft.com/en-us/server-cloud/products/system-center-2012-r2-configuration-manager`) can assist organizations with OS and software upgrades on their existing physical machines, if those machines lack the resources required, the hardware itself will still need replacement. Additionally, tools such as these often carry additional costs that must be factored into the cost of the migration.

Implementing Horizon View will not necessarily eliminate the need for tools to assist with our desktop migration. If we determine that these tools will provide some benefit, we must research whether the costs and resource requirements outweigh whatever that benefit that might be.

While many organizations might select to replace their existing physical computers with a thin or zero client tailored for use specifically with Horizon View or to rebuild the existing computer with just an OS and the Horizon View client software, there is no immediate need to do either of these unless we wish to prevent the user from continuing to use any existing applications on their physical desktop.

Keep in mind that, if we plan to reuse existing endpoints as VMware Horizon clients and are required to maintain vendor support for that equipment, replacing it outright might be more cost-effective.

Delivering applications instead of desktops

VMware Horizon View 6 introduced the capability to stream individual applications directly to the Horizon View client, a feature that is also known as **application remoting**. Using a **Microsoft Windows Remote Desktop Session Host** (**RDSH**) server, Horizon View can now deliver access to individual applications in addition to traditional virtual desktops.

VMware Horizon View 6 also offers the capability to directly deliver other applications, including those packaged with VMware ThinApp, streamed using **Citrix XenApp** (`http://www.citrix.com/products/xenapp/overview.html`) and even Web or SaaS applications using the included **Horizon Workspace Portal** (`http://www.vmware.com/products/workspace-portal`).

Application remoting enables organizations to distill the end user computing experience down to the smallest unit possible: individual applications. One scenario where application remoting can provide the most benefit is when a user uses only one or two applications; rather than providing them with their own virtual desktop, it might be more efficient to have them stream just these applications from a shared RDSH server.

Additionally, VMware created its own protocol provider for the RDSH servers so that application remoting clients can leverage the same **PC over Internet Protocol** (**PCoIP**) protocol used with virtual desktops; this is one of the key differentiating features of the Horizon View platform, offering high levels of performance using the minimum bandwidth required.

Chapter 11, Implementing Application Streaming Using Windows Remote Desktop Services, provides us with an overview on how to use VMware Horizon View and Microsoft Windows RDSH servers to enable the Microsoft Windows RDSH application remoting and streamed ThinApp applications.

No storage array needed thanks to VMware Virtual SAN

VMware Horizon View supports the **VMware Virtual SAN** (**VSAN**) hypervisor-converged storage platform. VMware Virtual SAN provides organizations that do not wish to invest in a traditional shared storage array for their Horizon View desktops with an additional option that can meet the capacity and performance needs that the desktops require.

With VMware VSAN, organizations need to only deploy vSphere servers that include additional dedicated local storage. This storage can be all flash disks or a combination of flash and spinning disks. The combination of flash and spinning disks, along with the automated data-tiering capabilities or VSAN, allows it to meet both the performance and capacity needs of almost any Horizon View environment. VMware VSAN can also be used to provide the storage required for the Horizon View infrastructure servers, if desired.

One advantage of using VMware VSAN is that it reduces the complexity of a VMware Horizon View deployment by reducing the overall number of infrastructure components required while also simplifying the management, as VSAN is managed using the **VMware vSphere Web Client**.

Chapter 10, Implementing VMware Virtual SAN for Horizon View, provides us with an overview on how to use VMware VSAN to provide storage for Horizon View.

Redefining office mobility

For many organizations, desktop mobility means providing users with a laptop and a **virtual private network** (**VPN**) connection that they can use to access company resources remotely. While this method of office mobility has worked, and continues to work, for many, managing these remote clients and their data can be challenging if organizations lack tools that are specifically designed to manage clients who are infrequently connected to an organization's private network. Organizations that cannot address these challenges might find themselves exposed to significant risks when it comes to the security of these remote physical endpoints, whether keeping them up-to-date with critical security patches or protecting and backing their data.

VMware Horizon View provides organizations with a number of different ways to rethink how they provide users with a mobile office:

- ▸ A VMware Horizon View Connection Server deployed as a specialized gateway, commonly referred to as a **View Security Server**, can be deployed in a perimeter network, also known as the **demilitarized zone** (**DMZ**), in order to provide secure access to Horizon View without needing to deploy a VPN. To further secure the user authentication process, Horizon View supports multifactor authentication platforms, such as RSA SecurID and others, that are supported by **RADIUS**, which is a network protocol that is most commonly used for authentication.

 Horizon View supports multiple methods in addition to VPN in order to secure remote client access connections, including **Secure Sockets Layer** (**SSL**) and encrypted PCoIP connections using a Horizon View PCoIP Secure Gateway or Horizon Workspace gateway.

- ▸ When paired with **VMware Horizon Workspace** and **VMware AirWatch Secure Content Locker** (http://www.air-watch.com/solutions/mobile-content-management), Horizon View clients gain access to a single portal that they can use to access desktops, streamed applications, applications packaged using ThinApp, and user data stored in AirWatch Secure Content Locker. AirWatch Secure Content Locker is a separate VMware product that integrates with the VMware Horizon Workspace portal and mobile devices in order to provide access to secure file storage.

- ▸ Using **Blast Adaptive UX**, a HTML5-compliant web browser is all that is required for Horizon View clients to access their desktops and applications. The software-based Horizon View client is also available for remote users, enabling greater flexibility.

- For organizations that wish to leverage VMware Horizon View in order to manage desktop images deployed to traditional physical desktops—beginning with Horizon View 6—you can manage images used by physical machines running **VMware Horizon Mirage** or as virtual machines running on **VMware Fusion Professional** (`http://www.vmware.com/products/fusion-professional`) or **VMware Player Plus** (`http://www.vmware.com/products/player`). *Chapter 9*, *Using VMware Mirage with Horizon View*, provides us with an overview on how to use VMware Horizon Mirage with Horizon View full clone desktops.

In summary, VMware Horizon View enables organizations to offer new virtual desktop mobility offerings without the need to provide additional mobile devices for remote access; train users on how to properly protect their mobile devices and their data; or explain to users how their experience differs when they are logging in remotely.

End user computing and security

Virtual desktops offer many potential benefits for enhancing end user computing security; however, but similar to traditional desktops, organizations must commit to the changes required for them to be effective. With the exception of remote desktops managed by VMware Horizon Mirage, Horizon View desktops are hosted in a data center where it is assumed that they will be more secure than traditional physical computers. In reality, with virtual desktops, there is no longer any physical hardware to steal, but securing the desktop OS and its applications is the same regardless of where it is located. The fact that a desktop is virtual does not automatically prevent the flow of data from that desktop to elsewhere, unless an organization takes steps to prevent it from using methods such as **Active Directory** (**AD**) group policies or various software tools.

Simply migrating desktops to VMware Horizon View or managing them using VMware Horizon Mirage does not mean that we do not need **data loss prevention** (**DLP**) platforms or organizational policies that are designed to protect our data. Horizon View and Horizon Mirage merely provide us with a tool that we can use to enhance or extend our data-protection goals.

VMware Horizon View supports a variety of options for controlling how USB devices access virtual desktops. The devices can be controlled based on a specific device (such as a USB Ethernet adapter), the type of device (such as the storage device), or even on the vendor product model. This feature is controlled using AD group policies and enables advanced control over how the desktop can be accessed.

The most common benefit of using Horizon View to provide virtual desktops is that their data remains in the data center, where we can protect it using whatever data center capabilities or protections are at our disposal. This includes tools such as vSphere-based backups of virtual desktop data, common storage array features such as snapshots and **Redundant Array of Inexpensive Disk** (**RAID**) protection, and even **VMware vShield Endpoint**, which provides **antivirus** (**AV**) protection at the hypervisor level rather than within each individual desktop.

VMware vShield also requires third-party scanning plugins to provide antivirus scanning capabilities. These plugins are currently offered by a number of different vendors including Trend Micro (`http://www.trendmicro.com/us/enterprise/cloud-solutions/deep-security/`) and McAfee (`http://www.mcafee.com/us/products/move-anti-virus.aspx`).

Each of these capabilities provides a more efficient means of protecting virtual desktops and their content than is possible with physical desktops. If physical desktops are still required, VMware Horizon Mirage can be used to provide similar levels of protection, namely the desktop contents and configuration.

VMware Horizon Mirage is discussed in greater detail in *Chapter 9*, *Using VMware Mirage with Horizon View*, but primarily, within the context of using it with Horizon View full clone virtual desktops. Consult the VMware Mirage website (`http://www.vmware.com/products/horizon-mirage`) for information on how Mirage can be used with physical desktops.

Simplifying the desktop support

One benefit of using virtual desktops is that they can dramatically change how an organization provides support to its end users. In scenarios where we are replacing our existing physical desktops with dedicated devices whose only purpose is to act as a client for Horizon View, with the exception of hardware failure, there is less of a need to provide support in person. The following is a list of key features and characteristics of VMware Horizon View:

- Horizon View application remoting using Microsoft Windows RDSH servers enables organizations to provide access to critical applications directly rather than deploying a physical or virtual desktop. Since the RDSH servers support multiple concurrent users, while a virtual desktop can only support one, fewer infrastructure resources might be needed.

- The VMware ThinApp application virtualization platform enables us to package and distribute applications independent of the desktop operating system. Horizon View and Horizon Workspace can also be used to provide access to ThinApp applications without the need to install them on each desktop.

- VMware Horizon View Persona Management enables us to centrally manage and protect the user profile data while delivering a personalized desktop experience regardless of where our users log in.

- Linked clone Horizon View desktops require far less storage capacity than physical or full clone desktops and can also be rapidly refreshed, thus discarding any changes that were made since the desktop was deployed or last recomposed.

These features are just a partial list of what Horizon View can offer, yet they alone offer us the opportunity to rethink how support is provided. With Horizon View, we don't have to expend resources that support individual desktops, as everything that makes these desktops unique can be abstracted or stored elsewhere. If everything that makes a desktop unique can be maintained in another location, such as custom applications and user persona data, our IT support staff can simply discard the problematic machine and provide the user with a fresh desktop free of any underlying issues.

With Horizon View, we can greatly reduce the support our desktops require and focus more on supporting the users. With linked clone desktops, when desktops need to be changed, these changes are applied to the desktop master image and rolled out to all users at our convenience.

> In this section, we referred to linked clone desktops that share a common master disk and write any changes to a dedicated delta disk. If we choose to use full clone desktops, we cannot use features such as a Horizon View desktop Refresh or Recompose. Due to this, full clone desktops are often managed using the same techniques as physical desktops; this also includes VMware Horizon Mirage.

Bring Your Own Device

The concept of having users use their own devices to access company resources is becoming more common as organizations move towards new ways of providing users access to their applications and data. With Horizon View, users can use their own endpoint as a client to access desktops, applications, or data hosted by Horizon View or other components of the VMware Horizon Suite.

Bring Your Own Device (**BYOD**) does not necessarily mean that users are spending their own money to purchase these devices. In some organizations, users are provided with a stipend to purchase whatever device they wish, preferably with some guidance from their IT department in terms of required client features or specifications. In some cases, by providing users with access to a wider variety of devices, they are more likely to end up with a device they are comfortable with, which might help make them more productive.

The concept of BYOD is most commonly seen with smartphones where employees use their own mobile device to access e-mail and other company resources, in many cases without being required to or without reimbursement.

Understanding the risks of end user computing

This recipe will discuss key topics that are important to keep in mind throughout our virtual desktop design and implementation. Each section represents a potential risk that can influence the perceived or realized success of our Horizon View project.

How it works...

Each of the topics discussed in this section has the potential to influence our design by extending the success or failure of our Horizon View environment. Due to the varying end user computing requirements from one organization to the next, this list represents just a starting point to assess what our organization must keep in mind when implementing virtual desktops.

Reducing costs is not priority number one

In many cases, the act of deploying virtual desktops will not be an organization's monetary concern. Additionally, if we continue to manage and support virtual desktops just like physical desktops, our virtual desktops might well end up costing us more. The following is a partial list of potential expenses that must be considered when determining whether cost savings are possible with virtual desktops:

- The cost of support, electricity, and maintenance of using existing physical desktops as Horizon View clients rather than implementing purpose-built clients that have a much smaller management footprint

- The cost required to upgrade our data center's **local area network** (**LAN**) and our company's **wide area network** (**WAN**) to provide sufficient bandwidth for Horizon View clients

- The additional amount of server **random access memory** (**RAM**) required to host virtual desktops that use traditional client-based firewalls and antivirus platforms rather than deploying platforms optimized for virtual desktop computing

- The cost of virtualizing desktops that require greater than average amounts of **central processing unit** (**CPU**) or RAM resources

- For organizations that do not regularly refresh or recompose their linked-clone-based virtual desktops, how that can impact the storage utilization over time

- For organizations that lack storage platforms that include deduplication capabilities, what storage resources are required to use full clone Horizon View desktops

- The labor costs when IT support personnel continue to spend time troubleshooting a linked clone desktop, rather than refreshing it to a just-deployed state and a known configuration

- The cost of deploying one virtual desktop for every user, rather than determining the actual maximum number of concurrent desktops needed overall

In most of these cases, ignoring these items will not make our virtual desktop environment a failure; however, the more we ignore them, the more difficult it will be for us to lower per-desktop support costs. Depending on what it costs to implement virtual desktops in our own organization, it might be that, even if we address all of these points, we still won't save money. This is why reducing costs should not be the first priority, as it cannot be guaranteed in all environments.

When designing our virtual desktop environment, we must consider everything involved with providing, managing, and supporting the desktops we have today. As mentioned earlier, if we operate and support our virtual desktops as we do for our physical desktops, we will make it very difficult to realize any cost savings. The topics we covered in this section are just an example of the types of things we must be conscious of if our goal is to attempt to reduce our costs associated with providing end user computing resources.

Knowing our use cases

A lack of understanding as to how our users interact with their desktops can have a significant impact on the success of our Horizon View deployment. It is about more than failing to appropriately size our virtual desktop infrastructure; it has to do with understanding what our users need in order to perform their duties. The following are just some examples we must consider when deciding who among our users is a suitable candidate for conversion to Horizon View virtual desktops.

Complex workstations

There will always be users whose workstations are not ideal candidates for conversion to a virtual desktop. This can include—but is not restricted to—workloads that require a significant amount of CPU or RAM resources; have a large number of peripherals; use applications unsuitable for virtualization or streaming that are also not common to other desktop users; use a multimonitor configuration that requires an unacceptable amount of Horizon View Client bandwidth; run graphics-intense applications such as **Computer Aided Design** (**CAD**) platforms; or have unique or resource-intensive storage requirements.

While CPU and RAM requirements will not prevent a desktop from being virtualized in all cases, when they are combined with any one of the other factors mentioned, it might be that the desktop is unsuitable to be deployed as a virtual desktop.

> Beginning with Version 6, VMware Horizon View supports **Virtual Shared Graphics Acceleration** (**vSGA**), which allows the virtual desktops to share a dedicated discrete card installed in each vSphere host (`http://www.vmware.com/files/pdf/techpaper/vmware-horizon-view-graphics-acceleration-deployment.pdf`). Support for vSGA might enable Horizon View to deliver the graphics performance that certain desktops require.

Application and services compatibility

Does all of our infrastructure support Horizon View? This includes telephone systems, video conferencing platforms, uncommon peripherals, and so on. It is crucial that organizations consult their vendors in order to ensure that their solutions are compatible with the proposed Horizon View environment.

Mobility inside the office

If we ask people to trade in laptops that never leave the office for a stationary Horizon View client without first researching how these laptops are used, we might not realize that they move around within the office itself. In a BYOD environment, this might not be an issue, as users will select whatever device best accommodates their workflow; if, however, our users have to use the devices provided to them, then there is a potential for problems. Depending on the needs of our users, it might be possible to solve this problem with tablets or other devices that are less costly than laptops but can still provide mobility within the office.

Understanding how our desktop configuration impacts our design

VMware Horizon View provides the capability to provision two different desktop types: **Horizon View Composer** linked clones and full clones. Before we discuss the differences between the two, let's outline what about them is the same:

- From the perspective of the end user, a linked clone and full clone desktop appear the same
- The master image is often prepared using the same tuning techniques

Deciding on which clone type to use is not always a simple task. While linked clones have certain advantages that we will review in this recipe, we should adopt different techniques of performing desktop maintenance in order to maintain that advantage. Additionally, using linked clones might require selecting software optimized for virtual environments, such as the antivirus platform, **vShield Endpoint**.

How it works...

In this section, we will review the characteristics of the different Horizon View desktop types and user assignment methodologies and how each of them impacts our View environment as a whole.

Full clone desktops

Full clone Horizon View desktops are created using a master image that has been converted into a vSphere template. VMware Horizon View clones this template to create a full clone desktop; from then on, this desktop is managed independently from all other desktops and the template itself. Apart from the fact that it was created from a vSphere template, the full clone desktop is very comparable to a physical desktop from a management standpoint. As a result, the full clone desktop is often managed using the same techniques used with a physical desktop.

Assuming that the infrastructure has adequate capacity to host the full clone desktops, the familiarity with their management might be enough of a reason to choose them over linked clone desktops. Additionally, with advancements in the storage technology—specifically, real-time deduplication—organizations can deploy full clone desktops that require very little physical storage when measured on a per desktop basis.

The following table shows us the results obtained when testing the actual per-desktop storage required for 2,500 Horizon View desktops when deployed on a storage array that includes the deduplication functionality. In this example, the master image was utilizing approximately 13 GB of the 24 GB virtual hard disk. To determine the physical storage required for each desktop, the amount of actual storage being used on the array was measured immediately after the desktop deployment, and then divided by the number of desktops deployed (2,500). The measurements were taken immediately after the desktops were deployed.

Desktop type	Total physical storage used for 2,500 desktops	Average per desktop storage used
Linked clone desktop	139.16 GB	57 MB
Full clone desktop	480.96 GB	197 MB

While the full clone desktop still used over three times the amount of physical storage as the linked clone desktop, the amount of storage required for the full clone desktops was reduced by over 95 percent due to the deduplication capabilities of the array. To deploy this number of desktops using an array that does not have deduplication capabilities would require approximately 32 TB of storage capacity as a minimum—the minimum providing no room for any growth beyond the 13 GB of disk space currently in use. This does not even take into account the IOPS required, a factor that influences the storage design as much as if not more, than, just the amount of capacity required.

If full clone desktops are a definite requirement, technologies such as arrays capable of deduplication or storage acceleration platforms might be required in order to meet the virtual desktop capacity and performance requirements while keeping storage costs reasonable.

VMware VSAN does not yet include deduplication capabilities. This does not prevent it from being used to host full clone desktops, but a careful analysis should be done to determine the amount of storage required across the VSAN cluster and ensure that the costs are not prohibitive.

Horizon View Composer linked clones

VMware Horizon View Composer linked clone desktops are also provisioned from a master image. While a full clone desktop is created from a vSphere template, a linked clone requires a master image that is in the standard vSphere virtual machine format.

A linked clone desktop has a number of advantages over a full clone desktop. Some of these advantages include the following:

- Linked clone desktops share the same parent virtual disk; therefore, the amount of disk space they require is greatly reduced. This relationship is shown in the following image:

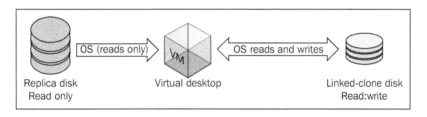

- Linked clone desktops can be recomposed, which replaces their replica disk with a new version that has software updates or other changes applied. Rather than applying updates to individual desktops, we should update the master image, and then use a Recompose operation to update the replica disks and apply these changes to the entire desktop pool.

 We cannot use a Recompose operation to upgrade the operating system version; it is not supported.

- Linked clone desktops can be refreshed, which returns them to the same condition they were in when initially deployed. When refreshed, any changes to the desktop OS disk that were made after the desktop was deployed are discarded. If a user-persistent data disk was used, the data on that disk will be retained.

- A linked clone desktop pool can be rebalanced, which redistributes the linked clone storage evenly across datastores. The individual linked clone disk utilization will vary over time, leading to an imbalance in storage utilization across all the datastores. A Rebalance operation addresses this by relocating the linked clone storage.

 Storage vMotion is not supported with linked clone desktops. Use a Horizon View Rebalance operation to relocate or rebalance the linked clone desktop storage.

Due to how a linked clone desktop works, there are specific considerations when it comes to client-based utilities and desktop management. If we were to treat linked clones like traditional physical desktops, we might find that the benefits of linked clone desktops begin to disappear. Some examples of this include the following:

- If we were to apply software patches to linked clones individually rather than updating the master image and then performing a Recompose operation, the linked clone virtual hard disks would grow significantly. This eliminates the storage efficiencies that are one of the primary reasons for choosing linked clones. Unless it is an emergency that requires immediate action, software patches should be applied only to the master image and rolled out to the desktops using a Recompose operation.

- Traditional client-based antivirus platforms require frequent virus pattern updates that can dramatically increase the linked clone storage utilization. A refresh might not address this issue, as the desktop will be forced to update the pattern files again when the refresh completes. Products such as vShield Endpoint address this issue by scanning for viruses at the hypervisor level rather than within the virtual machine. vShield Endpoint also provides the benefit of reducing desktop resource requirements, as traditional client-based AV software is not required.

- The Recompose, Refresh, and Rebalance operations all change the state of the linked clone virtual desktop, which can affect utilities such as indexing programs. If these operations lead to resource-intensive operations, such as a file index, every time they occur, it might be that they need to be disabled or their behavior altered. Tuning the master image can help alleviate this problem.

Whenever possible, we should approach managing linked clone desktops from the master image, as this helps preserve their benefits and minimize the amount of administrative effort required. Additionally, we should examine each of our client-based management tools and utilities to see whether there are versions optimized for virtual desktop use. These two recommendations can dramatically reduce the per-desktop resources required, which enables more desktops to run on the same infrastructure.

Many storage vendors provide the ability to create linked clones using the native features of their array. In many cases, these desktops can be provisioned more rapidly than Horizon View linked clones, enabling organizations to quickly deploy desktops that will still leverage Horizon View as a connection broker. While these desktops can be managed using Horizon View, since it did not create them, features such as refresh or recompose will not be available.

Consult the vendor documentation for information on what maintenance operations can be performed once the virtual desktops have been deployed using their native array features.

Floating versus dedicated user assignment

VMware Horizon View supports two options for assigning users to desktops: **floating** and **dedicated** user assignment. This section will define each of these options and discuss the optimal scenarios for each. Some of the terms used in this section, such as persistent and nonpersistent desktops, are defined in greater detail in the *Deciding between persistent and nonpersistent desktops* section.

Dedicated user assignment

Dedicated user assignment is when a Horizon View desktop is assigned to a single user. This user is the only one with permission to use that desktop, although the Horizon View administrator can alter the assignment, if required.

Dedicated user assignments are most commonly used in environments that use persistent desktops, as these desktops maintain their state as well as the user profile data between user sessions. Despite this, Horizon View also allows us to use dedicated assignment with nonpersistent linked clone desktops, although tools such as View Persona Management would be required to preserve the user profile data.

Horizon View can assign the desktops automatically when the user first logs in, or we can manually assign them ourselves using the **View Manager Admin console**.

Floating user assignment

Floating user assignment desktops have no owner; with floating user assignments, any desktops not currently in use in a desktop pool are accessible to anyone who has been granted access to the pool. A floating assignment is most common in environments that use nonpersistent desktops, as these desktops do not retain any unique personalization in between user sessions unless the pool is using linked clone desktops with user-persistent data disks.

One of the primary advantages of the floating user assignment is that it allows for the possibility of deploying only enough desktops to meet our maximum number of concurrent Horizon View clients, whereas, with dedicated user assignment, we are required to deploy a desktop for every Horizon View client. For organizations that maintain staff on multiple shifts, the floating user assignment might reduce the number of desktops required, as the number of concurrent Horizon View client sessions is likely to be much less than the total number of employees. Additionally, when combined with nonpersistent desktops, each worker will receive a freshly deployed desktop every time they log in, free of any changes that impact its functionality.

> When using the floating user assignment with persistent linked clone desktops, Horizon View hides the option to create a user-persistent data disk.

Deciding between persistent and nonpersistent desktops

VMware Horizon View provides organizations with the ability to manage desktop persistence automatically, without having to install additional software inside the base image. This section will discuss what differs between the two desktop persistence models. It is important to note that Horizon View does not refer to a desktop as **persistent** or **nonpersistent**; in using this term, we are referring to the act of refreshing a linked clone desktop or deleting and recreating a linked clone or full clone desktop after the user has ended their session.

Persistent desktops

Persistent desktops function just as the name indicates; they keep the contents of their virtual hard disks intact in between user logon sessions, reboots, or other common operations. As with full clone desktops, managing persistent desktops will be more familiar to the existing desktop administrators within an organization, as they retain their settings from one user session to the next.

For organizations that do not wish to use Horizon View Persona Management or any third-party tools to manage the user persona data, persistent desktops are the ideal selection when there is a need to maintain user files and settings between desktop sessions.

> Remember that linked clone desktops do not retain OS-level changes, including any applications that were installed, after a Refresh or Recompose operation. The user profile data can be retained by configuring a user-persistent data disk.

Nonpersistent desktops

VMware Horizon View supports the following scenarios when configuring nonpersistent desktops; they are selected by navigating to the **Add Pool | Pool Settings** page within the Horizon View Manager Admin console. Screenshots showing the configuration options for each scenario are also shown:

- ▶ **The linked clone dedicated assignment desktop**: Refresh upon logoff at the time indicated.

- ▶ **The linked clone floating assignment desktop**: Delete and redeploy or refresh immediately upon logoff.

- ▶ **The full clone dedicated assignment desktop**: Not supported as a nonpersistent desktop.

- ▶ **The full clone floating assignment desktop**: Delete and redeploy immediately upon logoff.

Whether we are refreshing or deleting and redeploying the desktop upon logoff, the impact is the same. Any changes made to the virtual desktop, with the exception of the optional linked clone user persistent data disk, are discarded and the desktop is returned to a just-deployed state.

The benefit of deleting the desktop upon logoff is that all of the space it was using is immediately freed up, whereas a refreshed desktop will not free up all of the space that was in use. If controlling the storage capacity utilization is a key requirement, deleting the desktop upon logoff might be the preferred setting.

The following is a list of items that we must consider when determining whether or not to use nonpersistent desktops:

> If required, the user persona data must be retained using persistent data disks with linked clone desktops or with persona management tools such as VMware Horizon View Persona Management or AppSense Environment Manager.

 We cannot configure user-persistent data disks on floating assignment linked clone desktop pools.

> If user-installed applications are required, consider virtualizing them with ThinApp and delivering them using Horizon View or VMware Horizon Workspace. Alternatively, consider streaming them using Microsoft Windows RDSH application remoting.

> Application caches such as Outlook should be disabled even if we are using persona management tools, as caches will need to be rebuilt every time the user logs in. This action can require significant resources.

> Programs such as client-based antivirus and file indexing will need to be updated every time the desktop is redeployed, which might require significant resources. In the case of AV, alternative solutions optimized for virtual desktops might be preferred; for indexing, either disable the feature or alter the setting to reduce its impact on the desktop.

> If large numbers of users were to log off at once, the spike in IO associated with a desktop refresh or delete and redeploy operations might impact the storage array performance. The impact of this will vary from one storage array to the next, and this should be considered during the Horizon View design phase.

> The frequent erasure of the desktop data might require that the `SCSI UNMAP` command be run to free up space on the storage array. The impact of this should be considered during the Horizon View design phase.

While there are some risks to be aware of, the combination of nonpersistent desktops and the floating user assignment is one of the most efficient means of providing EUC, as it can minimize the number of desktops required while providing desktops that are always in a *just-deployed* state.

Be smart – optimize your desktops!

There are two schools of thought when it comes to optimizing Windows for our Horizon View environment. One opinion is that the fewer resources Windows requires, the more desktops we can host on a given vSphere server. Additionally, we have probably made the desktop perform better, as there are no nonessential services running. We only need to talk to our desktop support team in order to learn the different tips and tricks they perform to make Windows run faster or with fewer errors.

The second school of thought says that you shouldn't have to optimize Windows. By doing this, you are degrading the Windows experience and introducing barriers to the adoption of your Horizon View implementation. File indexing is one example where this could be true, as some users might depend on the Windows search feature. Many other examples are less important, such as the various transparency features that Windows uses to make the user interface appear more attractive. Rather than blindly disabling every lesser-used feature we find, research should be done to identify how we can tune Windows without impacting the workflows our users depend on to perform their duties.

Even if you are fortunate enough to have the best of the best when it comes to storage technology, optimizing Windows also reduces virtual desktop vCPU and RAM needs, which can reduce our server requirements. Since Horizon View projects often deal with hundreds—if not thousands—of desktops, every reduction in virtual desktop resources requirements that you make is multiplied many times over.

Determining our Horizon View desktop infrastructure's requirements

Determining the resources required to host the Horizon View infrastructure is straightforward for the Horizon View and vCenter Servers but far more involved for vSphere servers that will host the virtual desktops. This recipe will focus primarily on determining virtual desktop resource requirements.

How it works...

The infrastructure resource requirements for VMware Horizon View can be broken down into two primary sections:

▸ Resources required by the virtual desktop itself, including compute, networking, and storage. This can vary based on the user workload, applications being used, and any other factors that distinguish one user from the next.

▸ The network bandwidth required for each Horizon View client connection; this will vary based on the workload profile of each client.

In this recipe, we review methods for measuring or determining what infrastructure resources we need for each of these items.

Key desktop resource requirements

One of the preferred methods to determine virtual desktop resource requirements is to use a commercial tool such as **Liquidware Labs Stratusphere FIT** (http://www.liquidwarelabs.com/products/stratusphere-fit). Stratusphere FIT can generate detailed reports concerning the compute resources required by each of the virtual desktops in our organization. This information can be used to determine the desktop resource requirements with a very high degree of precision.

For organizations that cannot justify the expense of Stratusphere FIT, and feel that a simpler approach to desktop resource utilization is sufficient, the Windows Performance Monitor tool can be used to measure the resource utilization of their virtual desktops.

While the Performance Monitor tool provides a useful insight into resource utilization, it cannot compare with commercial tools such as Stratusphere FIT. Given how important it is to accurately determine our Horizon View infrastructure requirements, we should consider using the best tools at our disposal in order to gather current desktop resource requirements.

When using Performance Monitor, the desktop should be measured during a period of normal use, and the data being measured should be saved into the comma-separated format in order to make it easier to analyze. This section will detail each of the counters that should be monitored using the Performance Monitor tool.

Due to differences in hardware and software configurations, Windows resource names will vary slightly from one system to the next. The performance monitor counter names provided in this section are just examples; when using the performance monitor, select the appropriate counter based on the target resource you wish to monitor. Ensure that you are monitoring the active resources, as a system might have some unused devices, such as hard disks or network adapters.

Network adapter bytes total/sec

This Windows counter represents the total network throughput of the specified desktop network adapter. The average of this value will help us calculate the network requirements of each virtual desktop on the vSphere Server. For Windows 7 and newer OSes, this counter is displayed as **Network Adapter\Bytes Total/sec–Network Adapter** in Windows Performance Monitor.

To determine the number of desktops a vSphere Server can host based on the information gathered, we use the following calculation:

> ▸ **Network**: The total server network bandwidth in MB/network total MB per second of reference desktop

> We must convert the network adapter line speeds from megabit to megabyte in order to match the output format of the Windows Performance Monitor data. The following formula can be used to perform the conversion: *Value in megabits / 8 = Value in megabytes*.

Physical disk – read/write bytes

Read/write bytes per second—the disk read and writes bytes of a desktop provide us with a starting point for sizing the storage network connection that will connect the vSphere hosts to the storage infrastructure. These counters are displayed as **PhysicalDisk\Disk Read Bytes/sec – 0 C:** and **PhysicalDisk\Disk Write Bytes/sec – 0 C:** in Windows Performance Monitor.

To determine the number of desktops a vSphere server can host based on the information gathered, we can use the following calculation:

> ▸ **Storage network**: The total server storage network bandwidth in MB (disk read MB per second + disk write MB per second) of the reference desktop

Physical disk – reads/writes

Reads/writes per second—the number of disk reads and writes on a desktop provide us a with starting point for sizing the virtual desktop storage platform. The storage design is impacted not only by the total amount of disk input/output (I/O), but also by the ratio of reads to writes. These counters are displayed as **PhysicalDisk\Disk Reads/sec – 0 C:** and **PhysicalDisk\Disk Writes/sec – 0 C:** in Windows Performance Monitor. These values can also be referred to as either read or write **I/O Operations per Second (IOPS)**.

To determine the number of desktops a vSphere Server can host based on the information gathered, we use the following calculation:

> ▸ *(Disk Reads per second + Disk Writes per second) * Total number of desktops = Total IOPS required by the virtual desktop storage solution*

> Regardless of which storage protocol our vSphere hosts will use, there will be some overhead involved. After you have measured your baseline disk bandwidth (disk read or write megabytes per second) or IO (disk reads or writes per second) from your reference desktop, add 15 percent to the value recorded prior to calculating your overall resource requirements.

The percent processor time

This counter measures the percentage of time for which the processor was busy. The average of this value will impact the number of virtual desktop processors we can host per vSphere Server CPU core. This counter is displayed as **Processor\% Processor Time - _Total** in Windows Performance Monitor.

To determine the number of desktops a vSphere Server can host based on the information gathered, we can use the following calculation:

> ▸ **Processor**: (Number of servers cores * 100) / % processor time of reference desktop

 When using the **_Total** counter, the total of all processor statistics will be returned, including those created by the **Intel HyperThreading** feature (if enabled).

Memory-committed bytes

This counter represents the total number of bytes allocated by Windows processes, including any that were paged to physical disk. The average of this value will help us calculate how much memory should be allocated to the virtual desktop master image and, by extension, how much memory will be required in each virtual desktop vSphere host. This counter is displayed as **Memory\Committed Bytes** in Windows Performance Monitor.

To determine the number of desktops a vSphere server can host based on the information gathered, we can use the following calculation:

> ▸ **Memory**: Total server memory in MB / (memory committed MB per second of reference desktop * 1.25)

 The 1.25 multiplier is used in this calculation to grant the desktop additional memory and reduce the likelihood that the Windows swap file will be utilized. In most cases, when a desktop is forced to use the swap file, a decrease in performance will occur as well as an increase in the amount of IO it generates, which is why the additional memory is important.

Horizon View Client's network bandwidth requirements

One of the easiest things to overlook when designing our Horizon View infrastructure is how much network bandwidth is required in order to support the client connections. The preferred protocol for Horizon View is PCoIP, although it also supports VMware HTML Access as well as **Microsoft Remote Desktop Protocol** (**RDP**).

PCoIP is a display protocol provided by VMware for use in the Horizon View product suite. The PCoIP protocol has multiple features that make it ideal for connecting to Horizon View desktops or streamed applications:

- It's capable of adapting to varying levels of connection latency and bandwidth
- It has multiple built-in techniques for optimizing and accelerating connections over a WAN
- It is able to achieve compression ratios of up to 100:1 for images and audio
- It uses multiple codecs that enable more efficient encoding and decoding of content between the virtual desktop and the remote client
- It is based on **User Datagram Protocol** (**UDP**), which eliminates the need for latency-inducing handshakes used in display protocols based on **Transmission Control Protocol** (**TCP**)

Microsoft RDP is a TCP-based display protocol that lacks many of the WAN optimization and acceleration techniques that are found in PCoIP. In addition, VMware Horizon View includes Microsoft **Group Policy Object** (**GPO**) templates that enable a very granular control over PCoIP connection characteristics. The Horizon View document *Setting up Desktop and Application Pools in View* (`https://pubs.vmware.com/horizon-view-60/index.jsp#com.vmware.horizon-view.desktops.doc/GUID-D90CC716-6CDA-4210-8AF2-9E75C729D847.html`) provides us with details on how to use the PCoIP GPO templates.

Client bandwidth estimates

The VMware Horizon *View Architecture Planning* guide (`https://pubs.vmware.com/horizon-view-60/index.jsp#com.vmware.horizon-view.planning.doc/GUID-5CC0B95F-7B92-4C60-A2F2-B932FB425F0C.html`) provides us with estimates for the PCoIP bandwidth utilization based on the application workload of the client. The following table is built upon this information:

User type	Workload characteristics	Bandwidth in Kbps
Task Worker	2D display and single monitor. Web and limited Office applications. Horizon View desktop and PCoIP settings optimized.	50–100 Kbps
Task Worker	2D display and single monitor. Web and limited Office applications. Horizon View desktop and PCoIP settings not optimized.	100–150 Kbps
Knowledge Worker (3D)	3D display (Windows Aero) and multiple monitors. Office applications.	400–600 Kbps

User type	Workload characteristics	Bandwidth in Kbps
Knowledge worker (3D): heavy video	3D display (Windows Aero) and multiple monitors. Office applications. Frequent bursts of large display changes and other imaging traffic.	500 Kbps–1 Mbps
Power user	3D display (Windows Aero) and multiple monitors. 480P video and images with frequent screen changes.	2 Mbps

Bandwidth utilization is heavily dependent on a number of factors, many of which can be controlled with the Horizon View PCoIP GPO settings or even Windows virtual desktops settings.

Even with a careful analysis of user desktop usage patterns, it is important to remember that there will be spikes in usage from time to time. A knowledge or task worker that has a need to use an application with a large amount of screen changes, such as viewing images in succession or watching a video, might cause a brief bandwidth spike between 500 Kbps and 1 Mbps or more, referenced as a *Heavy Video* user in the table. Preparing for these spikes in bandwidth utilization is important in order to preserve the quality of service for all of the Horizon View client connections.

Analyzing our Horizon with View environment

Measuring the resource requirements of our physical desktops and their users is a valuable exercise that will help us understand what will be required to transition them from the local desktop to the data center. While this is a valuable exercise, no amount of initial planning or analysis can ever replace a properly run pilot that validates the configuration of our master virtual desktop image, the performance of the Horizon View infrastructure, and the perceived end user experience.

How it works...

Ideally, our pilot should involve the same types of users on whom we performed our initial usage analysis but not necessarily the same users within each group. The following list includes a sample of the goals that our Horizon View pilot should attempt to achieve:

- Include multiple users from each user classification such as the task worker, knowledge worker, and power user
- Include fully remote users, including WAN-connected users at other company sites
- Run the pilot for the full duration of a business cycle so that recurring operations such as quarterly reporting or accounting functions can be observed

- Review the performance data from all layers of the Horizon View infrastructure including:

  - Storage

  - Network

  - vSphere host

  - Guest operating system

- Measure the impact of common scenarios such as:

  - **User logon storms**: These are large numbers of Horizon View clients logging on within a short time frame

  - **Steady state user load**: This measures the Horizon View infrastructure's performance during a period of steady desktop usage by a significant number of users

  - **Antivirus platform performance**: This measures the impact of common antivirus software tasks such as on-demand scans and pattern file updates

  - **Horizon View Refresh or Recompose**: This measures the impact of these common Horizon View maintenance operations

  - **A fully populated vSphere host**: This measures the host performance with higher than normal workloads, such as when a vSphere server fails, and the remaining vSphere servers must host its desktops in addition to their own

Performance issues at any layer of the Horizon View infrastructure will often result in a poor end user experience, usually in the form of longer-than-anticipated response times. This is one of the reasons why it is important to involve a large cross-section of our users in the pilot and seek their opinion throughout.

The performance data that we collect during the pilot can be used to determine our actual resource utilization, which can then be compared to the estimated resource utilization, as determined from our initial analysis of existing physical desktops. If the numbers differ by a significant amount, we will want to work to identify the cause and determine what would happen if any changes need to be made. Some potential issues that need to be looked out for include the following:

- The initial analysis of our users did not include a sufficient number or wide enough cross-section of users.

- The virtual desktop's master image was not properly optimized to reduce or stabilize the resource utilization. The VMware *Optimization Guide for Windows 7 and Windows 8 Virtual Desktops in Horizon with View* (http://www.vmware.com/resources/techresources/10157) technical paper provides common Windows desktop optimization techniques.

- ▶ A component of the Horizon View infrastructure was improperly configured.
- ▶ The pilot program is occurring during a period of higher than normal user workload, such as a recurring events unique to the organization, including quarterly or monthly reporting.

Summary

In summary, a pilot is our best time to learn about how virtual desktops will perform within our environment, both from a performance perspective and in terms of user acceptance. Use the pilot program to identity any potential barriers to a successful rollout, and make any changes that are required in order to minimize the risk of failure as the project moves forward into production.

2
Implementing a VMware Horizon View Cloud Pod

In this chapter, we will cover the following recipes:

- ▶ The VMware Horizon with View Cloud Pod overview
- ▶ Federated Pod Port requirements
- ▶ Configuring a Horizon View Federated Pod
- ▶ Entitling users or groups in a Horizon View Federated Pod
- ▶ Assigning users and groups to Horizon View sites
- ▶ Reviewing your Horizon View Federated Pod configuration
- ▶ Modifying Horizon View Federated Pod objects
- ▶ Removing objects from your Federated Pod or global entitlements
- ▶ Disabling the Horizon View Cloud Pod Architecture feature

Introduction

This chapter discusses how to enable, configure, and administer a VMware Horizon View Cloud Pod. The Horizon View Cloud Pod Architecture was first introduced in Horizon View 6 and allows administrators to deploy multisite, multipod environments that support global user entitlements. Additionally, when deployed in a multipod configuration, Horizon View 6 is capable of supporting up to 20,000 desktops or twice as many as previous versions. In this chapter, we will review the concepts behind a VMware Horizon View Cloud Pod and cover key areas related to the Cloud Pod functionality.

The VMware Horizon View Cloud Pod overview

A VMware Horizon View Cloud Pod, also known as a federated pod, consists of a set of Horizon View Connection Server instances, shared storage, a database server, and the vSphere and network infrastructures required to host desktop virtual machines.

In a traditional VMware Horizon View implementation, each pod is managed independently. With the Federated Pod Architecture feature introduced in Version 6, you can join together multiple pods to form a single Horizon View implementation called a pod federation.

A pod federation can span multiple sites or data centers and offers the following benefits over the previous single-pod model:

▸ It centrally manages Horizon View desktops located across multiple data centers.

▸ The desktop entitlement is managed globally, including the ability to assign desktops based on the location of the Horizon View client.

▸ It has the ability to balance the Horizon View Client load across multiple data centers using centralized rather than individual login portals and user entitlements.

▸ Users can be entitled to multiple desktop pools in up to four Horizon View pods across two sites. Rather than selecting which pool to use when logging into the Horizon View Client, the user is presented with only one pool, and the assignment of desktops is handled automatically, based on how the global entitlement is configured.

▸ Using federated Horizon View pods, we can enable native **disaster recovery** (**DR**) for the View infrastructure.

The following figure is an example of a basic Horizon View Cloud Pod Architecture:

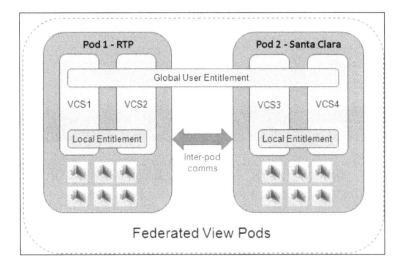

In the example topology, two previously standalone Horizon View pods in different data centers are joined together to create a pod federation. In a pod federation, an end user can connect to a Horizon View Connection Server instance in the **Research Triangle Park** (**RTP**) data center and can be assigned a desktop located in a completely different pod located in the **Santa Clara** data center.

Sharing key data in the global data layer

The Horizon View Connection Server instances in a pod federation use something called a global data layer to share the key data. The data that is shared includes information on the pod federation topology, user and group entitlements, Horizon View policies, and other information concerning the federated pod configuration.

In a Horizon View pod federation, the shared data is replicated between every member Horizon View Connection Server instance. The entitlement and topology configuration information stored in the global data layer determines where and how desktops are allocated across the pod federation.

When the Federated Pod feature is enabled, or additional pods are added to an existing pod federation, the global data layer is configured on each VHorizon View Connection Server instance.

Sending messages between pods

The Horizon View Connection Server instances in a federated pod communicate using an interpod communications protocol called the **View InterPod API** (**VIPA**).

Horizon View Connection Server instances use the VIPA interpod communication channel to launch new desktops, find existing desktops, and share health status data and other information. The VIPA interpod communications channel is configured when the Federated Pod feature is enabled.

Federated Pod's topology limits

A VMware Horizon View Federated Pod implementation consists of two or more Horizon View pods, which are linked together to create a pod federation. The following table details the configuration limits of a Horizon View Federated Pod:

Component	Limit
Desktops (per federated pod)	20,000
Pods	4
Sites	2
Horizon View Connection Servers	20
Desktops per each individual Horizon View pod	10,000

It is important to note that while a single pod can contain up to 10,000 desktops, a single Federated Pod comprised of up to four individual pods can contain 20,000 desktops at the most, even though individual pods support up to 10,000 desktops each.

 The topology limits of a federated pod are subject to change as new versions of Horizon with View are released. Consult the VMware Horizon with View documentation (`https://pubs.vmware.com/horizon-view-60/index.jsp`) for current information concerning platform limits.

A similar restriction exists for Horizon View Connection servers, where a single pod supports up to seven Connection servers in a five active plus two standby configuration, whereas a federated pod comprised of four individual pods supports a maximum of twenty Connection Servers.

Federated Pod's port requirements

A VMware Horizon View Federated Pod uses two different network ports to replicate the data and status information. This communication occurs between Horizon View Connection Servers located in different sites. The following table details the port numbers and their respective function within the Federated Pod:

Port	Service	Description
22389	Global data layer LDAP	The shared data is replicated on every Horizon View Connection Server instance in a pod federation. Each Connection Server instance in a pod federation runs a second LDAP instance to store the shared data.
8472	The View Interpod API (VIPA) interpod communication channel	Connection Server instances use the VIPA interpod communication channel to launch new desktops, find existing desktops, and share the health status data and other information.

Configuring a VMware Horizon View Federated Pod

A VMware Horizon View Federated Pod is configured using a command-line utility on Horizon View Connection Servers.

Getting ready

The Horizon View Federated Pod configuration process will require command-line access to at least one Connection Server in each pod that will be a member of the federated pod.

These commands can be executed remotely if you configure your Connection Servers to allow remote command access using tools such as **Microsoft PsExec** (`http://msdn.microsoft.com/en-us/library/bb897553.aspx`). If security policies or other concerns prevent this capability, you will need to run the commands directly within the console on the target View Connection Servers.

How to do it...

In this section, we will walk through the steps required to enable the View Federated Pod components, and then create a multisite Federated Pod. For this exercise, we will use the following resources:

- `VIEWCS01.vjason.local`: This is the Connection Server located in the **RTP** data center
- `VIEWCS03.vjason.local`: This is the Connection Server located in the **Santa Clara** data center
- `Svc-view`: This is the Microsoft **Active Directory** (**AD**) account that has administrative privileges to both pods used in this exercise
- `Vjason`: This is a single label name of the AD domain used in this exercise

For each command shown in this section, we will see both the command syntax as well as the resulting output when the command is executed in our own Horizon View environment. Refer to the following steps:

1. The first step in creating a new Federated Pod is to initialize the components that are required using the following command. We will execute this command on our Connection Server, which is `VIEWCS01.vjason.local`:

    - `lmvutil.cmd --initialize --authAs user --authDomain domain --authPassword password`

```
Administrator: C:\Windows\System32\cmd.exe                    _  □  X

c:\Program Files\VMware\VMware View\Server\tools\bin>lmvutil.cmd --initialize --
authAs svc-view --authDomain vjason --authPassword Password123
Please wait until the requested task is completed. This may take several minutes
.
Task is RUNNING (0%), waiting for completion...
Task is RUNNING (80%), waiting for completion...
Task is completed with result: SUCCESS
```

2. The next command joins our second Horizon View pod to the federated pod that we created in step 1 and must be executed on a connection server in that second pod. The `--joinServer` switch is used to specify a Connection Server located on the pod where the federated pod was created in step 1. We will execute this command on our Connection Server, which is `VIEWCS03.vjason.local`:

   ❑ `lmvutil.cmd --join --joinServer serverFQDN --authAs user --authDomain domain --authPassword password --userName domain\user --password password`

```
Administrator: C:\Windows\System32\cmd.exe            –  □  X

c:\Program Files\VMware\VMware View\Server\tools\bin>lmvutil.cmd --join --joinSe
rver viewcs01.vjason.local --authAs svc-view --authDomain vjason --authPassword
Password123 --userName vjason\svc-view --password Password123
Please wait until the requested task is completed. This may take several minutes
.
Task is RUNNING (0%), waiting for completion...
Task is RUNNING (40%), waiting for completion...
Task is RUNNING (95%), waiting for completion...
Task is completed with result: SUCCESS
```

3. In this step, we will verify that our standalone Horizon View pods have both been added to our new Federated Pod. By default, pods are assigned the same name as their first member Connection Server, but in the next step, we will change this name to something more meaningful, in this case, the pod geographical location. This command can be executed on any Connection Server located within the Federated Pod:

   ❑ `lmvutil.cmd --authAs user --authDomain domain --authPassword password --listPods`

```
Administrator: C:\Windows\System32\cmd.exe            –  □  X

c:\Program Files\VMware\VMware View\Server\tools\bin>lmvutil.cmd --authAs svc-vi
ew --authDomain vjason --authPassword Password123 --listPods
Pod: Cluster-VIEWCS03 [remote]
    Description: null
    Owning site: Default First Site
Pod: Cluster-VIEWCS01 [local]
    Description: null
    Owning site: Default First Site
```

4. Next, we will rename each of the pods in our federated pod. We will use the pod names obtained in step 3 for the `--podName` switch and supply new names for the `--newPodName` switch. The following optional command is run once for each pod in our federated pod and can be executed on any Connection Server located within the federated pod:

   ❑ `lmvutil.cmd --authAs user --authDomain domain --authPassword password --updatePod --podName "name" --newPodName "newName"`

5. In this step, we will create sites that can be used to control which desktops a user accesses. A user is entitled to a global pool that contains desktop pools located in multiple Horizon View pods using sites that we can control from which pod the user can receive a desktop. Creating sites does not by itself restrict the desktop access; these restrictions take place during the entitlement process described later in this chapter. These optional commands are run once for each pod in the federated pod and can be executed on any Connection Server located within the federated pod. The following example shows you both steps of the process, which include the `--createSite` and `--assignPodToSite` commands:

   ❑ `lmvutil.cmd --authAs user --authDomain domain --authPassword password --createSite --siteName "name"`

   ❑ `lmvutil.cmd --authAs user --authDomain domain --authPassword password --assignPodToSite --podName "name" --siteName "name"`

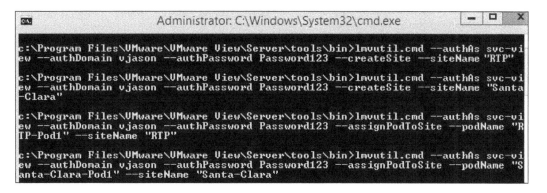

With these steps complete, our VMware Horizon View Federated Pod is ready to accept global entitlements, which we will explore in the next section of this chapter. The following screenshot shows you the updated Horizon View Manager Admin console with the new federated pod status section highlighted. In this example, we are viewing the console from the Santa Clara View Manager Admin console, which is why the RTP pod is displayed in the **Remote Pods** section. Were we using the RTP Horizon View Manager Admin console, the Santa Clara pod would be displayed under **Remote Pods**.

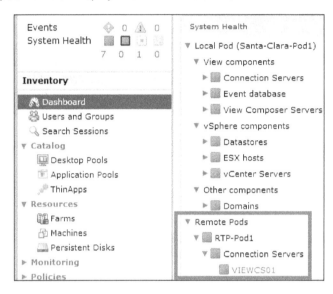

In addition to viewing the health of each of the Connection Servers that are members of the federated pod, you can also search for Client sessions based on the user, pod, or by which pod the connection is being brokered.

The following screenshot shows you the updated **Inventory** section in the **Search Sessions** window of the Horizon View Manager Admin console, where the option to search for sessions based on these additional parameters is found:

How it works...

The `lmvutil.cmd` command-line utility was first introduced in VMware Horizon View 6 and is used to configure and manage a Federated Pod. **Lmvutil** is installed as part of the Horizon View installation by default, although the services required to create a federated pod are not enabled until they are actually configured.

> The `lmvutil.cmd` utility is located in the following folder in the drive where the Connection Server software was installed:
>
> ▶ `Program Files\VMware\VMware View\Server\tools\bin`
>
> The path shown is the default installation path. If a different path was used, the `Server\tools\bin` directory structure will still be present in the new path.

The following table outlines the different `lmvutil` command-line switches that can be used when creating a new Federated Pod. These switches are only a subset of those available; additional ones will be detailed later on in this chapter. It is important to note that these and other `lmvutil` switches are case-sensitive, and each is preceded by two dashes.

Command-line switch	Description
`--assignPodToSite`	This is optional; it is used when assigning a pod to a specific site. This switch requires no additional information.
`--authAs`	This is a username with administrative permissions in the Connection Server pod.
`--authDomain`	This is a short version of the domain name the Connection Server is a member of.
`--authPassword`	This is the password for the user specified in the `--authAs` switch. If `"*"` is provided for this switch (including the quotes), you will be prompted for a password.
`--description`	This is optional; it is used to create a description for a pod.
`--help`	This is optional; displays information related to the use of the `lmvutil` command.
`--initialize`	This is used to initialize the first pod in a new pod federation. This switch requires no additional information.
`--listPods`	This is a list of the pods that are currently members of the pod federation.
`--newPodName`	This is used to specify the new name of a pod.
`--password`	This is the password for the username specified in the `--userName` switch.
`--podName`	This is used to specify the name of the target pod.

Command-line switch	Description
`--siteName`	This is optional; it is used to specify the name of the site. It is required when using site-based global entitlements.
`--updatePod`	This is used when updating the configuration of an existing pod. This switch requires no additional information.
`--userName`	This is used when joining a new pod to an existing pod federation; the username provided should have administrative permissions to the pod and the target federation. The name should be in the `domain name\username` format.
`--verbose`	This is optional; it displays a verbose output when executing `lmvutil` commands.

The `--authAs`, `--authDomain`, `--autoPassword`, `--help`, and `--verbose` commands are used with all commands related to Federated Pod configuration, entitlement, and management—examples of which are found later on in this chapter.

Entitling users or groups in a Horizon View Federated Pod

Once the VMware Horizon View Federated Pod has been created and desktop pools have been deployed in at least one pod, we can create a global entitlement. In this section, we will walk through the creation of a global entitlement. With a global entitlement, users see only one desktop pool in the Horizon View Client, yet they might be assigned desktops from any number of pods in the pod federation based on the entitlement configuration.

Getting ready

The following figure is a conceptual example of a global entitlement in a VMware Horizon View federation using the names of the objects used as an example later in this section. In this example, the sample user is a member of the global entitlement called **Global-Finance**. Global-Finance provides entitlement to two floating desktop pools, named **RTP-Finance-Floating** and **SantaClara-Finance-Floating**. The RTP-Finance-Floating pool is located in a pod named **RTP-Pod1** in the RTP data center, and the SantaClara-Finance-Floating pool is located in the pod named **Santa-Clara-Pod1** in the Santa Clara data center. While this example shows you only two pods in the pod federation, remember that up to four pods are supported. The user-entitlement process remains the same regardless of how many pods are there in the federation.

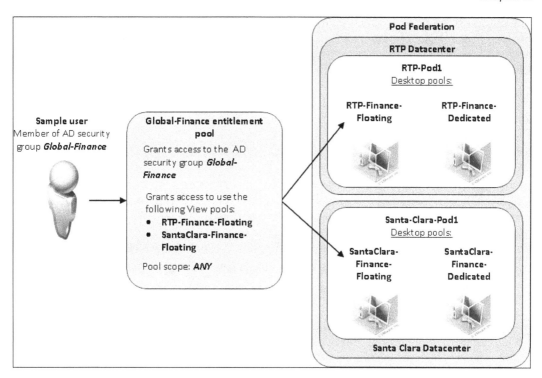

Since the Global-Finance pool has a scope policy of ANY, when a user requests a desktop, the Federated Pod Architecture feature looks for desktops from both the RTP and Santa Clara pods. While we have other pools available in each pod, they are not part of the Global-Finance pool, and as such, their desktops are not available for assignment to the Global-Finance pool users.

By default, a user will be provided with a desktop from a pod where they are located when they initiate the Horizon View Client logon process. If desktops are not available from any local entitled pods, yet other pods in other sites have desktops available, the user will automatically be assigned a desktop from the remote pod.

This section shows you the creation of a floating assignment global pool, which is the most logical choice, given that it provides the most flexibility for user assignment. While dedicated assignment global pools can be created, once a user has been assigned a desktop, they will continue to use it regardless of where they happen to be located. Additionally, were one pod to run out of desktops, large numbers of users might be permanently assigned desktops not local to them, which might lead to performance problems if there is insufficient bandwidth to support large numbers of remote users.

The advantage of the Federated Pod Architecture is that the user need only select a single desktop pool at login, and Horizon View will assign them whatever desktop is available from any pod specified in their global entitlement while still selecting local Horizon View pods by default, wherever possible.

To entitle AD users or groups access to resources in a federated pod, command-line access to one of the Connection Servers in the federated pod is required.

How to do it...

In this section, we will walk through the steps required to create a Horizon View Federated Pod global entitlement, including the assignment of both AD resources as well as Horizon View desktop pools. For this exercise, we will use the following resources:

- ▶ **Global-Finance**: This is the name of the new federated pod global entitlement.

- ▶ **RTP-Finance-Floating**: This is the floating assignment pool located in **RTP-Pod1**.

- ▶ **SantaClara-Finance-Floating**: This is the floating assignment desktop pool located in **Santa-Clara-Pod1**.

- ▶ **Vjason\Global-Finance**: This is the AD security group that will contain the users entitled to the **Global-Finance** global entitlement. When supplying the AD group name, you must include as well as show the domain name.

In this example, we have an AD security group named **Global-Finance** that contains nested AD security groups for each region. This type of hierarchy is common in global AD environments where security groups can be used differently from one region to the next. While Horizon View can identify nested security groups and grant the necessary access to the global desktop pool, the site assignment feature described in the next section cannot. Should you wish to assign AD security groups to specific Horizon View sites, you must first entitle each individual security group to the Horizon View global entitlement. The process used to entitle security groups is outlined in step 4 in this section.

For each command shown in this section, we will see both the command syntax as well as a demonstration of the command being executed in our own Horizon View environment. Refer to the following steps:

1. The first step is to create our global entitlement and make any changes to the default configuration. In this example, we will create a floating assignment entitlement with a scope of ANY, which enables Horizon View to assign users' desktops from any desktop pools added to the entitlement:

   ❑ ```lmvutil.cmd --authAs user --authDomain domain --authPassword password --createGlobalEntitlement --entitlementName "name" --isFloating --scope scope```

2. Next, using a command prompt in a Connection Server located in the `RTP-Pod1` pod, we will associate a previously created standard desktop pool with the global entitlement created in step 1. As we specified `--isFloating` in the previous example, only floating assignment desktop pools can be associated. The desktop pool ID that is used is the same one used when the desktop pool was first created:

   ❑ `lmvutil.cmd --authAs user --authDomain domain --authPassword password --addPoolAssociation --entitlementName "name" --poolId "id"`

3. Next, using a command prompt in a Connection Server located in the `Santa-Clara-Pod1` pod, we will repeat the process used in step 2, but this time, using the pool ID for a standard desktop pool located in that pod, as shown in the following screenshot:

Use the `lmvutil.cmd --listGlobalEntitlements` command to review all global entitlements that have been created.

4. Our final step is to assign an AD security group to the global entitlement. This step should be repeated as many times as necessary in order to add additional users or groups, and the format used should be `domain\name`, as shown in the following example:

   ❑ `lmvutil.cmd --authAs user --authDomain domain --authPassword password --addGroupEntitlement --entitlementName "name" --groupName "domain\name"`

```
Administrator: C:\Windows\system32\cmd.exe                          _  □  X

c:\Program Files\VMware\VMware View\Server\tools\bin>lmvutil.cmd --authAs svc-vi
ew --authDomain vjason --authPassword Password123 --addGroupEntitlement --entitl
ementName "Global-Finance" --groupName vjason\Global-Finance
```

5. The previous command can also be applied to individual AD user accounts using the following format:

   ❑ `lmvutil.cmd --authAs user --authDomain domain --authPassword password --addUserEntitlement --entitlementName "name" --userName "domain\name"`

With these steps complete, and assuming that all assigned desktop pools are ready, users will be able to log in to their newly created global desktop pool. The following screenshot shows you the appearance of the global desktop pool in the Horizon View Client, which is displayed as a single desktop pool even though the global entitlement is linked to two individual desktop pools located in wholly separate pods:

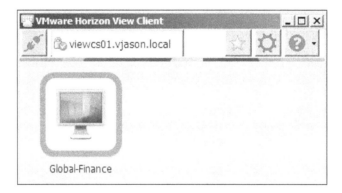

How it works...

The `lmvutil.cmd` command-line utility is again used to create global entitlements. The following table outlines additional command-line switches that are used to create a global entitlement and then associate it with users and desktop pools. As previously noted, these switches are case-sensitive, and each is preceded by two dashes.

Command-line switch	Description
`--addPoolAssociation`	This is used when associating a desktop pool with a global entitlement. This switch requires no additional information.
`--addGroupEntitlement`	This is used when adding an AD security group to a global entitlement.
`--addUserEntitlement`	This is used when adding an AD user to a global entitlement.
`--allowReset`	This is optional; it is used to grant users the ability to reset their Horizon View desktops.
`--createGlobalEntitlement`	This is used when creating a new global entitlement. This switch requires no additional information.
`--defaultProtocol`	This is optional; it is used to specify a default protocol. The options are either RDP or PCoIP.
`--description`	This is optional; it is used to create a description for a global entitlement.
`--disabled`	This is optional; It is used to create the global entitlement in a disabled state.
`--entitlementName`	This is used to specify the name of the entitlement.
`--fromHome`	This is optional; if a user has a home site, this switch instructs Horizon View to assign desktops from that site before looking at other sites.
`--userName`	This is used when assigning an AD security group to a global entitlement. The format used is `domain\ groupName`.
`--isDedicated`	This is optional; it is used to create a dedicated user entitlement.
`--isFloating`	This is optional; it is used to create a floating user entitlement.
`--multipleSessionsAutoClean`	This is optional; it automatically logs off any unused Horizon View sessions once a connection is established. This scenario typically occurs when a pod becomes unavailable. Then, the user establishes a new Client session that connects to a different pod, and then the original pod becomes available again. The user will be prompted for the client session to be used and the point at which the unused session will be logged off.
`--poolId`	This is used to specify the target Horizon View desktop pool ID.

Command-line switch	Description
`--preventProtocolOverride`	This is optional; it is used to prevent users from overriding the default display protocol.
`--requireHomeSite`	This is optional; it requires that the users be assigned a home site, else the entitlement will not be available. It must be used with the `--fromHome` switch.
`--scope`	This is used to set the scope of a global entitlement. Options are case-sensitive and include the following: ▸ `ANY`: This looks for desktops from any pod in the federation ▸ `SITE`: This looks for desktops only on pods located in the site where the user connects ▸ `LOCAL`: This looks for desktops only in the pod to which the user connects
`--userName`	This is used when assigning an AD user to a global entitlement. The format used is `domain\userName`.

Assigning users and groups to Horizon View sites

Previously in this chapter, we then about using Horizon View sites to control desktop assignments within a global entitlement. Using sites, Horizon View can restrict or prioritize the desktop assignment as follows:

▸ When the global entitlement has the `--requireHomeSite` option enabled, users are required to have a home site specified before they can be assigned a desktop

▸ When the global entitlement has the `--fromHome` option enabled, Horizon View will attempt to assign a desktop from their specified home site before assigning desktops located in other sites.

▸ Depending on the configuration of the global entitlement `--scope` setting, based on which pod they are connected to, they might be restricted to desktops in a specific site or even pod within a site (for sites that have more than one pod)

Getting ready

In the *Configuring a VMware Horizon View Federated Pod* section, we assigned our pods to sites named RTP and Santa-Clara. In this section, we will walk through assigning both AD security groups as well as individual users to a Horizon View site.

To assign AD users or groups to Horizon View Federated Pod sites, the command-line access to one of the Connection Servers in the federated pod is required.

How to do it...

In this section, we will walk through the steps required to assign both an AD user and security group. For this exercise, we will use the following resources:

- ▶ RTP and Santa-Clara: These are previously created Horizon View sites
- ▶ Global-Finance: This is a Horizon View global user entitlement
- ▶ ELehnsherr: This is an AD user account
- ▶ Santa-Clara-Finance: This is the AD security group

 If the --fromHome flag was not set when creating the global entitlement, Horizon View will ignore the AD user or group site assignments when assigning desktops to users. Refer to the *Modifying a Horizon View global entitlement* section of this chapter for instructions on updating the global entitlement settings after it has been created.

For each command shown in this section, we will see both the command syntax as well as a demonstration of the command being executed in our own Horizon View environment. Refer to the following steps:

1. To assign an AD user account to a site, we use the following command, which can be run on any Connection Server in the federated pod:

    ❑ lmvutil.cmd --authAs user --authDomain domain
      --authPassword password --createUserHomeSite --userName
      "domain\userName" --siteName "site" --entitlementName
      "name"

```
Administrator: C:\Windows\System32\cmd.exe                    _ □ X

c:\Program Files\VMware\VMware View\Server\tools\bin>lmvutil.cmd --authAs svc-vi
ew --authDomain vjason --authPassword Password123 --createUserHomeSite --userNam
e "vjason\elehnsherr" --siteName "RTP" --entitlementName "Global-Finance"
```

2. To assign an AD security group to a site, we use the following command, which can be run on any Connection Server in the federated pod:

   ❑ ```
     lmvutil.cmd --authAs user --authDomain domain
     --authPassword password --createGroupHomeSite
     --groupName "domain\groupName" --siteName "site"
     --entitlementName "name"
     ```

> As referenced earlier, prior to running this command, you would need to add the `Santa-Clara-Finance` AD security group to the global entitlement before assigning it to the `Santa-Clara` Horizon View site. If this is not done, an error will be displayed and the assignment will not be completed. Refer to step 4 in the previous section for instructions on how to add additional AD security groups to the global entitlement.

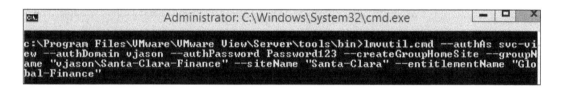

Since the AD user Horizon View site-assignment process must be performed using the command line one user at a time, it is much simpler to assign sites to the AD security groups instead and place the users in the appropriate security group based on their location or other requirements.

## How it works...

The `lmvutil.cmd` command-line utility assigns AD users and groups to Horizon View home sites. The following table outlines additional command-line switches that are used as part of the site assignment. As previously noted, these switches are case-sensitive and each is preceded by two dashes.

| Command-line switch | Description |
| --- | --- |
| `--createGroupHomeSite` | This is used when assigning a home site to an AD security group. |
| `--createUserHomeSite` | This is used when assigning a home site to an AD user account. |
| `--description` | This is optional; it is used to create a description for a Horizon View site. |
     ```

Command-line switch	Description
`--entitlementName`	This is optional; it is used to specify which global entitlement is to be associated with the Horizon View home site. If no entitlement name is provided, the assignment will be global and will apply to all global entitlements.
`--groupName`	This is used when assigning home sites to AD security groups. The group should be provided in the `domain\groupName` format.
`--siteName`	This is used to specify which Horizon View site will be assigned to the AD user or group.
`--userName`	This is used when assigning home sites to AD users. The group should be provided in the `domain\userName` format.

There's more...

Since a Horizon View home site can be set at both the AD user and security group level, it is important to understand what the effective home site is. Using the `lmvutil --resolveUserHomeSite` command-line switch, we can determine the effective home site. The full syntax for the command is as follows:

- `lmvutil.cmd --authAs user --authDomain domain --authPassword password --resolveUserHomeSite --entitlementName "name" --userName "domain\userName"`

In the following screenshot, we see the effective home site for a user whose AD account was set to the `RTP` home site, while the AD security group they are a member of is set to `Santa-Clara` as the home site. Based on the configuration, Horizon View has determined that the effective home site is `RTP`.

Reviewing your Horizon View Federated Pod configuration

In this recipe, we will review the syntax for several different commands used for Horizon View Federated Pod Administration. These commands build upon those reviewed earlier in this chapter, reusing many of the same command-line switches.

Getting ready

Several commands exist for viewing the configuration of our Federated Pod. Using these commands, we can verify that each of the commands used earlier in this chapter was completed successfully and accomplished what we meant to accomplish.

To view the configuration of a Federated Pod, command-line access to one of the Connection Servers in the federated pod is required.

How to do it...

In this section, we will demonstrate several different commands that are used to display the configuration of a Horizon View federated pod.

Viewing Horizon View global entitlements

The following command displays all of the global entitlements that have been created in our Horizon View federated pod:

- ```
  lmvutil.cmd --authAs user --authDomain domain --authPassword
  password --listGlobalEntitlements
  ```

Viewing desktop pools in a global entitlement

The following command displays all desktop pools that have been added to the specified global entitlement:

- ```
  lmvutil.cmd --authAs user --authDomain domain --authPassword
  password --entitlementName "name" --listAssociatedPools
  ```

Viewing AD group entitlements

The following command displays all of the global entitlements associated with the specified AD security group. The `--entitlementName` switch is optional:

- ```
  lmvutil.cmd --authAs user --authDomain domain --authPassword
  password --listEntitlements --entitlementName "name"
  --groupName "domain\groupName"
  ```
  ```

Viewing AD user entitlements

The following command displays all of the global entitlements associated with the specified AD user account. The `--entitlementName` switch is optional:

> ▸ `lmvutil.cmd --authAs user --authDomain domain --authPassword password --listEntitlements --entitlementName "name" --userName "domain\userName"`

Viewing AD user-dedicated user assignments

The following command displays dedicated Horizon View assignments associated with the specified AD user account. The `--listUserAssignments` switch is required, while one of the other switches (`--userName`, `--entitlementName`, `--podName`, and `--siteName`), at the minimum, are required:

> ▸ `lmvutil.cmd --authAs user --authDomain domain --authPassword password --listUserAssignments --userName "domain\userName" --entitlementName "name" --podName "name" --siteName "name"`

Viewing an AD user account's Horizon View home site

The following command displays the Horizon View home site assigned to the specified AD user account. The `--entitlementName` switch can also be supplied in order to refine the list of results returned:

> ▸ `lmvutil.cmd --authAs user --authDomain domain --authPassword password --showUserHomeSites --userName "domain\userName"`

The following screenshot shows you the sample output of this command. Were the user a member of additional global entitlements, they would also be displayed when this command is run:

Viewing an AD security group's Horizon View home site

The following command displays the home site assigned to the specified AD security group. The `--entitlementName` switch might also be supplied to refine the list of results returned:

> ▸ `lmvutil.cmd --authAs user --authDomain domain --authPassword password --showGroupHomeSites --groupName "domain\userName"`

The output of this command will be similar to that of the previous example where the home sites of an AD user account were displayed. Similar to that command, if the security group was a member of multiple global entitlements, each would be listed.

Viewing the Horizon View pods that are members of the federated pod

The following command displays the pods that have been added to the federated pod:

▸ ```
lmvutil.cmd --authAs user --authDomain domain --authPassword
password --listPods
```

### Viewing the Horizon View sites defined in the federated pod

The following command displays each of the sites that have been defined in the Federated Pod:

▸ ```
lmvutil.cmd --authAs user --authDomain domain --authPassword
password --listSites
```

How it works...

The following is a list of the `lmvutil.cmd` command-line switches and the accompanying description that were used in this section to view the configuration of objects in a Horizon View Federated Pod:

Command-line switch	Description
`--listAssociatedPools`	This lists desktop pools that have been added to the specified global entitlement.
`--listEntitlements`	This is used to display the entitlements assigned to a specific AD user or group.
`--listGlobalEntitlements`	This lists the global entitlements that have been created in the Federated Pod.
`--listPods`	This lists the pods that have been added to the federated pod.
`--listSites`	This lists the Horizon View sites defined in the Federated Pod.
`--listUserAssignments`	This lists the dedicated Horizon View assignments for a specific AD user.
`--showGroupHomeSites`	This displays the Horizon View home site assigned to a specific AD group.
`--showUserHomeSites`	This displays the Horizon View home site assigned to a specific AD user.

Modifying Horizon View Federated Pod objects

In this recipe, we will review how to modify various objects within a Federated Pod after they have been deployed. The objects include pods, global entitlements, and sites.

Getting ready

Multiple commands exist for modifying objects in a Federated Pod. Using these commands, we can make changes to the items we created earlier in this chapter.

To modify objects in a Horizon View Federated Pod, command-line access to one of the Connection Servers in the federated pod is required.

How to do it...

In this section, we will demonstrate several different commands that are used to modify the configuration of a Federated Pod.

Modifying Horizon View pods

The following command-line switches are used to update the configuration of a pod within a federated pod. The primary command-line switch that must be used to update the global entitlement is `--updatePod`, to which you add any additional switches that you might need. The following command is an example of how the `--updatePod` command-line option is used:

▶ ```
lmvutil.cmd --authAs user --authDomain domain --authPassword
password --updatePod --podName "name" --newPodName "newName"
```

### Modifying a Horizon View global entitlement

The following command-line switches are used to update a global entitlement after it has been created. The primary command-line switch that must be used to update the global entitlement is `--updateGlobalEntitlement`, to which you add any additional switches that you might need. The following command is an example of how the `--updateGlobalEntitlement` command-line option is used:

▶ ```
lmvutil.cmd --authAs user --authDomain domain --authPassword
password --updateGlobalEntitlement --entitlementName "name"
--enabled
```

Modifying Horizon View sites

The following command-line switches are used to update the configuration of a site within a federated pod. The primary command-line switch that must be used to update the global entitlement is `--editSite`, to which you add any additional switches that you might need. The following command is an example of how the `--editSite` command-line option is used:

▶ `lmvutil.cmd --authAs user --authDomain domain --authPassword`
`password --editSite --siteName "name" --newSiteName "newName"`

How it works...

The following is a list of the `lmvutil.cmd` command-line switches, and the accompanying description, that were used in this section to modify objects in a Horizon View Federated Pod:

Command-line switch	Description
`--disableFromHome`	This is used to disable the `--fromHome` option if it was previously enabled.
`--disableMultipleSessionAutoClean`	This is used to disable the `--multipleSessionAutoClean` option if it was previously enabled.
`--disableRequiredHomeSite`	This is used to disable the `--requiredHomeSite` option if it was previously enabled.
`--editSite`	This is required; it is used alongside other commands in order to edit the configuration of a Horizon View site.
`--enabled`	This is used to enable a global entitlement that is disabled or was created with the `--disabled` option.
`--newPodName`	This is used to specify a new pod name for a Horizon View pod.
`--newSiteName`	This is used to specify a new site name for a Horizon View pod.
`--updateGlobalEntitlement`	This is required; it is used alongside other commands to edit the configuration of a global entitlement.
`--updatePod`	This is required; it is used alongside other commands to edit the configuration of a Horizon View pod.

Removing objects from your Federated Pod or global entitlements

The commands referenced in this section focus on removing different objects from your federated pod or the global entitlements contained within it.

Getting ready

Multiple commands exist for removing objects in a Horizon View Federated Pod. Using these commands, we can undo changes to or remove objects that we have configured earlier in this chapter.

To remove objects from a Federated Pod, command-line access to one of the Connection Servers in the federated pod is required.

How to do it...

In this section, we will demonstrate several different commands that are used to remove objects from a Horizon View Federated Pod.

Removing a Horizon View pod from a pod federation

The following command is used to remove a pod from a pod federation. It must be run from a Connection Server located in the pod that is being removed:

▶
```
lmvutil.cmd --authAs user --authDomain domain --authPassword
password --unjoin
```

Removing a desktop pool from a global entitlement

The following command is used to remove a Horizon View desktop pool from a global entitlement:

▶
```
lmvutil.cmd --authAs user --authDomain domain --authPassword
password --removePoolAssociation --entitlementName "name"
--poolId "poolId"
```

Removing an AD user or group from a global entitlement

The following commands are used to remove an AD user account or security group from a global entitlement. The commands differ slightly based on whether or not a user or security group is being removed, so both are shown.

To remove an AD user account, use the following command:

- ► `lmvutil.cmd --authAs user --authDomain domain --authPassword password --removeUserEntitlement --userName "domain\userName" --entitlementName "name"`

To remove an AD security group, use the following command:

- ► `lmvutil.cmd --authAs user --authDomain domain --authPassword password --removeGroupEntitlement --groupName "domain\ groupName" --entitlementName "name"`

Removing an AD user or group Horizon View home site association

The following commands are used to remove the home site assignment from either an AD user or a security group. The commands differ slightly based on whether or not the site assignment is being removed from a user or a security group, so both are shown.

To remove a site assignment from an AD user account, use the following command:

- ► `lmvutil.cmd --authAs user --authDomain domain --authPassword password --deleteUserHomeSite --userName "domain\userName" --entitlementName "name"`

To remove a site assignment from an AD security group, use the following command:

- ► `lmvutil.cmd --authAs user --authDomain domain --authPassword password --deleteGroupHomeSite --groupName "domain\groupName" --entitlementName "name"`

Deleting a Horizon View home site

The following command is used to delete a site from a federated pod:

- ► `lmvutil.cmd --authAs user --authDomain domain --authPassword password --deleteSite --siteName "name"`

Deleting a global entitlement

The following command is used to delete a global entitlement from a federated pod:

- ► `lmvutil.cmd --authAs user --authDomain domain --authPassword password --deleteGlobalEntitlement --entitlementName "name"`

Forcibly removing a Horizon View pod from a Federated Pod

The following command is used to forcibly remove a pod from a pod federation and is typically only used when the pod is no longer available. It can be run from any Connection Server available so long as it is not one located in the pod that is being removed:

- ▸ `lmvutil.cmd --authAs user --authDomain domain --authPassword password --ejectPod --pod "podName"`

How it works...

The following is a list of the `lmvutil.cmd` command-line switches, and the accompanying description, that were used in this section to remove objects from a Horizon View Federated Pod:

Command-line switch	Description
`--deleteGlobalEntitlement`	This deletes a global entitlement.
`--deleteGroupHomeSite`	This removes a site assignment from an AD group.
`--deleteSite`	This deletes a Horizon View home site from the Federated Pod.
`--deleteUserHomeSite`	This removes a site assignment from an AD user account.
`--ejectPod`	This forcibly removes a pod from a pod federation.
`--removeGroupEntitlement`	This removes an AD group from a Horizon View global entitlement.
`--removePoolAssociation`	This removes a desktop pool from a Horizon View global entitlement.
`--removeUserEntitlement`	This removes an AD user account from a Horizon View global entitlement.
`--unjoin`	This removes a pod from a pod federation.

Disabling the Horizon View Cloud Pod Architecture feature

The following command is used to disable the Horizon View Cloud Pod Architecture feature. It is only required to be run on a single Connection Server across the entire pod federation.

Getting ready

To disable a Federated Pod, command-line access to one of the Connection Servers in the federated pod is required.

How to do it...

Use the following command:

- `lmvutil.cmd --authAs user --authDomain domain --authPassword password --uninitialize`

How it works...

The following is a list of the `lmvutil.cmd` command line switches, and the accompanying description, that were used in this section to disable a Horizon View Federated Pod:

Command-line switch	Description
`--uninitialize`	This is used to disable the Cloud Pod components on each Connection Server that is a member of the federated pod. This includes any and all configuration data related to the federated pod configuration, such as Horizon View global entitlements, individual AD user or group entitlements, and sites.

3
Horizon View Installation, Backup, and Recovery Using the CLI

In this chapter, we will cover the following recipes:

- ▸ Automating the installation of Horizon View Connection Servers
- ▸ Automating the installation of Horizon View Composer
- ▸ Performing Horizon View Connection Server backups
- ▸ Performing Horizon View Connection Server recoveries
- ▸ Performing a Horizon View Composer backup
- ▸ Performing Horizon View Composer recoveries

Introduction

This chapter discusses how to use the VMware Horizon View CLI to perform several key tasks involving the installation, backup, and recovery of different Horizon View components. Using the information provided in this chapter, we will be able to develop scripts that we can use to silently install View Connection, Security, and Composer servers as well as back up and restore critical configuration data.

This chapter is limited strictly to those commands that are unique to the Horizon View CLI tools and installation packages. This chapter discusses Horizon View command-line tools, such as the `vdmadmin.exe` application, which offers us some of the same capabilities that are also found in the **Horizon View PowerCLI cmdlets**. *Chapter 4*, *Managing Horizon View with PowerCLI*, will discuss the PowerCLI cmdlets at length, which is why this chapter focuses solely on commands that are unique to the CLI tools.

Automating the installation of Horizon View Connection Servers

The procedure for installing VMware Horizon View has not changed much over the last few years, even if the features of the product itself have. Other than the removal of the Horizon View Transfer Server option, starting with Horizon View Horizon View 6, the installation process is the same as it was with Horizon View 5.

Getting ready

In this section, we will learn how to install the Connection Server software using command-line options, which enables us to perform fully automated, silent installations. These commands can be used with automation platforms such as **vCloud Automation Center** (`http://www.vmware.com/products/vcloud-automation-center`) or **Microsoft System Center Configuration Manager** (`http://www.microsoft.com/en-us/server-cloud/products/system-center-2012-r2-configuration-manager/default.aspx`) to automate the deployment of new Horizon View pods or even to add replica Connection Servers to an existing pod.

This installation is performed directly on the Windows server that will host the Connection Server role using the Connection Server installation executable.

How to do it...

In this section, we will demonstrate how to perform an unattended installation of Horizon View standard, replica, and security servers.

The sample command-line installation of a standard Horizon View Connection Server

The following command shows us a sample syntax for a command-line installation of a standard Connection Server, which is also known as the first Connection Server in a pod. The highlighted text should be replaced with values that apply to our environment. Of the command-line options shown, only VDM_SERVER_RECOVERY_PWD_REMINDER is optional:

VMware-viewconnectionserver-x86_64-y.y.y-xxxxxx.exe /s /v"/qn VDM_SERVER_ INSTANCE_TYPE=1

VDM_INITIAL_ADMIN_SID=X-X-X-X-X-X VDM_SERVER_RECOVERY_PWD=Password

VDM_SERVER_RECOVERY_PWD_REMINDER="Password reminder""

Refer to the *Horizon View Connection Server command-line options* section of this chapter for an explanation of each command-line option.

Use the VMware-viewconnectionserver-x86_64-y.y.y-xxxxxx.exe /? command to display all of the command-line options, including ones not used or required during installation.

Note that if your Connection Server recovery password includes spaces, you will need to place the password value within quotes. In the example provided, the recovery password command-line switch will appear as follows: VDM_SERVER_RECOVERY_PWD="four word recovery password".

The following screenshot shows you this command being used to perform a silent installation of a standard Connection Server. In this example, we are granting administrative access to the AD security group whose SID we obtained in the *How to obtain Active Directory object security identifiers* section.

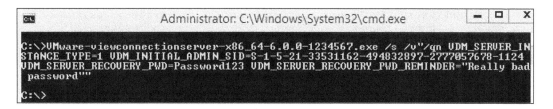

The sample command-line installation of a replica Horizon View Connection Server

The following command shows you a sample syntax for a command-line installation of a replica Connection Server. A replica server is used to provide high availability for the Connection Servers as well as support for additional Client connections. The text highlighted should be replaced with values that apply to our environment. In this example, we are using only those commands that are explicitly required to install a replica Connection Server:

```
VMware-viewconnectionserver-x86_64-y.y.y-xxxxxx.exe /s /v"/qn VDM_SERVER_
INSTANCE_TYPE=2
```

```
ADAM_PRIMARY_NAME=ExistingViewServerFQDN"
```

The following screenshot shows this command being used to perform a silent installation of a replica Connection Server. In this example, we are creating a replica of the `viewcs01.vjason.local` Connection Server:

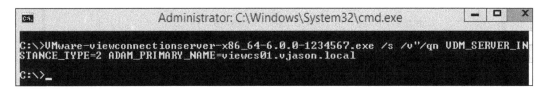

The sample command-line installation of a Horizon View Security Server

The following command shows us a sample syntax for a command-line installation of a Security Server. The highlighted text should be replaced with values that apply to our environment, although some values, such as ports and protocols, are shown set to their suggested values:

```
VMware-viewconnectionserver-x86_64-y.y.y-xxxxxx.exe /s /v"/qn VDM_
SERVER_INSTANCE_TYPE=3 VDM_SERVER_NAME=IPorFQDNofPairingConnectionS
erver VDM_SERVER_SS_EXTURL=https://ExternalFQDNofSecurityServer:443
VDM_SERVER_SS_PCOIP_IPADDR=X.X.X.X VDM_SERVER_SS_PCOIP_TCPPORT=4172
VDM_SERVER_SS_PCOIP_UDPPORT=4172 VDM_SERVER_SS_BSG_EXTURL=https://
ExternalFQDNofSecurityServer:8443
VDM_SERVER_SS_PWD=secret""
```

Refer to the *Horizon View Security Server command-line options* section of this chapter for an explanation of each command-line option.

If your security server password includes spaces, you will need to place the password value within quotes. In the example provided, the security server pairing the password's command-line switch will appear as follows:

▸ `VDM_SERVER_SS_PWD="`**`four word secret password`**`""`

Since this is the last value provided in the sample command, it would also need a second quote at the end, as shown.

The following screenshot shows this command being used to perform a silent installation of an additional Security Server. In this example, we are pairing the Security Server with the `viewcs01.vjason.local` Connection Server using a previously configured pairing password of `1234` and setting the PCoIP IP address and external URL as shown:

How it works...

The same Connection Server installer file is used to install both standard and replica Connection Servers as well as Security Servers. This section will focus on standard and replica Connection Servers only; Security Servers are discussed in *The sample command-line installation of a Horizon View Security Server* section of this chapter.

When we perform a silent installation of the Connection Server software, the data recovery password is logged in the installer's `vminst.log` file. This logfile should be edited to remove the password, and a global data recovery password set using the procedure outlined in the *How to set a global Horizon View recovery password* section of this chapter.

Horizon View Connection Server's command-line options

The following table provides a detailed list of the different command-line options that can be provided when performing a command-line installation of a standard or replica Connection Server. Note that some command-line options only apply to replica Connection Servers. These include the `ADAM_PRIMARY_NAME` and `ADAM_PRIMARY_PORT` properties.

Property	Description	Default Value
`ADAM_PRIMARY_NAME`	This is optional; it is used only when installing replica Connection Servers. It provides the hostname or IP address of the existing Connection Server instance to be replicated.	Not set
`ADAM_PRIMARY_PORT`	This is optional; it is used only when installing replica Connection Servers. It is the LDAP port of the existing Connection Server instance to be replicated.	Not set
`FWCHOICE`	This is optional; it is used to configure the Windows firewall for the Connection Server instance. Configure the firewall = 1 Do not configure = 2	1 (Configure firewall)

`INSTALLDIR`	This is optional; it is the path and folder in which the Connection Server software is installed.	`%ProgramFiles%\`
		`VMware\VMware`
		`View\Server`

`VDM_INITIAL_ADMIN_SID`	This is optional; it is the AD **security identifier (SID)** of the initial user or group that is authorized with full administration rights in Horizon View. The default value is the SID of the local administrators group on the Connection Server computer.	`S-1-5-32-544` (this is the SID of the local administrators' group on the target server)

Property	Description	Default Value
VDM_SERVER_INSTANCE_ TYPE	This is optional; it is a type of Horizon View server installation. Standard installation = 1 Replica installation = 2 Security server installation = 3	1 (this is a standard installation; it creates a new pod)
VDM_SERVER_RECOVERY_ PWD	This is the data recovery password. It is required only for replica Connection Servers if the global data recovery password is not set using the Horizon View global settings menu. The password must be between 1 and 128 characters in length.	This is not set, although the user must supply replica server installations if a global data recovery password is not set. It is required for standard Connection Servers.
VDM_SERVER_RECOVERY_ PWD_REMINDER	This is optional; it is the data recovery password reminder.	Not set

Horizon View Security Server's command-line options

While the Security Server is installed using the same installer as the standard and replica Connection Servers, only the following three command-line options apply to Security Server installations:

- ▶ FWCHOICE
- ▶ INSTALLDIR
- ▶ VDM_SERVER_INSTANCE_TYPE

Refer to the *Horizon View Connection Server's command-line options* section of this chapter for an explanation of each of these command-line options.

The following table provides a detailed list of the different command-line options that can be provided when performing a command-line installation of a Security Server. These command-line options apply only to Security Server installations.

Property	Description	Default Value
VDM_SERVER_NAME	This is the hostname or IP address of the existing Connection Server instance to be paired with the security server.	Not set
VDM_SERVER_SS_BSG_EXTURL	This is the Blast Secure Gateway's external URL. The URL must contain the HTTPS protocol, an externally resolvable security server name, and the port number (8443 by default).	Not set
VDM_SERVER_SS_EXTURL	This is the external URL of the security server. The URL must contain the protocol, externally resolvable security server name, and port number. HTTPS is the suggested protocol and 443 is the suggested port.	Not set
VDM_SERVER_SS_FORCE_IPSEC	This is optional; it forces IPsec to be used between the security server and its paired Connection Server instance. Force IPsec = 1 Allow pairing without IPsec = 2	1 (Force IPsec) If IPsec is forced but the pairing Connection Server does not have IPsec enabled, the installation will fail.
VDM_SERVER_SS_PWD	This the security server pairing password.	Not set
VDM_SERVER_SS_PCOIP_IPADDR	This is the hostname or IP address of the existing Connection Server instance to be paired with the security server.	Not set

Property	Description	Default Value
VDM_SERVER_SS_PCOIP_TCPPORT	This is the PCoIP Secure Gateway external TCP port number.	4172
VDM_SERVER_SS_PCOIP_UDPPORT	This is the PCoIP Secure Gateway external UDP port number.	4172

How to obtain Active Directory object security identifiers

When installing the Connection Server software using the command line, we have the option of specifying an Active Directory (AD) user or group that will have administrative access to the pod. This is done using the VDM_INITIAL_ADMIN_SID property and by supplying the AD SID of the user or group for which we wish to have administrative permissions. If this value is not supplied, administrative access will be granted to the local administrators group on the server where the Connection Server was installed.

While the SID can be viewed in the **Active Directory Users and Computers** console (**ADUC**), it cannot be copied, which makes creating scripts difficult, as the SID is a lengthy random string of characters that must be copied manually. Fortunately, we can use **Windows PowerShell** to obtain the SID, at which point, it can be copied straight from the PowerShell console.

The following two PowerShell commands can be used to display the SID of an AD user or security group. The highlighted text should be replaced with the AD user or group name of the object we wish to obtain the SID for:

```
$name="UserorGroupName"

(New-Object
System.Security.Principal.NTAccount($name)).Translate([System.Securit
y.Principal.SecurityIdentifier]).value
```

The following screenshot shows this command being used to obtain the SID for both a security group (View_Admins) and an AD user account (svc-view):

```
PS C:\> $name="View_Admins"
PS C:\> (New-Object System.Security.Principal.NTAccount($nam
e)).Translate([System.Security.Principal.SecurityIdentifier]
).value
S-1-5-21-33531162-494832897-2777057678-1124
PS C:\> $name="svc-view"
PS C:\> (New-Object System.Security.Principal.NTAccount($nam
e)).Translate([System.Security.Principal.SecurityIdentifier]
).value
S-1-5-21-33531162-494832897-2777057678-1108
PS C:\>
```

Only one SID can be granted administrative access to Horizon View when the software is being installed; additional administrators can be specified in the Horizon View Manager Admin console by navigating to **View Configuration | Administrators**, if required.

How to set a global Horizon View recovery password

By default, when installing the Connection Server software, we are asked to provide a recovery password, which that is used in the event that we need to restore the Horizon View **Active Directory Lightweight Directory Services** (**AD LDS**) database. To ensure consistency across our entire pod, we should set a global recovery password that is recorded in the Horizon View AD LDS database and subsequently replicated to all of the Connection Servers in the pod.

Once a global recovery password has been created, any additional Connection Servers that are added to the pod will not be required to provide a recovery password during the installation process.

To create a global recovery password, use the Horizon View Manager Admin console by navigating to **View Configuration | Global Settings | Change data recovery password**, as highlighted in the following screenshot:

Automating the installation of Horizon View Composer

In this recipe, we will learn how to perform a silent installation of Horizon View Composer, which is used in environments that will host linked-clone-based virtual desktops. One instance of Composer is required for each VMware vCenter Server linked to a pod.

Getting ready

When performing a silent installation of Horizon View Composer, the target server will be automatically rebooted. Ensure that this reboot operation will not impact the availability of any key services, particularly if Composer is being installed directly on the vCenter Server.

The installation of Horizon View Composer is performed directly on the Windows Server that will host the Composer role using the Horizon View Composer installation executable.

How to do it...

The following command shows you a sample syntax for a command-line installation of Horizon View Composer:

```
VMware-viewcomposer-y.y.y-xxxxxx.exe /s /v"/qn DB_DSN=DSNname
DB_USERNAME=DBusername DB_PASSWORD=DBpassword SSL_DEFAULTS=2
SSL_CERTIFICATE=CertificateThumbprint"
```

In this example, we have elected to use an existing SSL certificate already installed on the server which hosts our Composer Server. We can perform this by setting `SSL_DEFAULTS=2` and providing the thumbprint for the target SSL certificate to the `SSL_CERTIFICATE=` command-line option.

> As with the other command-line installations, if the password contains a space, you must place the password value within quotes. In the example provided, the Composer data password command-line switch will appear as follows:
>
> `DB_PASSWORD="four word db password"`

The SSL certificate must be installed in the **Personal** certificate store in **Certificates (Local Computer)**, as shown in the following screenshot. The certificate thumbprint can be obtained by double-clicking on the certificate, selecting the **Details** tab, and then selecting the **Thumbprint** field as shown:

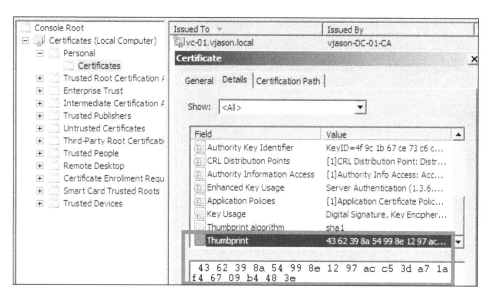

Refer to *Configuring SSL Certificates for View Servers* (https://pubs.vmware.com/horizon-view-60/index.jsp?topic=%2Fcom.vmware.horizon-view.installation.doc%2FGUID-80CC770D-327E-4A21-B382-786621B23C44.html) for additional information how to obtain and manage SSL certificates for both Horizon View Connection Servers and Horizon View Composer.

The following screenshot shows this command being used to perform a silent installation of a Horizon View Composer. In this example, we are configuring Composer to use a previously installed SSL certificate and have specified the required Composer database information. As shown in the screenshot, the spaces must be removed from the SSL thumbprint when including it in the command-line options:

In the event that we want to make Composer create and use a self-signed SSL certificate, we would simply need to exclude the SSL_DEFAULTS and SSL_CERTIFICATE command-line options.

How it works...

The following table provides a detailed list of the different command-line options that can be provided when performing a command-line installation on Horizon View Composer:

Property	Description	Default Value
DB_DSN	This is the Composer database data's source name (DSN).	Not set
DB_USERNAME	This is the Composer database's username.	Not set
DB_PASSWORD	This is the Composer database's password.	Not set
INSTALLDIR	This is the installation directory.	%ProgramFiles%\VMware\VMware View Composer\
SOAP_PORT	This is Composer's web access port.	Not set (18443 by default)
SSL_DEFAULTS	This generates a self-signed SSL certificate during the installation, which is equal to 1. It uses a previously installed SSL certificate (also requires the SSL_CERTIFICATE option) = 2.	1 (generates a new self-signed SSL certificate)

Property	Description	Default Value
SSL_ CERTIFICATE	This is used along with the SSL_ DEFAULTS option when selecting an existing SSL certificate. To use this, verify that the certificate is installed in the **Certificates** store by navigating to **Local Computer	Personal** and provide the thumbprint of the target certificate with any spaces removed.	Not set
UPGRADE_DB_ ACTION	This is used when upgrading an existing installation of Horizon View Composer. Upgrade the database = 1. Do not upgrade the database - 2.	1 (upgrade the database)

Performing Horizon View Connection Server backups

The data required to restore a Connection Server is stored in two different locations:

- The Horizon View Manager AD LDS database—replicated to each Connection Server in the pod
- The VMware vCenter Server database

Horizon View Composer also uses a database that contains critical configuration information related to linked clone desktops. Horizon View installations that utilize Composer will also need to back up the Composer database as part of their overall backup and recovery plan. Additionally, the Composer SSL certificates or RSA key container will also be required to be backed up. The procedure used to back up the Composer components is described in the *Backing up the Horizon View Composer SSL certificates* section of this chapter.

Getting ready

When planning backup strategies for federated Horizon View pods, remember that each pod within the pod federation must be backed up individually. While the pods replicate the entitlement information between them using a global AD LDS instance, that information alone is not enough to recover a single pod in the event of a disaster.

The backup process varies, depending on which specific component is being backed up.

This recipe will discuss two different backup operations, which include the vCenter Server database, the Horizon View AD LDS database, and the accompanying Composer database.

Backing up the vCenter Server database

The vCenter Server database should be backed up using whatever method is available within our environment. This includes options such as the following:

- Native backups based on the capabilities of the database platform, such as the **Microsoft SQL Server backup** or **Oracle Recovery Manager** (**RMAN**) backup.

- Third-party database backup solutions

There are no specific requirements with regard to database backup methodologies as long as we can recover the database to a previous state—either to the same database server or an alternate one. We should consult with our database server or backup software documentation if additional information on performing database backups is required.

Consult the VMware *vSphere Installation and Setup* guide (`http://pubs.vmware.com/vsphere-55/index.jsp#com.vmware.vsphere.install.doc/GUID-7C9A1E23-7FCD-4295-9CB1-C932F2423C63.html`) for additional information on how to back up the individual components of a vSphere installation.

Backing up the AD LDS database

The VMware Horizon View Connection Server AD LDS database contains key configuration data and should be backed up on a regular basis. By default, each Connection Server will perform a nightly backup of the AD LDS database at midnight (12:00 AM).

A limited number of changes to the Connection Server backup policy can be made within the Horizon View Manager Admin console. These changes include:

- The backup frequency

- The number of backups to be retained

- The backup folder location

- The data recovery password

The database backup time cannot be edited using the Horizon View Manager Admin console but only by manually editing the Horizon View AD LDS database. The procedure is described in the VMware KB article *1010285* (`http://kb.vmware.com/selfservice/microsites/search.do?language=en_US&cmd=displayKC&externalId=1010285`). Due to problems that can occur when manually editing the Horizon View AD LDS database, this value should not be changed unless there is an explicit need.

The following options can be configured using the following steps:

1. Navigate to **View Configuration | Servers | Connection Servers**.

2. Highlight the targeted Connection Server and click on **Edit** to open the **Edit Connection Server Settings** window.

3. Click on the **Backup** tab and make the desired changes. Refer to the following screenshot for an example:

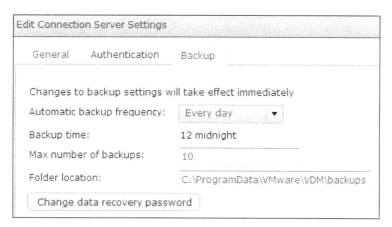

How it works...

The backup processes for the vCenter Server, Horizon View AD LDS, and Composer databases all rely on the native features of each respective database software. Due to the relationship between the data contained within each of these databases, it is important that these native backup features be used, rather than relying solely on traditional full backups of the servers that host them.

Additionally, the Horizon View AD LDS database is replicated to other Connection Servers. Were this server restored using anything other than native Horizon View AD LDS backups, the replication process might be corrupted.

Horizon View also includes a command-line utility named vdmexport.exe, which can be used to perform manual backups of the Horizon View AD LDS database only. To display options for this utility, execute it with a /? command-line switch such as vdmexport.exe /?. The following table shows you the command-line options available for the vdmexport.exe utility:

Command-line switch	Description
-f	This is required; it is the name of the encrypted backup file, for example, vdmexport.exe -f MyBackup.ldf.
-v	This is optional. It exports the data in a plain text format with no encryption; it cannot be used when the -c switch is used.
-c	This is optional. It exports the cleansed data in the plain text format; it cannot be used when the -v switch is used. When cleansed, the backup will not include passwords and other sensitive data and cannot be used to restore the Horizon View LDAP configuration, if required.

Performing Horizon View Connection Server recoveries

The process to restore a Connection Server varies based on what led to the need to perform a restore.

If we are restoring all of our Connection Servers in a pod from scratch, the Composer database will need to be restored as part of the recovery process, as its contents are tied to the information in the Horizon View AD LDS database.

Getting ready

In situations where it is required to restore multiple Horizon View-related databases at once, we should use backups that were taken as closely together as is possible when performing the restore. Ideally, backup plans for all Horizon View-related components, including the VMware vCenter Server database, should coincide as closely as possible to ensure that the data shared between them is consistent. The further apart the backups are taken, the less likely it is that the contents will match when a restore is required. This could lead to issues that require the assistance of VMware support, as items within one of more of the databases might need to be removed or edited.

How to do it...

In this recipe, we will discuss the how to restore the vCenter Server and Horizon View AD LDS databases. Additionally, we will discuss the proper method for fully removing a Connection Server from an existing pod.

Restoring a single Horizon View Connection Server

Horizon View configuration settings are stored in the local AD LDS database on each Connection Server. If the Connection Server software becomes corrupt and the pod contains at least one other functioning Connection Server, we can simply uninstall and reinstall it without having to perform any additional configuration.

If a Connection Server cannot be accessed due to a hardware or software failure and we need to replace it, we must remove it from the AD LDS replication set first. The following steps should be executed from one of the remaining functioning Connection Servers in the pod. In the example, we will remove the server named `viewcs02.vjason.local` from the AD LDS replication set using the `vdmadmin.exe` utility:

1. Navigate to the `%Program Files%\VMware\VMware View\Server\tools\bin` directory.

2. Execute the `vdmadmin.exe -S -r -s viewcs02.vjason.local` command.

The failed Connection Server `viewcs02.vjason.local` has been removed from the AD LDS replica set and can now be replaced.

To restore or replace the server, simply reinstall the Connection Server software on a new server, selecting the **View Replica Server** option when prompted, and the software will install and the server will be joined to the existing pod. We might also choose to silently install the Horizon View Composer software using the procedure described in *The sample command-line installation of a replica Horizon View Connection Server* section of this chapter.

Restoring the Horizon View Connection Server AD LDS database

The Connection Server's AD LDS database can be restored using the `vdmimport.exe` command-line utility, which is located in the Connection Server installation drive in the `%Program Files%\VMware\VMware View\Server\tools\bin` directory. The utility requires administrative access to the pod, so the AD user account that is used to run it must have administrative rights. If the AD account does not have sufficient rights, errors will be displayed during the restore operation.

The Horizon View AD LDS database is not usually restored unless all the Connection Servers were lost or if the AD LDS database was found to be corrupt. If we are only having problems with a single Connection Server, we should refer to the *Removing a Horizon View Connection Server* section of this chapter for instructions on how to restore or remove just that server.

The restore operation requires two commands:

1. Decrypt the AD LDS database backup titled `backup.ldf` to a file titled `decrypted.ldf`. Replace the password with the data recovery password specified during the installation of the first Connection Server or our global Horizon View recovery password if it was configured: `vdmimport -d -p password -f backup.ldf > decrypted.ldf`.

2. Restore the decrypted backup: `Vdmimport -f decrypted.ldf`.

Once the restore is complete, the remaining Connection Servers will replicate the restored data into their local Horizon View AD LDS databases.

> In the event that vSphere snapshots are used to restore a Horizon View Connection Server to a previous state, the Connection Server will stop replicating its AD LDS database to other Connection Servers. In the event that we wish to retain the configuration contained within the AD LDS database on the server where the snapshot was reverted, all other Connection Servers within the same View installation will need their Connection Server software and AD LDS database uninstalled and reinstalled from scratch. Refer to the VMware Horizon *View Upgrades* guide (`https://pubs.vmware.com/horizon-view-60/index.jsp#com.vmware.horizon-view.upgrade.doc/GUID-E3607442-8936-49A8-97B4-722D012FDF1E.html`) for additional information on what is required if a Connection Server is reverted to an earlier vSphere snapshot.

Restoring the VMware vCenter Server database

The VMware vCenter Server database is restored using the same tools that were used to perform the backup. We should consult with our database server or backup software documentation for information on how to perform the restore operation.

Refer to the VMware *vSphere Installation and Setup* guide (`http://pubs.vmware.com/vsphere-55/index.jsp#com.vmware.vsphere.install.doc/GUID-7C9A1E23-7FCD-4295-9CB1-C932F2423C63.html`) for additional information on how to restore the components of a VMware vSphere installation.

Removing a Horizon View Connection Server

The same `vdmadmin.exe` command should be used when we want to remove an existing Connection Server. To remove a Connection Server from our environment, perform the following steps:

1. Open Windows' **Programs and Features** control panel on the target server.
2. Uninstall the **VMware View Connection Server** software.
3. Uninstall the **AD LDS Instance VMwareVDMDS** software.

4. On any remaining Connection Server, execute the `vdmadmin.exe` command using the syntax provided in the *Restoring a single Horizon View Connection Server* section of this chapter. Supply the name of the server that we wish to remove in the command text.

These steps ensure that the target Connection Server has been removed from the Horizon View AD LDS database replication topology as well as the pod.

How it works...

The following table shows you the command-line options available for the `vdmimport.exe` utility:

Command-line switch	Description
`-f`	This is required; it is the name of the encrypted backup file to be decrypted or the decrypted backup file to be restored. Use it with the `-p` and `-d` command-line options when decrypting a backup file or by itself when performing a restore of a decrypted backup file. Encrypted backup files must be decrypted before they can be restored. Syntax: `-f MyBackup.ldf`.
`-p`	This provides the Horizon View recovery password; it is used to decrypt the backup prior to the restore; use it with the `-f` and `-d` command-line options. If the password includes spaces, you must place it within quotes. Syntax: `-p "two word password"`.
`-d`	This instructs the utility to decrypt the LDIF backup file; use it with the `-f` and `-p` command-line options.
`-i`	This is used to display information about a LDIF file; use it with the `-f` command-line option.

When using the `vdmimport.exe` utility to decrypt a Horizon View AD LDS backup LDIF file, you must specify an output file using the `> MyDecryptedBackupFile.ldf` format at the end of the command. A sample command used to decrypt an Horizon View AD LDS backup file would be as follows:

```
dmimport -d -p "View Restore Password" -f MyEncryptedBackup.ldf >
MyDecryptedBackup.ldf
```

With the backup file decrypted, we can now use the utility to restore it:

```
dmimport -f MyDecryptedBackup.ldf
```

Horizon View's `vdmadmin.exe` utility contains numerous options beyond the backup and restore operations described in this recipe. To learn about all of the options that the utility supports, either execute the utility with a `/?` command-line switch such as `vdmadmin.exe /?`, or refer to the VMware Horizon *View Administration* guide and section concerning *vdmadmin Command Options* (`https://pubs.vmware.com/horizon-view-60/index.jsp#com.vmware.horizon-view.administration.doc/GUID-360099AE-E0E3-49F7-9F4D-164A2F2C49D2.html`) for additional information on the different operations the utility can perform.

Performing a Horizon View Composer backup

The Connection Server backs up the Composer database as part of its own native backup process. This is the preferred method of backing up the Composer database, as it will be backed up at the same time as the Connection Server's AD LDS database. As these databases contain related information, it is critical that they be backed up at the same time.

Getting ready

The information required to restore Horizon View Composer is stored in two different locations:

▶ The Composer database

▶ The Horizon View Composer's SSL certificates or the RSA key container

The Composer database and SSL components should be backed up as part of a larger backup plan that includes the vCenter database, the Connection Server AD LDS database, and the Horizon View Event database. By default, each Connection Server backs up both the AD LDS database and the Composer databases to a folder on the Connection Server described in the *Backing up the AD LDS database* section of this chapter, which is `C:\ProgramData\VMware\VDM\backups`.

How to do it...

In this section, we will discuss how to back up the Horizon View Composer database, SSL certificates, and RSA key container.

Backing up the Horizon View Composer database

The default location for the Horizon View Composer database backups, which are performed by the Connection Server alongside the Horizon View AD LDS backup, is the `C:\ProgramData\VMware\VDM\backups` folder.

Each Connection Server in the pod performs the same backups and will have similar backup files. The Composer database's backups will have an `SVI` extension and will include the name of the Composer host server in the filename. In our example, the most recent Composer database backup file is titled `Backup-2014-0517000010-comp01_vjason_local.SVI`. `Comp-01` and is the name of the dedicated Horizon View Composer host server in our sample environment.

Backing up the Horizon View Composer SSL certificates

The process used to back up the default Composer SSL certificate requires that the Microsoft .NET Framework be installed on the Composer host server. The following steps explain how to back up the SSL certificates using the .NET `aspnet_regiis.exe` utility:

1. From a command prompt on the Composer host server, navigate to the `c:\Windows\Microsoft.NET\Framework\v2.0xxxxx` directory.

2. Execute the following command to export the Composer RSA key container to a local file named `keys.xml`:

   ```
   aspnet_regiis.exe -px "SviKeyContainer" "keys.xml" -pri
   ```

> The `keys.xml` file should be placed in an alternate folder rather than the Windows system folder in which the command was executed, as the Windows system folders are likely to be overwritten in the event of a restore. We can specify an alternative location by including the path in the `keys.xml` portion of the command, such as `c:\temp.keys.xml`.

The following screenshot shows you the expected output if the command was successful:

```
c:\Windows\Microsoft.NET\Framework\v2.0.50727>aspnet_regiis.exe -px "SviKeyConta
iner" "keys.xml" -pri
Exporting RSA Keys to file...
Succeeded!
```

The `keys.xml` file should be backed up on an alternative location to be used in the event that the Composer software needs to be installed on a new server.

 The VMware Horizon *View Installation* guide (`https://pubs.vmware.com/horizon-view-60/index.jsp#com.vmware.horizon-view.installation.doc/GUID-37D39B4F-5870-4188-8B11-B6C41AE9133C.html`) describes the process that is used to replace the SSL certificate of an existing Composer Server. During this process, we should have obtained a copy of the SSL certificate that can be used when restoring a Composer server from backups. If we choose to use a custom SSL certificate, we do not need to use the `aspnet_regiis` command to export the Composer RSA key container. During the creation of our custom SSL certificate, we should have been given a copy of it with the private key intact, which is what is required to perform a restore.

How it works...

Refer to the *Performing Horizon View Connection Server backups* section of this chapter or the *VMware Horizon View Administration* guide for additional information on how to configure the Horizon View backup process, which includes the Horizon View Composer database.

Refer to the Microsoft Developer Network article *ASP.NET IIS Registration Tool* (`http://msdn.microsoft.com/en-US/library/k6h9cz8h(v=vs.80).ASPX`) for a comprehensive list of the options for the `aspnet_regiis.exe` utility, which is used to back up the Composer RSA key container in the event that a custom Composer SSL certificate with accompanying private key is not used.

Performing Horizon View Composer recoveries

The same process is used either to recover or move Composer to a new host server. To retain the current settings, all that needs to be restored is the Composer database and either the RSA key container or the custom SSL certificate.

Getting ready

The Composer database should be restored using the native Horizon View command-line tool, which is `SviConfig.exe`. This tool is located within the Composer installation directory, which, by default, is in the following location on the drive where Composer was installed:

```
Program Files\VMware\VMware View Composer
```

We will need the following information to restore the database:

▸ **DSN**: This is the name of our DSN configured to use the Composer database on the Composer Server. In our sample server, the name is `composer`.

▸ **Composer database username**: In our sample server, the name is `composer`.

▸ **Composer database password**: In our sample server, the password is `Password123`.

▸ **Backup file path**: This is the location of the `Backup-2014-0517000010-comp01_vjason_local.SVI` file referenced in the *Backing up the Horizon View Composer database* section of this chapter. In our sample server, the file is located in `C:\Temp`.

As mentioned previously, when performing a Composer database restore, the Horizon View AD LDS database and VMware vCenter Server databases should also be restored using backups that were taken at similar times. If this is not done, inconsistencies across the databases might require the assistance of VMware Support in order to be fixed.

How to do it...

In this section, we will discuss how to restore the Horizon View Composer database, SSL certificates, and the RSA key container.

Restoring the Horizon View Composer database

The following steps outline the process used to restore the database using the information from our sample server:

1. Stop the **VMware Horizon View Composer** service.

2. From the command prompt, navigate to the Composer installation directory.

3. Execute the following command to restore the Composer database's backup:

```
Sviconfig.exe -operation=restoredata -dsnname=composer

-username=composer -password="Password123"

-backupfilepath="C:\Temp\Backup-2014-0517000010-
comp01_vjason_local.SVI"
```

4. The restore process should output several lines of status information. The last few lines of the output are shown in the following screenshot, the last of which indicates that the restore was successful:

```
Start processing the backup.
Object type AdConfigEntryDo found in the backup
Object type UcConfigEntryDo found in the backup
Object type AuthorizedUserDo found in the backup
Object type SequenceNumDo found in the backup
Object type VmNameDo found in the backup
Object type GuestComputerNameDo found in the backup
Object type ReplicaDo found in the backup
Object type DeploymentGroupDo found in the backup
Object type SimCloneDo found in the backup
Restoring data finished successfully.
```

5. Start the **VMware Horizon View Composer** service.

Horizon View Composer is now operating with the restored database.

Restoring the Horizon View Composer SSL certificates

The process to restore the Composer SSL certificates varies depending on the scenario. The following sections explain the procedure to be used based on whether or not we plan to reuse an existing SSL certificate.

Both of these procedures assume that we have already restored our Composer database and have also configured a DSN connection to that database on our Composer's host server.

Restoring Horizon View Composer with a new default SSL certificate

Prior to installing the Composer software, restore the RSA key container that was backed up in the *Backing up the Horizon View Composer SSL certificates* section. The following steps outline the full restore process:

1. Copy the `keys.xml` backup file to a location on the new Composer host server, preferably not a Windows system folder that can be overwritten in the event of a restore.

2. From the command prompt on the new Composer host server, navigate to the `c:\Windows\Microsoft.NET\Framework\v2.0xxxxx` directory. The xxxxx portion of the folder path will need to be updated to match whatever version of .NET 2.0 is installed on our Composer host server.

3. Execute the following command to import the Composer RSA key container. The following screenshot shows the expected output if the command was successful:

```
aspnet_regiis.exe -pi "SviKeyContainer" "keys.xml" -exp
```

```
c:\Windows\Microsoft.NET\Framework\v2.0.50727>aspnet_regiis.exe -pi "SviKeyConta
iner" "keys.xml" -exp
Importing RSA Keys from file..
Succeeded!
```

4. Reinstall Horizon View Composer using the procedure outlined in the *VMware Horizon View Installation* guide. Since this is a new server, Composer will note that no SSL certificates were found and will create a new one. We can also choose to silently install the Composer software.

Horizon View Composer is now ready to be linked to the Connection server using the steps provided in the VMware Horizon *View Administration* guide (`https://pubs.vmware.com/ horizon-view-60/index.jsp#com.vmware.horizon-view.installation.doc/ GUID-37D39B4F-5870-4188-8B11-B6C41AE9133C.html`).

Restoring Horizon View Composer with a custom SSL certificate

The process used to restore a Connection server with a custom SSL certificate requires the Microsoft Certificate MMC Snap-in, configured to access the **Certificates (Local Computer) | Personal** certificate store. The remaining options are configured during the installation of Composer. The following steps outline the full restore process:

1. Install the custom SSL certificate on the new Connection server using the procedure outlined in the *VMware Horizon View Installation* guide.

2. Reinstall Composer using the steps provided in the *VMware Horizon View Installation* guide. Since the SSL certificate has already been installed, select the **Use an existing SSL certificate** option, and select the designated certificate. We can also choose to silently install the Composer software using the procedure described in the *Automating the installation of Horizon View Composer* recipe of this chapter.

3. Complete the installation and reboot the Composer host server.

 Since we are reusing the same SSL certificate, it is important to remember that the new Composer host server should have the same computer name as the old one. As mentioned earlier, our certificate must have the private key intact in order for us to restore it.

Horizon View Composer is now ready to be linked to the Connection server using the procedure outlined in the VMware Horizon *View Administration* guide (`https://pubs.vmware.com/horizon-view-60/index.jsp#com.vmware.horizon-view.administration.doc/GUID-7EABB558-29DC-4F14-826A-B7FB6D7131B3.html`).

How it works...

Refer to the VMware Horizon View installation, administration, and upgrade guides for a comprehensive list of the features of the `SviConfig.exe` command-line utility, including those options discussed in this section related to the restore of the Horizon View Composer database.

Refer to the Microsoft Developer Network article *ASP.NET IIS Registration Tool* (`http://msdn.microsoft.com/en-US/library/k6h9cz8h(v=vs.80).ASPX`) for a comprehensive list of options for the `aspnet_regiis.exe` utility, which is used when using a new default self-signed Composer certificate when reinstalling Composer and using an existing Composer database.

4
Managing VMware Horizon View with PowerCLI

In this chapter, we will cover the following major recipes:

- ▶ Enabling remote management on a Horizon View Connection Server so that PowerShell can be used remotely
- ▶ Establishing a remote PowerShell session
- ▶ Viewing all the PowerCLI commands and their options
- ▶ Managing desktop pools with PowerCLI
- ▶ Creating an automatically provisioned linked-clone desktop pool
- ▶ Creating an automatically provisioned full-clone desktop pool
- ▶ Creating a manually provisioned desktop pool
- ▶ Creating a manual unmanaged desktop pool
- ▶ Creating a Microsoft Windows Remote Desktop Services (RDS) Pool
- ▶ Updating the Horizon View pools
- ▶ Creating a network label specifications
- ▶ Exporting network label specifications for linked-clone pools
- ▶ Exporting network label specifications for full-clone pools
- ▶ Retrieving the Horizon View Composer Server information
- ▶ Retrieving a list of the Horizon View desktop pools
- ▶ Removing desktop pools
- ▶ Entitling a desktop pool

- ▸ Entitling or unentitling an individual desktop
- ▸ Reviewing the desktop pool entitlement
- ▸ Refreshing a linked-clone desktop or pool
- ▸ Recomposing a linked-clone desktop pool
- ▸ Rebalancing a linked-clone desktop pool
- ▸ Updating the Horizon View global settings
- ▸ Updating the Horizon View connection broker settings
- ▸ Adding a vCenter Server to Horizon View
- ▸ Removing a vCenter Server from Horizon View
- ▸ Updating the settings of vCenter Server that is linked to Horizon View
- ▸ Monitoring the remote Horizon View sessions
- ▸ Resetting a Horizon View desktop
- ▸ Disconnecting the Horizon View Client session
- ▸ Logging Off the Horizon View Client Session
- ▸ Configuring the Horizon View license
- ▸ Retrieving the global Horizon View configuration data
- ▸ Retrieving the Horizon View connection broker information
- ▸ Retrieving a list of virtual machines that are managed by Horizon View
- ▸ Retrieving a list of physical machines
- ▸ Retrieving AD user or group Information
- ▸ Retrieving information about persistent data disks
- ▸ Retrieving the Horizon View event reports and their descriptions
- ▸ Retrieving the Horizon View event reports
- ▸ Retrieving the Horizon View infrastructure health monitors and their status
- ▸ Retrieving a list of the vCenter Servers linked to the Horizon View environment
- ▸ Retrieving a list of the Windows RDS Servers registered with Horizon View

Retrieving the Horizon View license information

VMware Horizon View provides 45 different PowerShell commands that you can use to configure, manage, and monitor the Horizon View environment. These commands are known as **Horizon View PowerCLI**, and they enable administrators to do everything from automating repetitive operations to using existing IT infrastructure management platforms in order to perform common tasks. While not every aspect of the Horizon View environment can be managed or configured using PowerCLI, most of the common settings can.

The Horizon View PowerCLI commands can only be executed against a single pod at a time; if you have multiple distinct pods, you must use separate PowerShell sessions for each. While each of these commands uses capital letters to identify individual words within the command, PowerCLI itself is not case-sensitive. You do not need to capitalize any part of the PowerCLI commands or the command options.

Using the information provided in this chapter, you should be able to reduce the time you spend in the **Horizon View Manager Admin** console by building scripts that can perform the actions more quickly.

The following values will be used to create our sample PowerCLI commands later in the chapter. Some portions of the text are in **bold**; these represent objects that are created automatically within vCenter but are not visible to the end user (such as **vm** or **Resources**) or objects that are unique to each environment (such as **host**, referring to a vSphere server hostname). These objects must be included in the PowerCLI command or it will not work.

Configuration object	Sample value
The AD domain name	vjason.local
The AD group used for example commands	Finance_View_Users
The AD user used for example commands	Erik Lensherr (vjason\elensherr)
The destination vCenter folder for Horizon View desktops, including the path	/RTP/Desktops
The linked-clone's OS disk storage	/RTP/**host**/DT-Cluster1/Datastore1
The linked-clone's persistent (user) data disk storage	/RTP/**host**/DT-Cluster1/Datastore2
The linked-clone's replica disk storage	/RTP/**host**/DT-Cluster1/Datastore3
For full-clone desktops, each datastore serves the same role. We still need to specify a destination datastore for our desktops, but only one is explicitly required with full-clones.	
Linked-clone desktops' parent VM, including the path	/RTP/**vm**/Master/Win81x32-LC
The vCenter datacenter	RTP
The vCenter server name	VC-01.vjason.local
The Horizon View vCenter AD service account	vjason\svc-view
The Composer Server AD account	vjason\svc-composer
The Composer AD domain	vjason.local
The Connection Server used	VIEWCS01.vjason.local
Horizon View Finance Users AD Group	Finance_View_Users
The Horizon View folder for Finance Pool	Finance
Virtual machine snapshot 1 name	0522
Virtual machine snapshot 2 name	0525

Configuration object	Sample value
The virtual machine template for full-clone desktops with the path	/RTP/**vm**/Master/Win81x32-FC
The vSphere cluster for desktops with the path	/RTP/**host**/DT-Cluster1
The vSphere resource pool for desktops with the path	/RTP/**host**/DT-Cluster1/**Resources**
vSphere Windows customization specification	View_Full_Clones

Enabling remote management on Windows

Unlike vSphere PowerCLI, VMware Horizon View does not include a standalone installer that is used to remotely manage Horizon View using PowerCLI. The PowerCLI commands will only work when executed from a Connection Server. To enable remote management, we must enable **Windows Remote Management** (**WinRM**) on at least one Connection Server in each pod that we want to manage.

WinRM is based on the **WS-Management Protocol**, which is a SOAP-based protocol that is used to enable interoperability between hardware and OSs from different vendors. We will use WinRM to establish remote PowerShell connections to a Connection Server; this will enable us to run commands from that server without actually having to log in to the server console.

How to do it...

In this recipe, we will configure WinRM to use HTTPS for an added measure of security. This ensures that, if we need to pass sensitive information over a WinRM session, it cannot be read in clear text. Consult Microsoft KB's article 2019527 (http://support.microsoft.com/kb/2019527) for information on how to obtain the SSL certificate required to enable WinRM HTTPS connections.

The following steps outline how to enable WinRM in Windows in the event that it has not been previously enabled:

1. Log in to the Connection Server that you will use for your remote sessions.

2. Enable and start the **Windows Remote Management (WS-Management)** service. This service should be set to start automatically.

3. From a Windows command prompt on the server, execute the following command in order to enable inbound WinRM requests over HTTPS:

```
winrm quickconfig -transport:https
```

4. When prompted, answer **y** to approve the operation, and verify that the operation succeeded, as shown in the following screenshot:

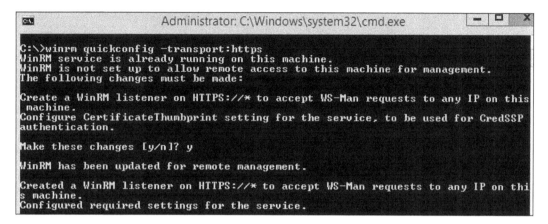

5. If the Windows firewall is enabled on the Connection Server, create a firewall rule that allows TCP port 5986 inbound. This is the port that is used when connecting to WinRM over SSL. If you wish to block WinRM over HTTP to ensure that only HTTPS can be used, block TCP port 5985 inbound using an additional firewall rule.

WinRM is now configured and is available to any users with local administrative access to the server.

Establishing a remote Horizon View PowerCLI session

Once WinRM is enabled, you can connect to the Connection Server remotely over a PowerShell session.

How to do it...

The following steps outline how to establish a remote PowerShell session, and then enable the Horizon View PowerCLI commands:

1. Open a PowerShell window on the computer that you will use to remotely manage Horizon View.

2. Use the following command to initiate a remote PowerShell session. You will need to provide the FQDN of the Connection Server, a user ID that has administrative access to both the Horizon View and Connection Server, and the **-UseSSL** option:

```
Enter-PSSession -ComputerName "ConnectionServerFQDN" -UseSSL
-Credential "domain\username"
```

The following screenshot shows you the previous step in action:

3. A **Windows PowerShell Credential Request** window will open as shown in the following screenshot; provide the password for the user account specified in the **-Credential** option of the previous step and click on **Ok**:

4. The PowerShell window will now display a command prompt that includes the name of the Connection Server as shown in the following figure. You are now running a PowerShell session on this server from the local drive indicated in the console. You can change drives by selecting another drive letter exactly as you would if you were logged on directly using the console on the Connection Server.

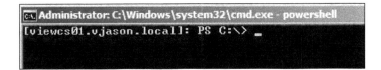

5. Switch to the following directory on the Connection Server; this folder path assumes that Connection Server was installed in the default `Program Files\VMware\ VMware View\Server\extras\PowerShell` directory

6. Execute the following command to run the script that will load the Horizon View PowerCLI commands:

`.\Add-snapin.ps1`

Once the script has run completely, **Welcome to VMware View PowerCLI** should appear, as shown in the following figure. You are now able to use PowerCLI to remotely manage the Connection Server.

```
Administrator: C:\Windows\system32\cmd.exe - powershell
[viewcs01.vjason.local]: PS C:\Program Files\V
werShell> .\add-snapin.ps1
Loading VMware View PowerCLI

            Welcome to VMware View PowerCLI

[viewcs01.vjason.local]: PS C:\Program Files\V
werShell> _
```

Viewing all the PowerCLI commands and their options

In this recipe, we will review all of the current VMware Horizon View PowerCLI commands and provide examples of how they are used.

How to do it...

The Horizon View PowerCLI commands must be enumerated using either a local or remote PowerCLI session. To establish a remote session, refer to the *Establishing a remote Horizon View PowerCLI session* recipe found earlier in this chapter.

Listing all PowerCLI commands

The `Get-Command` PowerShell command is used to display all of the commands available in the specified PowerShell snap-in. To display a current list of PowerCLI commands available in the version of the Horizon View you are working with, use the following command:

```
Get-Command -PSSnapin VMware.View.Broker | more
```

Displaying the options for a single Horizon View PowerCLI command

The `Get-Help` PowerShell command is used to display the command-line options for the specified PowerShell or Horizon View PowerCLI command. To display a list of command options and examples, use the following command:

```
Get-Help command | more
```

To display more detailed information about any of the Horizon View PowerCLI commands, append the `Get-Help` command with either of the following switches:

- ▶ The `-detailed` switch: This displays additional information about the command
- ▶ The `-examples` switch: This displays examples of how the command is used
- ▶ The `-full` switch: This displays additional technical information about the command

The following is an example of how these switches are used with the `Get-Help` command:

```
Get-Help command -full | more
```

Managing desktop pools with PowerCLI

The Horizon View PowerCLI provides a number of different commands that the administrators can use to provision and administer desktop pools. Many administrative tasks can be performed using PowerCLI, which enables administrators to build their own scripts in order to automate common tasks.

How to do it...

We will need to determine the configuration that we will use for our desktop pool. The different options are described in greater detail in the *How it works...* section of this recipe.

How it works...

The following options are supported when creating desktop pools using PowerCLI. Options that are specific to linked-clone desktop pools or virtual desktops are indicated:

- ▶ The `AllowMultipleSessions` option: This specifies whether a single user can have multiple concurrent client sessions within the same desktop pool. This setting only applies when using floating assignment pools.
- ▶ The `AllowProtocolOverride` option: This specifies whether users can override the default display protocol; this is allowed by default.
- ▶ The `AutoLogoffTime` option: This specifies whether desktops will log off after getting disconnected, and if so, after how long (in minutes).
- ▶ The `Composer_ad_id` option: This specifies the ID of the composer server to be used when provisioning linked-clone desktops.

Rather than using this option, use the `Get-ComposerDomain` command as shown in the examples in order to provide the required value. This method makes completing commands much simpler, as the `Composer_ad_id` value is a long string that is easily mistyped.

▸ The `CustomizationSpecName` option: This specifies the name of the vSphere customization specification to be used when customizing desktops using Windows **Sysprep**. When creating full-clone desktop pools, a customization specification is required, or the Windows customization will need to be performed manually after the desktops have been deployed.

▸ The `DataDiskLetter` option: This specifies the drive letter for the linked-clone persistent (user) data disk. The letter `D` will be used by default.

Once the desktops have been deployed, the data disk letter cannot be changed without deleting and recreating the desktops.

▸ The `DataDiskSize` option: This specifies the size in MB of the linked-clone persistent (user) data disk. The disk is 2048 MB by default.

Once the desktops have been deployed, the data disk size cannot be changed without deleting and recreating the desktops.

▸ The `DataStorePaths` option: This specifies which datastores are to be used to provision full-clone desktops. The full path to the datastore must be provided, multiple datastores should be separated using semicolons, and the entire value should be contained within quotes, for example, `"/RTP/host/DT-Cluster1/Datastore1;/RTP/host/DT-Cluster1/Datastore2;/RTP/host/DT-Cluster1/Datastore3"`.

▸ The `DatastoreSpecs` option: This specifies which datastores are to be used to provision linked-clone desktops, their storage overcommit level, and their functions. The storage overcommit level options are `None`, `Moderate`, `Aggressive`, and `Conservative` (the default). The `datastore` functions are `replica`, `data`, and `OS`. Separate datastores—using semicolons—and multiple datastores can be specified for a single configuration type. The full path to the datastore must be provided, and the entire value should be contained within quotes, for example, `"[Aggressive,OS]/RTP/host/DT-Cluster1/Datastore1;[Aggressive,data]/RTP/host/DT-Cluster1/Datastore2;[Aggressive,replica]/RTP/host/DT-Cluster1/Datastore3"`.

The storage overcommit levels are explained in detail in the VMware document *Setting up Desktop and Application Pools in View* (`https://pubs.vmware.com/horizon-view-60/topic/com.vmware.horizon-view.desktops.doc/GUID-6CD0B342-74D4-4D95-A190-52A87E946599.html`).

▶ The `Description` option: This is used to provide a more detailed description of the desktop pool. This setting is optional, and when provided, the value should be contained within quotes.

▶ The `DefaultProtocol` option: This specifies the default display protocol from either RDP or PCoIP (the default).

▶ The `DeletePolicy` option: This specifies whether a desktop will be deleted or refreshed when the user logs off. By default, the desktops are not deleted. The options include `DeleteOnUse` or `RefreshOnUse`. The `RefreshOnUse` option applies to linked-clone desktops only.

▶ The `DisplayName` option: This is the display name of the desktop pool for the Horizon View Client. When provided, the value should be contained within quotes.

▶ The `Disabled` option: This is used to enable or disable the desktop pool, preventing clients from logging in.

▶ The `FlashQuality` option: This specifies the maximum quality allowed for Adobe Flash content. The options include `HIGH`, `LOW`, `MEDIUM`, and `NO_CONTROL` (the default).

▶ The `FlashThrottling` option: This specifies how often Adobe Flash should refresh what it's displaying. The options include `AGGRESSIVE` (2500 ms), `CONSERVATIVE` (100 ms), `MODERATE` (500 ms), and `DISABLED` (the default).

▶ The `FolderId` option: This specifies the folder in which the desktop pool needs to be placed within Horizon View; this is often used when delegating administrative access at the Horizon View folder level.

▶ The `HeadroomCount` option: This specifies the minimum number of desktops that have powered on and are available at all times.

▶ The `IsProvisioningEnabled` option: This specifies whether the pool will provision desktops when it is created. The options are `$true` or `$false`.

▶ The `IsUserResetAllowed` option: This specifies whether users can restart their virtual desktops. Users cannot reset their desktops by default. The options are `$true` or `$false`.

▶ The `LogoffScript` option: This specifies a script that is run when someone logs out of a linked-clone desktop. Provide the full path to the script on the desktop drive that is contained within quotes.

- The `MaximumCount` option: This specifies the maximum number of desktops to be created.

- The `MaxVMsPerNetworkLabel` option: This specifies the maximum number of desktops that can be created on each virtual machine network. They are used when creating a network label specification file.

- The `MinimumCount` option: This specifies that desktops should be provisioned on demand, in amounts equal to the number provided. To provision all desktops upfront, use the same value that is specified for `MaximumCount`.

- The `MinProvisionedDesktops` option: This specifies the minimum number of linked-clone desktops that should be provisioned and available during Horizon View Composer's maintenance operations. This value must be smaller than the `MinimumCount` value.

- The `NamePrefix` option: This specifies the name of the virtual desktops; the value should be contained within quotes. For example, `"ViewDesktop{n}"` or `"ViewDesktop{n:fixed=3}"`.

 The `fixed=3` option: This specifies that the number must contain three digits, which means that two digit numbers would be prepended with a single zero and one digit number with two zeroes.

- The `NetworkLabelConfigFile` option: This is used to configure the desktop virtual machine network as well as the number of desktops per virtual machine network based on the specified network label specification file. The configuration file must have been previously exported from an existing desktop pool. Network label configuration files are discussed in greater detail in the *Creating a network label specification* recipe later in this chapter.

- The `OrganizationalUnit` option: This is the AD DN of the OU in which you need to place the AD computer accounts. Do not include the DN of the domain itself, for example, `"OU=ViewDesktops,OU=Corporate"`.

- The `ParentSnapshotPath` option: This is the path to the snapshot that is relative to the linked-clone parent VM. You must insert it before/after the snapshot name, for example, `/0522`.

- The `ParentVmPath` option: This is the path to the linked-clone parent VM. You must include the full path, including the `vm` folder that is invisible within vCenter, for example, `/RTP/vm/Master/Win81x32-LC`.

- The `Persistence` option: This specifies whether the linked-clone desktops will be persistent or nonpersistent. The options are `persistent` or `nonpersistent`:

    - When specifying `nonpersistent`, you cannot specify any of the options for persistent (user) data disks, as they cannot be used with nonpersistent desktops. The pool will also be assigned with the floating user assignment.

▶ The `Pool_id` option: This is the desktop pool ID. Spaces are not allowed when specifying the pool ID.

▶ The `PostSyncScript` option: This specifies a script that is run when linked-clone desktops are provisioned, refreshed, or recomposed. Provide the full path to the script on the desktop drive, contained within quotes.

▶ The `PowerPolicy` option: This specifies the power state of desktops when they are not in use. The options include `RemainOn`, `PowerOff`, `Suspend`, and `Always On` (the default).

▶ The `ResourcePoolPath` option: This is the path to the resource pool that will contain the virtual desktops. If resource pools are not being used, simply specify the vSphere cluster. You must include the full path contained within quotes, including the host and resources folder that are invisible within vCenter, for example, `"/RTP/host/DT-Cluster1/Resources"`.

▶ If you are using a resource pool, specify it after the resources in the path name, for example, `"/RTP/host/DT-Cluster1/Resources/ResourcePool1"`.

▶ The `RefreshPolicyDays` option: This specifies when the linked-clone refresh after logoff is enabled and also specifies how often it will occur (in days).

▶ The `RefreshPolicyType` option: This specifies whether or not a linked-clone refresh will occur when a user logs off. The options are `Always`, `Conditional`, and `Never` (the default). When selecting `conditional`, you must set either the `RefreshPolicyDays` or `RefreshPolicyUsage` parameters.

▶ The `RefreshPolicyUsage` option: When the liked clone refresh after logoff is enabled, this option specifies how full the OS disk must be in percent before a refresh will be performed. Do not include the percentage sign when specifying a value.

▶ The `SeSparseThreshold` option: This specifies how much unused space in GB must exist on a linked-clone desktop before Horizon View will attempt to reclaim the space. The threshold is 1 GB by default.

▶ The `SuspendProvisioningOnError` option: This specifies whether Horizon View will suspend the provisioning of desktops within a pool if an error is encountered. The options are `$false` and `$true` (the default).

▶ The `TempDiskSize` option: This specifies the size in MB of the linked-clone temp (disposable) disk. The disk is 4096 MB by default.

▶ The `TemplatePath` option: This is the path to the template that is used to create full-clone virtual desktops. You must include the full path, including the `vm` folder that is invisible within vCenter, for example, `"/RTP/vm/Master/Win81x32-FC"/`.

- ▶ The `UseSeSparseDiskFormat` option: This specifies whether the space-efficient sparse virtual disks will be used; these enable Horizon View to reclaim stale or stranded data in the virtual machine disks and subsequently reduce the storage space utilization.

- ▶ The `UseTempDisk` option: This specifies whether or not to use a linked-clone temp (disposable) disk. The options are `$false` and `$true` (the default).

- ▶ The `UseUserDataDisk` option: This specifies whether or not to use a linked-clone persistent (user) data disk. The options are `$false` and `$true` (the default).

- ▶ The `Vc_id` option: This specifies the ID of the vCenter Server to be used when provisioning the desktops. Rather than using this setting, use the `Get-ViewVC` command, as shown in the examples.

- ▶ The `VmFolderPath` option: This specifies the vCenter folder in which you need to create the virtual machines. If no folder is specified, Horizon View will create the folder for the desktop pool in the root of the vCenter folder hierarchy. The full path to the folder must be specified, including the invisible `vm` folder, for example, `/RTP/vm/Desktops`

Creating an automatically provisioned linked-clone desktop pool

The commands used to create a (persistent) dedicated assignment and (nonpersistent) floating assignment desktop pool are similar, and both are shown in this recipe.

Getting ready

A desktop pool that will be created using PowerShell has the same requirements as one that is created using the Horizon View Manager Admin console. This means that we must supply the required pool configuration options, including the path to our virtual desktop master image. Since we are creating a linked-clone desktop pool, our master image must have a snapshot taken too.

How to do it...

To create a desktop pool, we will first need to determine the configuration options as described in the *How it works...* section of the *Managing desktop pools with PowerCLI* recipe in this chapter.

The dedicated assignment persistent linked-clone pool

Not all of the values in the following example command are mandatory; the `FolderId`, `DataDiskLetter`, `DataDiskSize`, `TempDiskSize`, and `VmFolderPath` values can all be omitted and the defaults will be used. The remaining values are all required in order to create a linked-clone pool using the `Add-AutomaticLinkedClonePool` PowerCLI command:

```
Get-ViewVC -serverName "VC-01.vjason.local" | Get-ComposerDomain
-domain "vjason.local" -username "vjason\svc-composer" | Add-
AutomaticLinkedClonePool -Pool_id "FinanceLC1" -DisplayName
"Finance Desktops" -NamePrefix "FinanceLC{n:fixed=4}"
-VmFolderPath "/RTP/vm/Desktops" -ResourcePoolPath "/RTP/host/
DT-Cluster1/Resources" -ParentVmPath "/RTP/vm/Master/Win81x32-LC"
-ParentSnapshotPath "/0522" -DatastoreSpecs "[Aggressive,OS]/RTP/
host/DT-Cluster1/Datastore1;[Aggressive,data]/RTP/host/DT-Cluster1/
Datastore2;[Aggressive,replica]/RTP/host/DT-Cluster1/Datastore3"
-MaximumCount 100 -MinProvisionedDesktops 25 -HeadroomCount 90
-MinimumCount 100 -DataDiskLetter D -DataDiskSize 1536 -TempDiskSize 3072
-FolderId "Finance" -NetworkLabelConfigFile "d:\LCConfigFile"
```

The floating assignment (non-persistent) linked-clone pool

To create the linked-clone desktop pool floating assignment (nonpersistent), the following changes would need to be made to the example command from the previous section of this recipe:

1. Omit the options for `DataDiskLetter` and `DataDiskSize`.
2. The OS and data disks must be the same datastore, so adjust the datastore specifications to read `[Aggressive,data,OS]`.
3. Add the `-Persistence NonPersistent` option.

Based on these requirements, the updated command is as follows. The items that were added or changed are in bold; the items that were removed are not shown:

```
Get-ViewVC -serverName "VC-01.vjason.local" | Get-ComposerDomain
-domain "vjason.local" -username "vjason\svc-composer" | Add-
AutomaticLinkedClonePool -Pool_id "FinanceLC1" -DisplayName "Finance
Desktops" -NamePrefix "FinanceLC{n:fixed=4}" -VmFolderPath "/RTP/
vm/Desktops" -ResourcePoolPath "/RTP/host/DT-Cluster1/Resources"
-ParentVmPath "/RTP/vm/Master/Win81x32-LC" -ParentSnapshotPath
"/0522" -DatastoreSpecs "[Aggressive,data,OS]/RTP/host/DT-
Cluster1/Datastore1;[Aggressive,data,OS]/RTP/host/DT-Cluster1/
Datastore2;[Aggressive,replica]/RTP/host/DT-Cluster1/Datastore3"
-MaximumCount 100 -MinProvisionedDesktops 25 -HeadroomCount 90
-MinimumCount 100 -TempDiskSize 3072 -FolderId "Finance" -Persistence
NonPersistent
```

How it works...

The `Add-AutomatedLinkedClonePool` command is used to create linked-clone desktop pools. Some desktop pool options, such as **Horizon View Storage Accelerator** settings or some of the advanced options for **SeSparse reclamation**, cannot be configured using PowerCLI. These settings must be configured after the pool has been created using the Horizon View Manager Admin console.

The example commands created a linked-clone desktop pool with the following characteristics:

- The desktop pool will be created using the `VC-01.vjason.local` vCenter Server.
- The desktop pool's display name is `Finance Desktops`.
- The desktop pool ID is `FinanceLC1`.
- The desktop names will start with `FinanceLC`, and then will be followed by a four-digit number using leading zeroes if required, for example, `FinanceLC0023`.
- The desktops will be created in the vSphere cluster named `DT-Cluster1`. This cluster has no resource pools created within it, so the cluster itself will be used as the resource pool.
- The desktop pool folder will be placed in the `Desktops` folder within vCenter.
- The desktop pool will be placed in the `Finance` folder within the Horizon View Manager Admin console.
- The pool will contain `100` provisioned desktops, a minimum of `25` desktops will be available during Composer's maintenance operations, and `90` desktops will be powered on and will be available at all times.
- The Composer Server is standalone in the test environment, so the dedicated user account for Composer is specified in the `Get-ComposerDomain` command (`vjason\svc-composer`). If Composer is installed directly on the vCenter Server, the vCenter Server user will be used instead (`vjason\svc-view`).
- The parent virtual machine, also known as the virtual desktop master image, is named `Win81x32-LC`, and the snapshot used to create the desktop pool is named `0522`.
- A network label configuration file will be used. This file is located in the location specified on the virtual machine where the PowerCLI command is executed from.
- Since a vSphere Windows Customization Specification template is not named, the desktops will be customized using VMware QuickPrep.
- The disposable data disk is `3072` MB in size.

▶ The following options apply only to the persistent linked-clone desktop pool:

 ❑ Since no option is specified, the pool will be created as persistent desktops

 ❑ A different datastore is used for the OS, persistent (user) data disks, and replica disks, and the overcommit policy is set to `Aggressive` for each

 ❑ The persistent (user) data disk uses the letter `D` and is `1536` MB in size

> When creating linked-clone desktop pools, you must specify the vCenter and Composer domain in separate commands prior to beginning the command that actually creates the pool, for example:
>
> ```
> Get-ViewVC -serverName "VC-01.vjason.local"
> | Get-ComposerDomain -domain "vjason.local"
> -username "vjason\svc-composer" | ...
> ```
>
> The | character is used to feed the results of one PowerCLI command to the next command, which is an operation known as **piping**.

Creating an automatically provisioned full-clone desktop pool

The `Add-AutomaticPool` command is used to create full-clone desktop pools. Some desktop pool options, such as Horizon View Storage Accelerator, cannot be configured using PowerCLI. These settings must be configured after the pool has been created using the Horizon View Manager Admin console.

Getting ready

Creating a desktop pool using PowerCLI requires all of the same information that is required when using the Horizon View Manager Admin console as well as a virtual desktop master image that has been converted into the vSphere template format.

How to do it...

To create a desktop pool, we first need to determine the configuration options as described in the *How it works... section of the Managing desktop pools with PowerCLI* recipe in this chapter.

Not all of the values in the following example command are mandatory; the `FolderID` and `CustomizationSpecName` values can both be omitted, and the defaults can be used. The remaining values are all required in order to create a full-clone pool using the `Add-AutomaticPool` PowerCLI command:

```
Get-ViewVC -serverName "VC-01.vjason.local" | Get-ComposerDomain -domain
"vjason.local" -username vjason\svc-composer" | Add-AutomaticPool
-Pool_id "FinanceFC1" -DisplayName "Finance Desktops" -NamePrefix
"FinanceFC{n:fixed=4}" -VmFolderPath "/RTP/vm/Desktops" -ResourcePoolPath
"/RTP/host/DT-Cluster1/Resources" -TemplatePath "/RTP/vm/Master/
Win81x32-FC" -DatastorePaths "/RTP/host/DT-Cluster1/Datastore1;/
RTP/host/DT-Cluster1/Datastore2;/RTP/host/DT-Cluster1/Datastore3"
-MaximumCount 100 -HeadroomCount 90 -MinimumCount 100 -FolderId "Finance"
-CustomizationSpecName "View_Full_Clones"
```

How it works...

The example command created a full-clone desktop pool using many of the same settings as the dedicated assignment persistent linked-clone pool in the previous recipe with the following changes:

- The desktop pool's display name is `Finance Desktops`
- The desktop pool ID is `FinanceFC1`
- The desktop names will start with `FinanceFC`, and then will be followed by a four-digit number, for example, `FinanceFC0023`
- The parent vSphere template, also known as the virtual desktop master image, is named `Win81x32-FC`
- A vSphere Windows Customization Specification template named `View_Full_Clones` was specified, so Windows Sysprep will be used to customize the virtual machines
- Three datastores will be used to store the full-clone desktops

Creating a manually provisioned desktop pool

Manually provisioned desktop pools are typically used when the desktops are created outside the Horizon View environment using tools such as vSphere or an array-based virtual machine cloning tool. These manually provisioned desktops must be available in vCenter in order for them to be added to the manually provisioned desktop pool.

Getting ready

Prior to creating the manually provisioned desktop pool, at least one supported virtual machine with the Horizon View agent installed must be available within vCenter. This desktop must not be assigned to any existing desktop pools, as it will be added to the new manually provisioned desktop pool during the pool-creation process.

How to do it...

To create a desktop pool, we first need to determine the configuration options as described in the *How it works...* section of the *Managing desktop pools with PowerCLI* recipe in this chapter.

The following example command will create a manually provisioned desktop pool and add the virtual machine named `Desktop-01` to it:

```
Add-ManualPool -Pool_id "Manual1" -Id (Get-DesktopVM -Name "Desktop-01").
id -Vc_name "VC-01.vjason.local"
```

The `Get-DesktopVM` option was run within the command in order to obtain the value for the virtual machine ID (`id`). By placing the command within parentheses and appending it with `.id`, it returns the value we require in order to complete our `Add-ManualPool` command.

How it works...

Manual desktop pools support most of the same configuration options as linked-clone or full-clone pools as well as the following additional options:

- The `Id` option: This is the vCenter machine ID for the virtual machine to be added to the pool
- The `VC_name` option: This is the hostname of the vCenter Server that manages the pool VMs
- The `Vm_id_list` option: This is the ID for multiple virtual machines to be added to the pool, separated by semicolons

The `Add-ManualPool` command requires at least these options to be specified in order to create a pool: `Pool_id`, `VC_name` or `Vc_id`, and `Id`.

Creating a manual unmanaged desktop pool

Manual unmanaged desktop pools are typically used when the target desktops are created outside the Horizon View and vSphere environments, such as physical desktops or virtual desktops created using storage-array-based cloning features. Regardless of where these desktops are physically located, they must have the Horizon View agent installed in order to be added to manual unmanaged desktop pools.

Getting ready

Prior to creating the manual unmanaged desktop pool, at least one supported desktop with the Horizon View agent installed must be available. This desktop must not be assigned to any existing desktop pools, as it will be added to the new manual unmanaged desktop pool during the pool-creation process.

How to do it...

To create a desktop pool, we first need to determine the configuration options as described in the *How it works...* section of the *Managing desktop pools with PowerCLI* recipe in this chapter.

The following example command will create a manual unmanaged desktop pool and add the virtual machine named `Desktop-01` to it:

```
Add-ManualUnmanagedPool -Pool_id "Manual2" -Pm_id (Get-
DesktopPhysicalMachine -Name "Desktop-01").sid
```

The `Get-DesktopPhysicalMachine` option was run within the command in order to obtain the value for the Windows SID (`Pm_id`).

 Desktops that are added using this command must have the Horizon View agent software installed and should be registered with a Connection Server.

How it works...

Manual desktop pools support most of the same configuration options as linked-clone or full-clone pools as well as the following additional options:

- The `Pm_id` option: This is the physical machine ID that is used to identify the physical desktop
- The `Pm_id_list` option: This is the physical machine ID that is used to identify multiple physical desktops, separated by semicolons

The `Add-ManualUnmanagedPool` command is similar to the `Add-ManualPool` command, but it relies on Windows **System Identifiers** (**SIDs**) rather than vCenter machine IDs.

Creating a Microsoft Windows Remote Desktop Services (RDS) pool

Windows **Remote Desktop Services** (**RDS**) pools are pools that provide access to Windows RDS hosts rather than individual Horizon View desktops.

Getting ready

Prior to creating the Windows RDS pool, at least one supported Windows RDS Server with the Horizon View agent installed must be available. This RDS Server must not be assigned to any existing Windows RDS pools, as it will be added to the new Windows RDS pool during the pool-creation process.

How to do it...

To create a desktop pool, we will first need to determine the configuration options as described in the *How it works...* section of the *Managing desktop pools with PowerCLI* recipe in this chapter.

The following example command will create a Windows RDS desktop pool and add the RDS server named `TermServ-01` to it:

```
Add-TerminalServerPool -Pool_id "TermServ1" -Pm_id (Get-
DesktopPhysicalMachine -Name "TermServ-01").sid
```

The `Get-DesktopPhysicalMachine` option was run within the command in order to obtain the value for the Windows SID (`Pm_id`).

> Windows RDS servers that are added using this command must have the Horizon View agent software installed and should be registered with a Connection Server.

How it works...

The `Add-TerminalServerPool` command uses options that are similar to the `Add-ManualUnmanagedPool` command.

Updating the Horizon View pools

There are five different PowerCLI commands that are used to update the configuration of an existing desktop pool:

- **The Update-AutomaticLinkedClonePool command**: This is used to update the configuration of an existing linked-clone pool.
- **The Update-AutomaticPool command**: This is used to update the configuration of an existing full-clone pool.
- **The Update-ManualPool command**: This is used to update the configuration of an existing manually provisioned pool.
- **The Update-ManualUnmanagedPool command**: This is used to update the configuration of an existing manually provisioned unmanaged pool.
- **The Update-TerminalServerPool command**: This is used to update the configuration of an existing Windows RDS pool.

How to do it...

To update the configuration of an existing desktop pool, we first need to determine what configuration option we wish to change, as described in the *How it works...* section of the *Managing desktop pools with PowerCLI* recipe in this chapter.

Updating a linked-clone pool

In this example, we will update the linked-clone desktop pool configuration using the `Update-AutomaticLinkedClonePool` command. The only option required is the value for `Pool_id` apart from any other options you wish to change:

```
Update-AutomaticLinkedClonePool -Pool_id "FinanceLC1"
-AllowProtocolOverride $false
```

Updating an automatically provisioned full-clone pool

In this example, we will update the full-clone desktop pool configuration using the `Update-AutomaticPool` command. The only option required is the value for `Pool_id` apart from any other options you wish to change:

```
Update-AutomaticPool -Pool_id "FinanceFC1" -DefaultProtocol RDP
```

Updating a manually provisioned pool

In the following example, we will update the manually provisioned pool configuration using the `Update-ManualPool` command. The only option required is the value for `Pool_id` apart from any other options you wish to change:

```
Update-ManualPool -Pool_id "Manual1" -FlashQuality HIGH
```

Updating a manually provisioned unmanaged pool

In the following example, we will update the manual unmanaged pool configuration using the `Update-ManualUnmanagedPool` command. The only option required is the value for `Pool_id` apart from any other options you wish to change:

```
Update-ManualUnmanagedPool -Pool_id "Manual2" -FlashThrottling AGGRESSIVE
```

Updating a Windows RDS pool configuration

In the following example, we will update the Windows RDP configuration using the `Update-TerminalServerPool` command. The only option required is the value for `Pool_id` apart from any other options you wish to change:

```
Update-TerminalServerPool -Pool_id TermServ1 -AutoLogoffTime 15
```

How it works...

Each of the commands demonstrated in this recipe supports the same configuration options as their associated `Add-` commands that are used to create the desktop pools. For example, the `Update-AutomaticLinkedClonePool` command supports the same options as the `Add-AutomaticLinkedClonePool` command that is used to create linked-clone pools.

Creating a network label specification

A network label specification is used to configure desktop pools that need to automatically place desktops on one of multiple available virtual machine networks, often for network capacity reasons. This feature is currently available only when using PowerCLI.

Getting ready

In this example, the vSphere cluster where your desktop desktops will be deployed has two virtual machine networks named `VLAN10` and `VLAN20`, and each virtual machine network can support no more than 250 desktops. We are going to create a desktop pool that has 500 desktops. To do this using the desktop Manager Admin console, we will need two virtual desktop master images, one connected to each virtual machine network. You will then need to create two desktop pools, one for each virtual desktop master image.

How to do it...

When you use network label specification files, you need only one virtual desktop master image and one desktop pool. In this recipe, we will create network label specification files that we can use when creating desktop pools.

The following code shows you the contents of a network label configuration file that will create 250 desktops at most in each of the two virtual machine networks (VLAN10 and VLAN20):

```
#Network Label Configuration Spec

#WARNING! Setting enabled flag to false will
#turn off the automatic network label assignment
#for newly provisioned desktops.
enabled=true

#Parameter Definition for NIC
nic1=Network adapter 1

#Parameter Definition for Network
network01=VLAN10
network02=VLAN20

#Network Label Attribute Definition
#Expected format:
#<nic_param>.<network_param>.maxvm=<max vm for network label>

nic1.network01.maxvm=250
nic1.network02.maxvm=250
```

While it is possible to manually create a network label specifications file, the recommended method for the created file is to export it from an existing desktop master image. The export process is described in the next two recipes in this chapter.

How it works...

The network label specification file contains the following fields that should be edited based on the needs of our desktop pool and infrastructure configuration:

- The enabled field: This can be set to true or false; it is used to enable or disable the network label configuration for new desktops.

- The maxvm field: This defines the maximum number of desktops that will be placed in the specified virtual machine network.

- The nic1 field: This defines the network adapter of the desktop that will be configured.

- The networkXX field: This defines each of the vSphere virtual machine networks where the desktops will be placed. One parameter will be created for each virtual machine network used, and the network name should match the name of the virtual machine network on the vSphere host where the desktop will be deployed.

Once all of these fields have been defined, they are combined to create network label attribute definitions using the following format:

```
nic1.network01.maxvm=250
nic1.network02.maxvm=250
```

Exporting network label specifications for linked-clone pools

In this recipe, we will demonstrate how to create a network label specification file by exporting the configuration of an existing virtual desktop master image.

Getting ready

To export the network label specification file that will be used to create linked-clone pools, we need a virtual desktop master image that is configured with our desired virtual machine network settings. The virtual machine should also have a snapshot taken, as this is a prerequisite for images that will be used to create linked-clone desktop pools.

How to do it...

The following example command reads the network labels of the virtual machine networks for the specified linked-clone parent VM, which is located in the specified vSphere cluster and vCenter Server. The maximum number of VMs that will be created per network label is `250`, and the network label specification file will be created on the `D` drive:

```
Export-NetworkLabelSpecForLinkedClone -ClusterPath "/RTP/host/DT-
Cluster1" -vc_id (Get-ViewVC -ServerName "VC-01.vjason.local").vc_id
-ParentVmPath "/RTP/vm/Master/Win81x32-LC" -ParentSnapshotPath "/0522"
-MaxVMsPerNetworkLabel 250 -NetworkLabelConfigFile "d:\LCConfigFile"
```

The `Get-ViewVC` command is run within the preceding command to obtain the `vc_id` value. You can also add the `FailIfNoNetworkFound` command option, which will cause the command to fail if no suitable network labels are found in the vSphere cluster. The options are `$false` and `$true` (the default).

 Since we are running a PowerCLI command on a remote system, the network label specification file will actually be created on the D drive of the Connection Server.

How it works...

The `Export-NetworkLabelSpecForLinkedClone` command requires several options in order to create the network label specification file including the following:

- The `ClusterPath` option: This is the full path to the vSphere cluster

- The `MaxVMsPerNetworkLabel` option: This is the maximum number of desktops to be placed on each virtual machine network

- The `ParentVmPath` option: This is the full path to the parent VM used to export the network label data from

- The `NetworkLabelConfigFile` option: This is the location and filename of the exported network label specification file

- The `ParentSnapshotPath` option: This is the path to the parent VM snapshot including

- The `Vc_id` option: This is the vCenter Server ID

Exporting network label specifications for full-clone pools

In this recipe, we will demonstrate how to create a network label specification file by exporting the configuration of an existing virtual desktop master template.

Getting ready

To export the network label specification file that will be used to create full-clone pools, we need a virtual desktop master image that is configured with our desired virtual machine network settings. The virtual machine should also be converted into the vSphere template format, as this is a prerequisite for images that will be used to create full-clone desktop pools.

How to do it...

The following example command uses the same parameters as the `Export-NetworkLabelSpecForLinkedClone` command:

```
Export-NetworkLabelSpecForFullClone -ClusterPath "/RTP/host/DT-
Cluster1" -vc_id (Get-ViewVC -ServerName "VC-01.vjason.local").vc_id
-TemplatePath "/RTP/vm/Master/Win81x32-FC" -MaxVMsPerNetworkLabel 250
-NetworkLabelConfigFile "d:\FCConfigFile"
```

The `Get-ViewVC` option was run within the command in order to obtain the vCenter ID (`vc_id`).

How it works...

The `Export-NetworkLabelSpecForFullClone` command requires the same input as the `Export-NetworkLabelSpecForLinkedClone` command, but since we will be working with virtual desktop master images in the vSphere template format, we are required to use the `TemplatePath` option and not the `ParentVmPath` and `ParentSnapshotPath` options.

The `TemplatePath` option is the full path to the parent vSphere template that is used to provision the full-clone virtual desktops, including the invisible `vm` folder.

Retrieving the Horizon View Composer Server information

The `Get-ComposerDomain` command can be used to obtain the Composer information using the `Vc_id`, `Domain`, or `Username` options.

How to do it...

The following example command retrieves the Composer information based on which vCenter the Server Composer is linked to:

```
Get-ComposerDomain -Vc_id (Get-ViewVC -Name "VC-01.vjason.local").vc_id
```

How it works...

The `Get-ViewVC` command is run within the command to obtain the `vc_id` value, which is easier than attempting to type in the value manually, as it is a series of random letters and numbers. This technique will be used in many of the examples for this chapter, as it makes working with certain values much easier. Omit the options in order to retrieve a list of all Composer information.

Retrieving a list of the Horizon View desktop pools

The `Get-Pool` command can be used to retrieve a list of all the Horizon View pools or simply those that match the supplied specifications.

How to do it...

The following command will retrieve a list of the Horizon View pools that have the `PCoIP` protocol enabled:

```
Get-Pool -Enabled $true -Protocol PCoIP
```

Omit the options to retrieve a list of all the Horizon View pools.

How it works...

The `Get-Pool` command can be used to obtain information on desktop pools based on these options: `Description`, `DisplayName`, `Enabled` (`$true` or `$false`), `Pool_id`, `PoolType`, `Protocol`, and `VcServerName`. The `VcServerName` option is simply the name of the vCenter Server that hosts the desktop pool's virtual machines.

Removing desktop pools

The `Remove-Pool` command is used to remove desktop pools from the pod.

How to do it...

The only option required for this command is the desktop pool ID using the `-Pool_ID` switch, which can be obtained using the `Get-Pool` command described in the previous recipe.

The command also supports the following options:

▶ The `-DeleteFromDisk` switch: The default value is `$false`, which removes the pool but does not delete the desktops. Use `-DeleteFromDisk $true` to delete the desktops as well as the desktop pool.

▶ The `-TerminateSession` switch: The default value is `$false`, which means that desktops in use as well as the desktop pool itself will not be deleted until the Horizon View client logs off. Use `-TerminateSession $true` to terminate any existing View client sessions, and proceed with the pool creation.

How it works...

In this example, we will remove the desktop pool we created earlier using the `Remove-Pool` command. The only option required is the value for `Pool_id`, although, in this example, we are also including the `-DeleteFromDisk $true` option that will also delete the desktops during the pool deletion process:

```
Remove-Pool -Pool_id "FinanceLC1" -DeleteFromDisk $true
```

Entitling a desktop pool

Entitling is the act of granting AD users or groups access to the Horizon View pools. In this recipe, we will demonstrate how to either add or remove user and group's Horizon View pool entitlements.

How to do it...

Perform the following steps to entitle a desktop pool:

1. The following `Add-PoolEntitlement` command will entitle the `Finance_View_Users` group to the `FinanceLC1` desktop pool:

   ```
   Add-PoolEntitlement -Pool_id FinanceLC1 -sid (Get-User -Name
   "Finance_View_Users").sid
   ```

2. To entitle individual users, simply provide the first and last name of the user:

   ```
   Add-PoolEntitlement -Pool_id FinanceLC1 -sid (Get-User -Name "Erik
   Lensherr").sid
   ```

    The `Get-User` command accepts wildcards, but be careful while using them, as the wrong user might be returned. If in doubt, use the Get-User command by itself to verify that you are selecting the correct user.

3. The `Remove-PoolEntitlement` command uses the same format as the `Add-PoolEntitlement` command; however, if you are removing the last entitlements from the desktop pool, you must add the `-ForceRemove $true` option for the command to succeed. This prevents you from accidentally removing all entitlements from a desktop pool, for example:

   ```
   Remove-PoolEntitlement -Pool_id "FinanceLC1" -sid (Get-User -Name
   "Finance_View_Users").sid -ForceRemove $true
   ```

How it works...

The `Add-PoolEntitlement` and `Remove-PoolEntitlement` commands require you to specify the user or group AD's **system identifier** (**SID**) in order to add or remove desktop pool entitlements. For this, use the `Get-User` command within the `PoolEntitlement` command. Despite the name, the `Get-User` name is used to obtain both AD users and groups.

Entitling or unentitling an individual desktop

Entitling an individual desktop is similar to entitling a desktop pool, except that, in this case, we need both the user SID as well as the machine ID.

How to do it...

For the following example command, we will nest two commands, `Get-DesktopVM` and `Get-User`, within the `UserOwnership` command:

```
Update-UserOwnership -Machine_id (Get-DesktopVM -Name "ViewLC0001").
machine_id -Sid (Get-User -Name "Jason Ventresco").sid
```

 The `Get-User` command accepts wildcards, but be careful while using them, as the wrong user might be returned. If in doubt, use the `Get-User` command by itself to verify that you are selecting the correct user.

The `Remove-UserOwnership` command requires only the desktop machine ID:

```
Remove-UserOwnership -Machine_id (Get-DesktopVM -Name "ViewLC0001").
machine_id
```

Reviewing the desktop pool entitlement

The `Get-PoolEntitlement` command can be used to review the AD users and groups that have been granted access to the specified pool ID.

How to do it...

The `Get-PoolEntitlement` command supports only one option: `Pool_id`. The following example command retrieves the entitlement settings for the desktop pool with the `FinanceLC1` ID:

```
Get-PoolEntitlement -Pool_id "FinanceLC1"
```

Omit the options in order to retrieve a list of user entitlements for all desktop pools. If the pool does not have an entitlement, the command will return an exception.

Refreshing a linked-clone desktop or pool

The `Send-LinkedCloneRefresh` command is used to refresh either a specific linked-clone desktop or an entire desktop pool.

How to do it...

1. The following example command selects all the desktops in the `FinanceLC1` pool and schedules them to refresh at the indicated time. In addition, the operation will continue even if an error occurs but will not force users to log off:

   ```
   Get-Pool -Pool_id "FinanceLC1" | Get-DesktopVM | Send-
   LinkedCloneRefresh -schedule "2014-07-25 18:00" -StopOnError
   $false -ForceLogoff $false
   ```

2. To refresh just a single desktop, you can use a simpler version of the command that requires only the machine ID and the schedule:

   ```
   Send-LinkedCloneRefresh -Machine_id (Get-DesktopVM -Name
   "ViewLC0001").machine_id -schedule "2014-07-25 18:00"
   ```

   This command will refresh only the desktop named `ViewLC0001`.

How it works...

When using the `Send-LinkedCloneRefresh` command to refresh an entire pool, the command requires us to specify each desktop within the pool, so we will be piping the output of the `Get-Pool` and `Get-DesktopVM` commands into the `Send-LinkedCloneRefresh` command.

We must also specify the time to begin the refresh using the `-schedule` option in the `YYYY-MM-DD HH:MM` format using a 24-hour format for the hour. We must remember that any time specified will be executed based on the time on the Connection Server itself.

Other options for the command include `StopOnError`, which is enabled by default and halts the refresh if errors occur, and `ForceLogoff`, which is disabled by default and will force users to log off. Both of these options accept either `$true` or `$false` as options.

Recomposing a linked-clone desktop pool

The `Send-LinkedCloneRecompose` command is used to recompose either a specific linked-clone desktop or the entire desktop pool.

How to do it...

1. In the following example, we will be recomposing to a new snapshot of the same parent VM; the snapshot is named `0525`. Since this VM now has two snapshots, the `ParentSnapshotPath` will now be in the `/0522/0525`, format, where `0522` is the name of the original snapshot used to create the pool. The remainder of the command follows a format that is similar to the `Send-LinkedCloneRefresh` command:

    ```
    Get-Pool -Pool_id "FinanceLC1" | Get-DesktopVM | Send-
    LinkedCloneRecompose -ParentVMPath "/RTP/vm/Master/Win81x32-LC"
    -ParentSnapshotPath "/0522/0525" -schedule "2014-07-25 18:00"
    ```

    The command will recompose all desktops in the pool to the snapshot named `0525` at the indicated time. You can also select a different parent VM when performing a recompose, but remember that the VM must be running the same OS as the existing desktops.

2. You can also recompose a single desktop using the `-machine_id` option and the `Get-DesktopVM` command:

    ```
    Send-LinkedCloneRecompose (Get-DesktopVM -Name "ViewLC0001").
    machine_id -ParentVMPath "/RTP/vm/Master/Win81x32-LC"
    -ParentSnapshotPath "/0522/0525" -schedule "2014-07-25 18:00"
    ```

How it works...

The `Send-LinkedCloneRecompose` command requires you to specify multiple options, including `Schedule`, `ParentVMPath`, and `ParentSnapshotPath`. The command also supports the `StopOnError` and `ForceLogoff` options.

Rebalancing a linked-clone desktop pool

The `Send-LinkedCloneRebalance` command is used to rebalance either a specific linked-clone desktop or an entire desktop pool.

How to do it...

1. The following example command selects all the desktops in the `FinanceLC1` pool and schedules them to rebalance at the indicated time:

   ```
   Get-Pool -Pool_id "FinanceLC1" | Get-DesktopVM | Send-
   LinkedCloneRebalance -schedule "2014-07-25 18:00"
   ```

2. To rebalance just a single desktop, you can use a simpler version of the command that requires only the machine ID and the schedule:

   ```
   Send-LinkedCloneRebalance -Machine_id (Get-DesktopVM -Name
   "ViewLC0001").machine_id -schedule "2014-07-25 18:00"
   ```

3. This command will rebalance only the desktop named `ViewLC0001`.

How it works...

The `Send-LinkedCloneRebalance` command uses the same format as the other linked-clone maintenance commands. All that is required is the desktop pool ID and the schedule. The command also supports the `StopOnError` and `ForceLogoff` options.

Updating the Horizon View global settings

The `Update-GlobalSetting` command can be used to update a number of different Horizon View global settings.

How to do it...

The following example command enables and configures the `Force Logoff` and `Pre Login` messages:

```
Update-GlobalSetting -DisplayPreLogin $true -PreLoginMessage
"Unauthorized users prohibited" -DisplayLogoffWarning $true
-ForcedLogoffMessage "You will be logged off"
```

How it works...

The following settings can be set using the `Update-GlobalSetting` command:

- ▶ The `DisplayLogoffWarning` setting: This displays a warning to the Horizon View Client prior to a forced logoff; this value should be contained within quotes.

- ▶ The `DisplayPreLogin` setting: This displays a login message prior to the Horizon View Client logging into the Connection Server; this value should be contained within quotes.

- ▶ The `ForceLogoffAfter` setting: This sets how long you need to wait in minutes after the warning message appears to force logoff of the Horizon View Client.

- ▶ The `ForceLogoffMessage` setting: This is the text for the force logoff message; this value should be contained within quotes.

- ▶ The `MessageSecurityMode` setting: This sets the security level for communication between Horizon View components. The options include `Disabled`, `Mixed`, and `Enabled` (the default).

- ▶ The `PreLoginMessage` setting: This is the text for the pre-login message; this value should be contained within quotes.

- ▶ The `ReauthenticateOnInterrupt` setting: This will force the Horizon View Client to reauthenticate after connection interruption. The options are `$true` or `$false` (the default).

- ▶ The `SessionTimeout` setting: This is the timeout value in minutes for inactive Client sessions.

- ▶ The `UseSslClient` setting: This forces SSL Client connections. The options are `$true` or `$false` (the default).

- ▶ The `WidgetPolling` setting: This enables automatic status updates in the Horizon View Manager Admin console. The options are `$true` (the default) or `$false`.

Updating the Horizon View connection broker settings

The `Update-ConnectionBroker` command supports a number of options in order to configure Connection brokers, which includes both Connection Servers and Security Servers.

How to do it...

The following example command updates the external PCoIP URL of the Horizon View Security Server named `VIEWSEC-01`:

```
Update-ConnectionBroker -Broker_id "VIEWSEC-01" -ExternalPCoIPUrl
"192.168.0.1:4172"
```

How it works...

The following options are supported when using the `Update-ConnectionBroker` command:

- ▶ The `Broker_id` option: This is the name of the Horizon View connection broker.

- ▶ The `DirectConnect` option: This will enable direct connections to the Horizon View desktops. The options are `$true` or `$false` (the default).

- ▶ The `DirectPCoIP` option: This will enable direct PCoIP connections to the Horizon View desktops. The options are `$true` (the default) or `$false`.

- ▶ The `ClearNodeSecret` option: This will clear the existing RSA SecurID node secret (if in use).

- ▶ The `ExternalURL` option: This is the external URL for the Connection Server home page.

- ▶ The `ExternalPCoIPUrl` option: this is the external URL for PCoIP access using the secure gateway.

- ▶ The `LdapBackupFolder` option: This is the folder that is used for the Horizon View LDAP backups.

- ▶ The `LdapBackupFrequency` option: This is the frequency of LDAP backups. The options are `EveryHour`, `Every6Hour`, `Every12Hour`, `EveryDay` (the default), `Every2Day`, `EveryWeek`, `Every2Week`, and `Never`.

- ▶ The `LdapBackupMaxNumber` option: This is the maximum number of LDAP backups that need to be retained. The default is `10`.

- ▶ The `LogoffWhenRemoveSmartCard` option: This will log off the Horizon View Client sessions when the user's smart card is removed. The options are `$true` or `$false` (the default).

- ▶ The `NameMapping` option: This will enforce RSA SecurID and Windows name matching. The options are `$true` or `$false` (the default).

- ▶ The `SecureIDEnabled` option: This will enable RSA SecurID authentication. The options are `$true` or `$false` (the default).

- ▶ The `SmartCardSetting` option: This will enable smart card authentication. The options are `Required`, `Off`, or `Optional` (the default).

- ▶ The `Tags` option: This will set Connection Server tags, used to restrict connections to desktop pools to specific Connection Servers.

- ▶ The `PCoIPBandwidthLimit` option: This will configure the per-session PCoIP bandwidth limit in Kbps.

Adding a vCenter Server to Horizon View

The `Add-ViewVC` command is used to add a VMware vCenter Server to Horizon View so that it can be used to manage and provision the Horizon View desktops.

How to do it...

The following example links the `VC-01.vjason.local` vCenter Server to Horizon View:

```
Add-ViewVC -ServerName "VC-01.vjason.local" -Username "vjason\svc-view"
-Password "Password123" -CreateRampFactor 8 -UseComposer $true
```

How it works...

The `Add-ViewVC` command requires several options be specified in order to link a vCenter Server to the Horizon View environment. These include the following:

- ▶ The `CreateRampFactor` option: This is the maximum of concurrent vCenter desktop provisioning operations.

- ▶ The `Password` option: This is the password for the `-Username` account. The password should be contained within quotes.

- ▶ The `ServerName` or `Name` option: This is the FQDN of the vCenter Server. Either option can be specified.

- ▶ The `Username` or `User` option: This is the user who has appropriate permissions within vCenter in the `domain\username` format. Either option can be specified.

Additional options can be specified. These include the following:

- ▶ The `ComposerPort` option: This is the port that needs to be used with the Horizon View Composer Server.

- ▶ The `DeleteRampFactor` option: This is the maximum of concurrent desktop power operations.

- ▶ The `Description` option: This is the description for vCenter Server in the Horizon View Manager Admin console. This value should be contained within quotes.

- ▶ The `DisplayName` option: This is the display name for vCenter Server in the Horizon View Manager Admin console. This value should be contained within quotes.

- ▶ The `Port` option: This is the port to be used with vCenter Server.

- ▶ The `UseComposer` option: This is for using the Composer Server installed on vCenter Server. The options are `$true` or `$false` (the default).

▶ The `UseComposerSsl` option: This is for using SSL when connecting to the Composer Server. The options are `$true` (the default) or `$false`.

▶ The `UseSpaceReclamation` option: This will enable the **SeSparse** space reclamation on vSphere hosts managed by the vCenter Server. The options are `$true` or `$false` (the default).

▶ The `UseSsl` option: This is for using SSL when connecting to the vCenter Server. The options are `$true` (the default) or `$false`.

Options such as port numbers and whether or not to use SSL (enabled by default) will use their default values if not specified and should not be changed under most circumstances. A number of vCenter options cannot be configured when linking a vCenter Server using PowerCLI. These include Horizon View Storage Accelerator, standalone Composer Servers, dedicated users for the Composer, the Composer domains, and others. These options must be configured after using the Horizon View Manager Admin console.

If your vCenter Server or Composer Server SSL certificate is not trusted by the Connection Servers, the `Add-ViewVC` operation will fail. This is different from adding a vCenter Server using the Horizon View Manager Admin console, which allows you to accept an untrusted certificate. To use this command, you must replace the default vCenter Server SSL certificate with one signed by a trusted certificate authority.

Removing a vCenter Server from Horizon View

The `Remove-ViewVC` command can be used to remove a vCenter Server that is currently linked to Horizon View.

How it works...

The `Remove-ViewVC` requires only the vCenter Server name in order to unlink it from Horizon View. The vCenter Server cannot be removed if desktops are currently deployed.

How to do it...

The following example command will remove the `VC-01.vjason.local` vCenter Server from Horizon View:

```
Remove-ViewVC -ServerName "VC-01.vjason.local"
```

Updating the settings of vCenter Server that is linked to Horizon View

The `Update-ViewVC` command can be used to update the settings of a vCenter Server that is currently linked to Horizon View.

How to do it...

The following example command updates the `DeleteRampFactor` as well as the description of the vCenter Server named `VC-01.vjason.local`:

```
Update-ViewVC -ServerName "VC-01.vjason.local" -DeleteRampFactor 10
-Description "VC-01 vCenter Server"
```

How it works...

This command supports the same options as the `Add-ViewVC` command. Specify the vCenter Server to be updated using the `ServerName` or `Name` option, and then update the options as required.

Monitoring the remote Horizon View sessions

The `Get-RemoteSession` command is used to obtain information about any current Horizon View client sessions. The command supports several options that can be used to return only those sessions that match the specified criteria.

How to do it...

The following example command retrieves all the remote Horizon View client sessions for the `FinanceLC1` desktop pool:

```
Get-RemoteSession -Pool_id FinanceLC1
```

How it works...

The `Get-RemoteSession` command supports multiple options for listing client connections. Only one option is required in order to retrieve session information. The options include the following:

> ▸ The `Username` option: The username is in the `FullDomainName\username` format, for example, `vjason.local\elensherr`

▶ The `Pool_id` option: This is the desktop pool ID, for example, `FinanceLC1`

▶ The `Session_id` option: This is the Horizon View client session ID

▶ The `Duration` option: This is the duration in the format "dd day(s) hh hour(s) mm minute(s) ss second(s)", for example, `2 days 1 hour 15 minutes 1 second`

▶ The `DnsName` option: This is the DNS name of the virtual desktop

▶ The `State` option: This is the state of the desktop (`Connected` or `Disconnected`)

▶ The `Protocol` option: This is the protocol being used in the session (`PCoIP` or `RDP`)

▶ The `StartTime` option: This is the time at which the session was started, including the day, time, time zone, and year, for example, `Mon Jul 25 16:00:15 EST 2014`

Resetting a Horizon View desktop

The `Send-VMReset` command can be used to reset a desktop, for example, when it is in an unresponsive state.

How to do it...

The following example command will reset the desktop named `ViewLC0001`:

```
Send-VMReset -Machine_id (Get-DesktopVM -Name "ViewLC0001").machine_id
```

How it works...

The `Send-VMReset` command requires the machine ID in order to identify the desktop.

Disconnecting the Horizon View Client session

The `Send-SessionDisconnect` command disconnects users based on the session ID.

How to do it...

The following example command will disconnect the session belonging to the `vjason.local\elensherr` AD user:

```
Send-SessionDisconnect -Session_id (Get-RemoteSession -Username "vjason.local\elensherr").session_id
```

How it works...

The Horizon View client session ID is a really long value that is difficult to work with, so we will use the `Get-RemoteSession` command within the `Send-SessionDisconnect` command instead in order to disconnect the target user.

Logging Off the Horizon View Client Session

The `Send-SessionLogoff` command disconnects users based on the Horizon View client session ID.

How to do it...

The `Send-SessionLogoff` command uses the same format as the `Send-SessionDisconnect` command. Additionally, we will use the `Get-RemoteSession` command to retrieve the target session ID.

The following example command will log off the session belonging to the `vjason.local\elensherr` AD user:

```
Send-SessionLogoff -Session_id (Get-RemoteSession -Username "vjason.
local\elensherr").session_id
```

Configuring the Horizon View license

The `Set-License` command is used to license a Horizon View pod.

How to do it...

The `Set-License` command requires only one option: `-key`. Do not remove the dashes from the license key, for example:

```
Set-License -Key "11111-AAAAA-22222-BBBBB-33333"
```

Retrieving the global Horizon View configuration data

The `Get-GlobalSetting` command is used to retrieve information about the Horizon View global settings.

How to do it...

The `Get-GlobalSetting` command has no options; simply execute the command by itself in order to obtain the configuration data.

Retrieving the Horizon View connection broker information

The `Get-ConnectionBroker` command is used to retrieve information about Horizon View connection brokers, which include both Connection Servers and Security Servers.

How to do it...

The following example command retrieves information about the `VIEWCS01` Connection Server:

```
Get-ConnectionBroker -Broker_id "VIEWCS01"
```

How it works...

The `Get-ConnectionBroker` command supports only one option, which is `Broker_id`. This is the computer name of the Connection or Security Server you wish to retrieve. Omit the options in order to retrieve all the Horizon View connection brokers.

Retrieving a list of virtual machines managed by Horizon View

The `Get-DesktopVM` PowerCLI command can be used to return a list of the virtual desktops that meet the specified criteria.

How to do it...

The following example command retrieves a list of desktops that currently have a refresh operation scheduled:

```
Get-DesktopVM -ComposerTask refresh
```

Omit the options in order to retrieve a list of all virtual machines.

How it works...

The `Get-DesktopVM` command supports multiple options that enable you to return desktops based on very specific criteria. The criteria include the following:

- ▶ The `ComposerTask` option: This retrieves desktops with the specified scheduled composer tasks. The options are `attachUdd`, `detachUdd`, `mkChkPoint`, `rebalance`, `refresh`, `replaceUdd`, and `resync`. The `Udd` term stands for user data disk.

 A full description of each of these options is available in the VMware document *View Integration* (`https://pubs.vmware.com/horizon-view-60/topic/com.vmware.view.integration.doc/view_integration_powershell.5.5.html`)

- ▶ The `GetNetworkLabel` option: This retrieves the network label settings. The options are `$true` or `$false`.

- ▶ The `IsInPool` option: This retrieves desktops based on whether or not they are in a desktop pool. The options are `$true` or `$false`.

- ▶ The `IsLinkedClone` option: This retrieves desktops based on whether or not they are linked clones. The options are `$true` or `$false`.

- ▶ The `Name` option: This displays the name of the desktop in vCenter.

- ▶ The `Pool_id` option: This is the desktop pool ID.

- ▶ The `PoolType` option: This will only list VMs that will work with the specified pool type. The only option is `Manual`.

- ▶ The `Vc_id` option: This is the vCenter Server ID.

Retrieving a list of physical machines

The `Get-DesktopPhysicalMachine PowerCLI` command can be used to return a list of physical desktops managed by Horizon View and that meet the specified criteria.

How to do it...

The following example command retrieves a list of all desktops running the Windows 7 OS:

```
Get-DesktopPhysicalMachine -OS Win7
```

Omit the options to retrieve a list of all physical machines.

How it works...

`Get-DesktopPhysicalMachine` supports multiple options that enable you to retrieve physical desktops based on very specific criteria. The criteria include the following:

- ▸ The `Description` option: This is the description of the physical machine. This value should be contained within quotes.
- ▸ The `DisplayName` option: This is the display name of the physical machine. This value should be contained within quotes.
- ▸ The `Hostname` option: This is the DNS name of the target physical desktop.
- ▸ The `Sid` option: This is the Windows machine SID.
- ▸ The `State` option: This is the machine state. The options include `AgentUnreachable`, `Available`, `Connected`, `Disconnected`, `ConfigurationError`, or `Validating`.
- ▸ The `OS` option: This is the operating system. The options include `XP`, `Vista`, `Win7`, or `Win8`.

Retrieving the AD user or group Information

The `Get-User` command is typically used to pipe user or group names into other Horizon View PowerCLI commands.

How to do it...

The following example returns only those AD groups that start with `View`:

```
Get-User -IncludeUser $false -Name "View"
```

Omit the options to retrieve a list of all users and groups.

How it works...

The following options are available when using the `Get-User` command:

- ▸ The `IncludeUser` option: This sets whether the results include AD user accounts. The options are `$False` and `$True` (the default).
- ▸ The `IncludeGroup` option: This sets whether the results include AD groups. The options are `$False` and `$True` (the default).
- ▸ The `Name` option: This is the name of the user or group to be returned. This value should be contained within quotes. If quotes are not used, partial matches are allowed based on the start of the name.
- ▸ The `Domain` option: This will return users or groups from a specific domain.

Retrieving information about persistent data disks

The `Get-ProfileDisk` command can be used to retrieve information about the desktop's persistent data disks that are registered with Horizon View.

How to do it...

The following example command will retrieve information about the persistent disk that belongs to the specified user:

```
Get-ProfileDisk -Username "vjason.local\elensherr"
```

Omit the `-Username` option in order to retrieve details about all of the persistent data disks registered with Horizon View.

How it works...

The `Get-ProfileDisk` command supports several options in order to retrieve information about the persistent disks registered with Horizon View:

- The `Name` option: This is the name of the persistent disk.
- The `Username` option: This is the full domain\username of the owner of the persistent disk.
- The `VmName` option: This is the name of the VM that is using the persistent disk.
- The `LastPool` option: This is the desktop pool that contains the persistent disk.
- The `DataStore` option: This is the datastore where the persistent disk is stored.
- The `Status` option: This is the status of the persistent disk. The options include `In Use`, `Archiving`, and `Detached`.

Retrieving the Horizon View event reports and their descriptions

The `Get-EventReportList` command is used to retrieve a list of event report names and their description.

How to do it...

The `Get-EventReportList` command has no options; simply execute the command by itself.

Retrieving the Horizon View event reports

The `Get-EventReport` command is used to retrieve a list of events from the specified event report.

How to do it...

The following example command retrieves all event data about user events:

```
Get-EventReport -ViewName user_events
```

How it works...

The `Get-EventReport` command supports the following three options:

- ▶ The `ViewName` option: This is the name of the event report to output. The options include `config_changes`, `user_auth_failures`, `user_count_events`, and `user_events`.
- ▶ The `Start-Date` option: This is the start date for the report, for example, `2014-07-25 18:00`.
- ▶ The `End-Date` option: This is the end date for the report, for example, `2014-07-26 18:00`.

Retrieving the Horizon View infrastructure's health monitors and their status

The `Get-Monitor` command is used to retrieve Horizon View's health-monitoring data from all or specific monitors.

How to do it...

The following example command retrieves all the health-monitoring data for the `VIEWCS01` Connection Server:

```
Get-Monitor -Monitor_id "VIEWCS01"
```

Omit the options to retrieve a list of all the monitoring data.

How it works...

The `Get-Monitor` command supports two different options:

- The `Monitor_id` option: This is the ID of the monitor. You can provide the specific monitor ID itself, as obtained from the `Get-Monitor` command, or you can specify a Horizon View server name; all monitors for that server will be returned.

- The `Monitor` option: This is the name of the monitor. The possible values include the following:

  - The `CBMonitor` option: This is the Connection Server monitor

  - The `DBMonitor` option: This is the Horizon View event database monitor

  - The `DomainMonitor` option: This is the domain connection monitor

  - The `SGMonitor` option: This is the Security Server monitor

  - The `VCMonitor` option: This is the vCenter Server monitor

Retrieving a list of the vCenter Servers linked to the Horizon View environment

The `Get-ViewVC` command retrieves the Horizon View Composer Server information for the specified Composer server.

How to do it...

The following is an example of how the `Get-ViewVC` command is used:

```
Get-ViewVC -Name "VC-01.vjason.local"
```

Omit the `-Name` option in order to retrieve a list of all vCenter Servers.

How it works...

The `Get-ViewVC` command supports the use of multiple options in order to retrieve the vCenter Server information. These options include the following:

- The `ComposerPort` option: This is the port to be used with the Composer Server.

- The `ComposerURL` option: This is the Composer URL in the `https://ComposerFQDN:Port` format.

- The `ComposerUsername` option: This is the Composer username in the `domain\username` format.

- ▶ The `Description` option: This is the description for the vCenter Server in the Horizon View Manager Admin console. This value should be contained within quotes.

- ▶ The `DisplayName` option: This is the display name for the vCenter Server in the Horizon View Manager Admin console. This value should be contained within quotes.

- ▶ The `Name` option: This is the Composer Server's name.

- ▶ The `Port` option: This is the port to be used with vCenter Server.

- ▶ The `ServerName` option: This is the Composer Server's name.

- ▶ The `Username` option: This is the Composer's username in the `domain\username` format.

Retrieving a list of the Windows RDS Servers registered with Horizon View

The `Get-TerminalServer` PowerCLI command can be used to return a list of Windows RDS Servers used with Horizon View.

How to do it...

The following example command will retrieve information about the Windows RDS Server named `TermServ-01.vjason.local`:

```
Get-TerminalServer -Hostname "TermServ-01.vjason.local"
```

Omit the option to retrieve a list of all Windows RDS Servers.

How it works...

The `Get-TerminalServer` command uses similar options to the `Get-DesktopPhysicalMachine` command.

Retrieving the Horizon View license information

The `Get-License` command is used to retrieve the Horizon View license status.

How to do it...

The `Get-License` command has no options; simply execute the command by itself.

5
Implementation of Horizon View Persona Management

In this chapter, we will cover the following major recipes:

- ▶ Implementing Horizon View Persona Management
- ▶ Configuring Horizon View Persona Management's advanced options

Introduction

VMware Horizon View Persona Management is a feature that is included with all Horizon View license levels; its purpose is to preserve Windows user profile data by dynamically replicating it back and forth between the desktop and a remote profile repository, typically referred to as a Horizon View Persona Management repository.

Horizon View Persona Management improves upon Microsoft roaming profiles by only loading profile data when it is required, synchronizing profile changes back to the persona management repository at specified intervals, enabling persistent user application settings and data, and providing other benefits described in this chapter. Horizon View Persona Management might, in some cases, eliminate the need for a virtual desktop's persistent data disk or the use of assigned Horizon View desktops, as all critical user data and settings are maintained in the persona management repository and provided to the user on demand.

Horizon View Persona Management was first introduced in Horizon View 5 in order to provide Administrators with an option to manage Windows user profile data. Unlike Horizon View Persona Management, when a user who has traditional Windows roaming profiles enabled logs in or out of a desktop, the entire contents of their profile must be copied between the desktop and the remote profile repository regardless of how much of the profile data will actually be required during the session. This method of profile management is resource-intensive as compared to techniques used by Horizon View Persona Management, particularly when the profile contains large amounts of data that must be copied.

Horizon View Persona Management provides a much more optimized method for managing user profile data, as it uses multiple techniques that are not supported by Windows' roaming profiles. The following are some of the key features that distinguish Horizon View Persona Management from Windows roaming profiles:

- The user's profile data is loaded only when it is needed rather than all at once during the logon process, thus minimizing the network traffic and the disk IO required to support a user logon session.

- Changes to the user profile data are synchronized to the profile repository at configurable intervals rather than all at once as with Windows roaming profiles. This method provides enhanced profile data protection while enabling faster logoffs, as less data will need to be saved upon logoff.

- Implementing Horizon View Persona Management requires no changes to Active Directory user accounts, is compatible with existing Windows roaming profile repositories, and is configured using Group Policies that are applied only to the Horizon View desktops AD computer accounts.

- Horizon View Persona Management can eliminate the need to use persistent data disks with linked-clone desktops, as it enables user profile persistence independent of the desktop.

- It enables a persistent user experience even when using non-persistent or floating assignment Horizon View desktops, where the profile data would otherwise be discarded when the user session ends.

- It provides additional capabilities that are not available with Windows roaming profiles such as **user interface** (**UI**) elements unique to Horizon View Persona Management, expanded user profile folder redirection support, and advanced logging capabilities useful for troubleshooting.

- It can be used to import existing user profiles into the Horizon View Persona Management repository by installing the standalone Persona Management software on the user's source desktop.

- It provides tools that can be used to migrate existing Windows XP V1 format profiles to the V2 version used by Windows 7 and newer Microsoft OSs. This feature is discussed in the document *View User Profile Migration* (`https://pubs.vmware.com/horizon-view-60/index.jsp#com.vmware.horizon-view.profilemigration.doc/GUID-0A0EBBF7-53F8-48D3-8E98-28AF658149A6.html`).

While Windows roaming profiles can provide some of the same basic features, as Horizon View Persona Management, they are not optimized for virtual desktop environments and, as such, require more resources when servicing user logon and logoff requests.

Understanding Horizon View Persona Management

Horizon View Persona Management is not configured or administered using the Horizon View Manager Admin console; it is implemented using Windows group policies. To enable Persona Management, we require the following three things:

- A CIFS-based file share that can store the profile data.

- The `ViewPM.adm` group policy template, available in the Horizon View GPO Bundle ZIP file on the **Horizon View downloads** page (`https://my.vmware.com/web/vmware/info/slug/desktop_end_user_computing/vmware_horizon_with_view/6_0`).

  If available, place the `ViewPM.adm` file in the Group Policy AD domain, **Central Store**, where it will be replicated to the different domain controllers and will be available for use when creating group polices. The procedure to implement a Central Store is described in the Microsoft TechNet article *How to Implement the Central Store for Group Policy Admin Templates, Completely* at `http://blogs.technet.com/b/askpfeplat/archive/2011/12/12/how-to-implement-the-central-store-for-group-policy-admin-templates-completely-hint-remove-those-adm-files.aspx`.

- A desktop that has the Horizon View Agent and the Persona Management option installed or a physical desktop that has the standalone Persona Management software installed.

Horizon View Persona Management is configured using the `ViewPM.adm` AD group policy template, which can be applied using either of the following methods:

- Applied directly to the virtual desktop master image prior to the deployment

- Applied using the **AD Group Policy Management Console** to an **organizational unit (OU)** that contains the computer objects where Horizon View Persona Management will be used

Once enabled, Horizon View Persona Management will be used for all users' profile management on desktops where the group policies are applied and which have the Persona Management software installed, even if Windows roaming profiles are enabled within the users AD account.

The *Implementing Horizon View Persona Management* recipe later in this chapter will provide detailed information on how to configure each of the items required to implement and configure Persona Management.

Features of Horizon View Persona Management

Horizon View Persona Management includes a number of options for customizing how the user profile data is retained and accessed. These options include:

▶ The profile folder redirection for additional Windows profile directories beyond what is available with native AD group policies alone

▶ The ability to download specific user profile folders in the background after the user logs on

▶ The ability to exclude specific user profile folders from roaming, which can be used to prevent unnecessary profile data from roaming

▶ The ability to exclude the files from specific desktop Windows processes from roaming with the user, such as the antivirus application data

Details on how to configure the various options for Horizon View Persona Management will be provided in the *Configuring Horizon View Persona Management's advanced options* recipe later in this chapter.

Implementing Horizon View Persona Management

This recipe will discuss the steps that are required to deploy and enable Horizon View Persona Management. This section will focus on just those steps that are required to implement Persona Management. To learn about the advanced configuration options contained in the `ViewPM.adm` group policy template, see the *Configuring Horizon View Persona Management's advanced options* recipe later on in this chapter.

Getting ready

The article *VMware View Persona Management Deployment Guide* at `http://www.vmware.com/files/pdf/view/VMware-View-Persona-Management-Deployment-Guide.pdf` recommends that the Horizon View infrastructure meet certain minimum requirements in order to ensure optimal performance when transferring persona data. These recommendations include:

▶ One file server with 8 GB of RAM for every 1000 View Persona Management clients or a **Network Attached Storage** (**NAS**) platform capable of handling the total number of expected clients

▶ At least 1 Gbps network connectivity between the Persona Management clients and the file servers that host the Persona Management repository, although a faster connection is recommended in order to ensure optimal performance during periods of heavy load, such as a large number of users logging into their desktops simultaneously

These recommendations are a good starting point for a Persona Management implementation but, ultimately, requirements for each environment will vary, and we might find that we need either more or fewer resources to host the Persona Management repository. Some factors that impact the Persona Management file server and infrastructure requirements include the average user profile size, how often the user profile is accessed, the storage capacity and performance characteristics, and the network speed and latency.

The performance of the file server that hosts the Persona Management repository should be monitored at all times in order to ensure that it is performing optimally.

Horizon View Persona Management uses the Microsoft **Volume Shadow Service** (**VSS**) to freeze and then back up the user profile data to the Persona Management repository. Do not back up the user profile data using client-based utilities that also use this feature, as this might corrupt the profile. To back up the user profile data, back it up directly from the Persona Management repository.

The Horizon View Persona Management repository

Horizon View Persona Management requires a CIFS-based file share with the following permissions set at the folder and share levels.

If Horizon View Persona Management is replacing existing Windows roaming profiles, the same user profile repository can be used, as the format is the same. However, if the user profile directory name's format changes when switching to Horizon View Persona Management, a new blank profile folder will be created and used.

NTFS permissions required for the Horizon View Persona Management repository's parent folder are as follows:

User account	Minimum permissions required
Administrator	None
Creator owner	Full control, subfolders, and files only
Everyone	No permissions
Local system	Full control, this folder, subfolders, and files
Active Directory Security Group, which contains Persona Management users	List folder/read data, create folders/append—this folder only
The backup software service account (if applicable)	Consult the vendor documentation for your backup solution

These settings might need to be adjusted in order to ensure that the folder can be backed up. Consult your backup vendor for the minimum permissions required for your backup program, and implement any changes as required.

The share permissions required for the Persona Management repository share are as follows:

User account	Minimum permissions required
Everyone	No permissions
Active Directory Security Group, which contains Persona Management users	Full control
The backup software service account (if applicable)	Consult the vendor documentation for your backup solution

When a new user logs in to a computer with the Horizon View Persona Management software enabled, it will automatically create their profile folders.

 If the users use both traditional desktops and Horizon View desktops concurrently, it is recommended that you standardize one solution in order to manage user profiles rather than using roaming profiles and Horizon View Persona Management concurrently. Should you choose to use Horizon View Persona Management, which is the optimal choice for this scenario, you will need to use the standalone Persona Management installer in order to install the software on the physical desktops.

How to do it...

In this section, we will review in detail the steps required to install Horizon View Persona Management, the techniques used to enable the Windows services it requires, and the minimum group policy settings required to enable it.

It is assumed that we have already configured a suitable Persona Management repository based on the requirements listed previously in this recipe.

 Horizon View Persona Management is not supported on Microsoft Windows RDS Servers.

Configuring the Horizon View Persona Management components

Perform the following steps to ensure that Persona Management functions properly:

1. Enable Horizon View Persona Management using either of the following techniques:

    ❑   Install Persona Management using the standalone installer; the 32-bit installer will have a name similar to `Vmware-personamanagement-x.x.x-yyyyyy.exe` while the 64-bit installer will be named similar to `Vmware-personamanagement-x86_64-x.x.x-yyyyyy.exe`

    ❑   Remove and reinstall the Horizon View Agent software, verifying that the **VMware Horizon View Persona Management** option is enabled, as shown in the following figure:

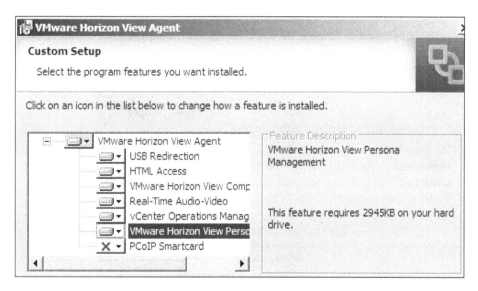

2. If the **Microsoft Software Shadow Copy Provider** and **Volume Shadow Copy** options were disabled, enable them using the following Windows PowerShell commands that are executed from a PowerShell command prompt:

    ```
    Powershell Set-Service 'VSS' –startuptype "automatic"

    Powershell Set-Service 'swprv' –startuptype "automatic"
    ```

Enabling VMware Horizon View Persona Management

In this section, we will be implementing the settings directly in the virtual desktop master image by launching the local group policy manager tool, which is `gpedit.msc`. Alternatively, you can also implement the required settings with the AD **Group Policy Management Console** (**GPMC**) or **Advanced Group Policy Management** (**AGPM**) using a group policy that is applied to the OU that contains the target AD computer accounts.

The procedure used to implement group policies can vary from one environment to the other, so we should consult our AD administrators for the preferred method to implement the changes that we require.

The following steps explain how to enable Persona Management using the `ViewPM.adm` group policy template:

1. Run **gpedit.msc** on the virtual desktop master image in order to launch **Local Group Policy Editor**.

2. Navigate to **Local Computer Policy | Computer Configuration | Administrative Templates**, and select **Add/Remove Templates**.

3. In the **Add/Remove Templates** window, click on the **Add** button.

4. Obtain and extract the `ViewPM.adm` group policy template from the Horizon View GPO Bundle ZIP file, highlight the template file, and click on **Open** to import the template and return to the **Add/Remove Templates** window.

5. Click on the close button to close the **Add/Remove Templates** window and return to the **Local Group Policy Editor** window.

6. Navigate to **Local Computer Policy | Computer Configuration | Administrative Templates | Classic Administrative Templates (ADM) | VMware View Agent Configuration** and expand the **Persona Management** folder to display all the Persona Management policy folders, as shown in the following screenshot:

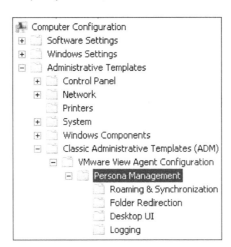

7. Select the **Roaming & Synchronization** node.

8. Double-click on the **Manage user persona group policy** setting in the right pane to open the policy configuration window.

9. Click on the **Enabled** radio button to enable Persona Management as shown in the following screenshot. **Profile upload interval** can also be changed in this window; by default, this is set to upload profile changes every 10 minutes. Click on **Ok** when done with the configuration.

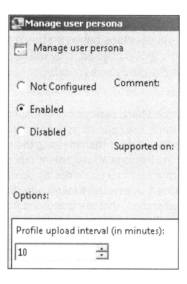

10. Double-click on the **Persona repository location group policy** setting in the right pane to open the policy configuration window.

11. Click on the **Enabled** radio button and populate **Persona Share Path** with the path to the Persona repository. In the following screenshot, the Share Path is set to `\\dc-01.vjason.local\$profiles\%username%\profile`. Click on **Ok** when done with the configuration. If your Persona Management repository will store profiles for users in multiple AD domains, you might want to include the `%userdomain%` variable in the share path like this: `\\dc-01.vjason.local\$profiles\%username\profile`.

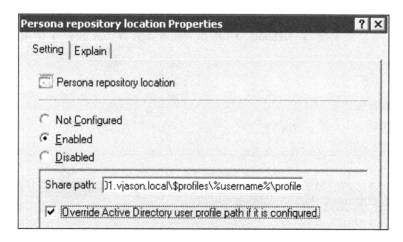

12. Verify that the **VMware Horizon View Persona Management** service is installed on the virtual desktop master image.

13. Verify that the **Microsoft Software Shadow Copy Provider** and **Volume Shadow Copy** services on the virtual desktop master image are set to **Automatic** and are started.

Horizon View Persona Management has now been enabled and will manage the user profiles of anyone who logs on to the virtual desktops based on this master image. If the policies were applied using Active Directory group policies, they will apply to any computer accounts contained within the OU to which the policy was linked.

In step 11, the **Share path** profile repository that we used contained the `%username%` variable in the path to the profile directory. Rather than creating the profile directory in the root of the Persona Management repository, this creates the profile directory in a subfolder. By doing this, we can reuse the root `%username%` folder later for features such as folder redirection, that are discussed in the *Configuring Horizon View Persona Management's options* recipe later in the chapter. Had we created the profile directory within the root of the Persona Management repository, we would have had to create an additional folder to store any profile folders that we want to redirect.

The following figure shows us a profile directory that was created upon logging in to a desktop with Persona Management enabled. Since we used the `%username%` variable in the Persona Management repository path, the user profile's folder was actually created inside another folder named after the user's AD login.

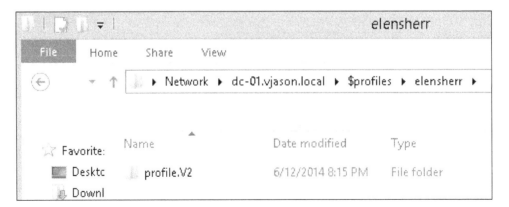

The next recipe will provide information about additional group policy settings that can be used to further customize Persona Management.

How it works...

By default, Horizon View Persona Management will use the Active Directory user profile path if that setting has been configured in either the user's Active Directory account or using the group policies. The same repository should not be used if the target user is using both Windows roaming profiles and Horizon View Persona Management.

To override any existing Windows user profile path settings, click on the **Override Active Directory user profile path if it is configured** checkbox in the **Persona repository location** group policy setting. Enabling this option will not affect the operation of Windows roaming profiles.

 The VMware document *View User Profile Migration* (https://pubs.vmware.com/horizon-view-60/index.jsp#com.vmware.horizon-view.profilemigration.doc/GUID-0A0EBBF7-53F8-48D3-8E98-28AF658149A6.html) provides examples on how existing profiles can be imported into Horizon View Persona Management; this is a process that varies depending on the source desktop OS and the profile location.

The Persona Management group policies are located in a group policy template file named `ViewPM.adm` and are located in the Horizon View GPO Bundle ZIP file. Both the zip file and the standalone Persona Management installers are available on Horizon View's download page (https://my.vmware.com/web/vmware/info/slug/desktop_end_user_computing/vmware_horizon_with_view/6_0).

Configuring Horizon View Persona Management's advanced options

Horizon View Persona Management's `ViewPM.adm` group policy template contains settings that are arranged in the following four categories:

- ▸ Roaming and Synchronization
- ▸ Folder redirection
- ▸ Desktop UI
- ▸ Logging

The purpose and usage of each of these settings will be explained in this recipe.

Getting ready

The settings reviewed in this recipe are used to further customize the Horizon View Persona Management feature. While the previous recipe focused only on those settings that were explicitly required to enable Persona Management, this recipe covers all options, such as Persona folder redirection, Advanced Persona synchronization and roaming options, notification preferences, and logging settings.

Understanding the full capabilities of the Horizon View Persona Management feature is important to any deployment, as the default settings might not be optimal in all cases. Consider the following examples:

▶ If large amounts of data are kept in user profile folders, profile folder redirection might be a better choice than using Persona Management to replicate the data back and forth between the Persona Management repository and the local computer

▶ If the contents of specific profile folders are not required to be retained in between Horizon View client sessions, they can be excluded from the Persona Management replication

The next section of this recipe will discuss each of the Persona Management options and will help us understand why we might want to use them in our environment.

How do to it...

The Horizon View Persona Management settings described in this section are all implemented using the same group policy template referenced in the previous *Implementing Horizon View Persona Management* recipe. The instructions provided in this recipe assume that you have already imported Persona Management's `ViewPM.adm` group policy template as described in the previous recipe and are ready to configure the feature.

Roaming and Synchronization

The Roaming and Synchronization node is used to enable and configure the core Persona Management features.

> By default, Administrators will not have permission to access the user profile folders created by View Persona Management. The Microsoft TechNet article *Group Policy Recommendations for Roaming User Profiles* (`http://technet.microsoft.com/en-us/library/cc781862` provides information on how to enable the **Add the Administrators security group to the roaming user profile share** policy, which will grant this access.

The following steps outline how to configure the core Persona Management settings located in the Roaming and Synchronization node. Unless otherwise indicated, all settings are disabled or are blank by default:

1. Enable the **Manage user Persona** setting to activate Persona Management, configuring the following optional setting, if required:

    ❑ **Profile upload interval**: This option is measured in minutes, and it specifies how often changes to the local user profile are copied back to the Persona Management repository. The default value is 10; the acceptable values range from 1 to 9999.

2. Configure the **Persona repository location** setting with the **Universal Naming Convention** (**UNC**) path to the Persona Management repository share, configuring the following optional setting, if required:

    ❑ The **Override Active Directory user profile path if it is configured** checkbox: This is used to override any existing Active Directory settings that set the user profile path and can be used to ensure that Persona Management is using the share indicated in **Share path**

3. Enable the optional **Roam local settings folders** setting to enable the synchronization of the users' Local Settings or AppData\Local folders, which contain the application data for applications such as Outlook. These folders should be synchronized in the event that these settings are maintained across multiple desktops.

The following tips explain some characteristics of the Windows local settings folders and how they impact Horizon View Persona Management:

> ▸ This setting should be enabled when using Windows 8 or 8.1 in order to ensure that critical user profile data is maintained between desktop sessions.
>
> ▸ This setting can place additional load on Persona Management as some applications might place large amounts of data in these folders. Due to the resources required to store and replicate these folders, it is not recommended that you roam these folders when using dedicated desktops. If these or other large files need to be preserved across user sessions, consider options such as redirecting the user profile folder or reconfiguring the application to use a network drive if the vendor supports it.
>
> ▸ Microsoft Outlook's OST files are used to store a copy of a user's Exchange mailbox on the local desktop, often for Outlook performance reasons, and are one of the primary concerns when using any Persona Management solution. If we are using Outlook and Exchange, we should consult our messaging administrators in order to help understand our options for preserving e-mail client performance in a virtual desktop environment.

4. Enable the optional **Remove local persona at log off** setting to delete the locally stored user profile when the user logs off a computer with Persona Management enabled. The following are common reasons why this setting would be enabled:

    ❑   This setting is typically used to reduce desktop storage requirements when using pooled desktops.

    ❑   This setting is generally not used with dedicated desktops that include persistent data disks, as their users will require it again the next time they log in. Since the desktops are dedicated to a single user, there is simply no need to remove the profile data.

    ❑   This setting should not be used when a desktop pool is configured to refresh or delete the desktop upon logoff, as the Persona will be deleted during that operation.

5. If not required, disable the **Delete 'Local Settings' or 'AppData\Local' when persona is removed** option of the **Remove local persona at log off** setting, as it is enabled by default. This option enables the removal of the `Local Settings` or `AppData\Local` folders upon logout. These folders contain the application data that is retained by Persona Management when the **Roam local settings folders** option is enabled. If disabled, some user profile folders will remain on the desktop upon logoff.

6. Configure the optional **Files and folders to preload** setting to specify any files and folders that should be fully downloaded when a user logs in. This setting is typically used to enhance the desktop performance by preloading specified folders or files that we know will be required upon login. Note the following details when using this feature:

    ❑   This setting will delay the logon process while the specified files and folders are being downloaded

    ❑   By default, the list includes **<Start Menu|\Programs\Startup**, which cannot be removed

    ❑   An additional setting, **Folders to background download**, provides similar functionality without impacting logon times

    ❑   Files and folder names are specified using paths relative to the root of the local user profile, such as **My Documents\Preload**

7. Configure the optional **Files and folders to preload (exceptions)** setting to exclude files or folders specified in the related **Files and folders to preload** policy from preloading. The following is an example of how this setting is used:

    ❑   Using the example from the **Files and folders to preload** policy to exclude a folder within the `My Documents\Preload` folder, the format would be `My Documents\Preload\Exclude`, where `Exclude` is the target folder name

8. Enable the optional **Windows roaming profiles synchronization** setting to force the specified files and folders to be managed by standard Windows roaming profiles rather than Horizon View Persona Management. With this policy, the specified files and folders are fully downloaded when the user logs in and fully uploaded when they log out. Note the following details regarding the use of this feature:

   ❑ By default, the list includes **<Roamed Application Data|\Microsoft\ Windows** and **Themes\Custom.theme and <Roamed Application Data|\ Microsoft\SystemCertificates**, which cannot be removed

   ❑ Files and folder names are specified using paths that are relative to the root of the local user profile

9. Configure the optional **Windows roaming profiles synchronization (exceptions)** setting to exclude files or folders located within the folders specified in the **Windows roaming profiles synchronization** policy from getting preloaded.

10. Configure the optional **Files and folders excluded from roaming** setting to exclude specified files and folders within the local user profile from being copied to the Persona Management repository. Note the following details regarding the use of this feature:

    ❑ By default, the list includes the `temp` folder for the profile, the `ThinApp` cache folder, and the `cache` folders for Internet Explorer, Firefox, Chrome, and Opera

    ❑ This setting is typically used to exclude data that is not required to roam with the user

    ❑ Files and folder names are specified using paths relative to the root of the local user profile

11. Configure the optional **Files and folders excluded from roaming (exceptions)** setting to prevent the specified files or folders that are located within the folders specified in the **Files and folders excluded from roaming** policy from being excluded from roaming.

12. Configure the optional **Folders to background download** setting to enable the background-download of specified folders upon user logon while still allowing the user logon process to complete:

    ❑ This setting is typically used in addition to or in place of the **Files and folders to preload** setting in scenarios where the folders are required on the local computer but not immediately

    ❑ Unlike the **Files and folders to preload** policy, this setting does not delay the user logon process

❑ This setting is frequently used to background-download the `ThinApp Sandbox` directory, which is recommended in order to prevent the Sandbox corruption that can occur if the ThinApp application is opened before the complete contents of Sandbox have been copied to the local disk

❑ Folder names are specified using paths that are relative to the root of the local profile

13. Configure the optional **Folders to background download (exceptions)** setting to exclude files or folders located within the folders specified in the **Folders to background download** policy from being downloaded in the background.

14. Enable the optional **Cleanup CLFS Files setting to instruct View Persona Management** setting to delete the files created by the **Common Log File System** (**CLFS**) for the roaming profile `ntuser.dat` and `usrclass.dat` files. This setting should only be enabled when problems occur with either of these files.

15. Enable the optional **Enable background download for laptops** setting to instruct Persona Management to download all Persona Management profile data remote repositories to the laptop where the logon occurs. This ensures that the laptop logon process can proceed without having to wait for all of the profile data to download. Note that the target laptop must be running the Horizon View Persona Management software.

16. Configure the optional **Excluded Processes** setting to instruct Persona Management to avoid copying files from the repository to the desktop that was requested by the specified processes. This feature is typically required when the processes in question cannot be configured to disable offline file retrieval. This option prevents files from being unnecessarily copied from the Persona Management repository.

Information on the default settings for many of the policies described in this section can be found in the article *VMware View Persona Management Deployment Guide* (`http://www.vmware.com/files/pdf/view/VMware-View-Persona-Management-Deployment-Guide.pdf`).

Folder Redirection

The Folder Redirection node enables us to redirect user profile folders to a network share using Horizon View Persona Management rather than replicating them. In the *Using the Horizon View Persona Management Group Policies* section of this recipe, we created a group policy that will create a folder structure specific to each user. In the example shown, a folder has been created with the `\\dc-01.vjason.local\$profiles\elensherr` path. As discussed in the section, we will use that folder to provide an example of how to use the Persona Management folder redirection policies. The following steps outline how to enable folder redirection using Horizon View Persona Management:

1. Identify the folders to be redirected from the following list:

   ❏ Application data (Roaming)

   ❏ Contacts

   ❏ Cookies

   ❏ Desktop

   ❏ Downloads

   ❏ Favorites

   ❏ History

   ❏ Links

   ❏ My documents

   ❏ My music

   ❏ My pictures

   ❏ My videos

   ❏ Network neighborhood (also known as My Network Places)

   ❏ Printer neighborhood

   ❏ Recent items

   ❏ Saved games

   ❏ Searches

   ❏ Send to

   ❏ Start menu

   ❏ Startup items

   ❏ Templates

   ❏ Temporary Internet Files (also known as Internet Cache)

> The `Temporary Internet Files` (Internet Cache) folder cannot be shared between desktops.

2. Enable each folder as required and provide the UNC path to the redirection target. The following example can be used to redirect the `desktop` folder using the existing Persona Management share:

   ❏ `\\dc-01.vjason.local\$profiles\%username%\desktop`

3. Repeat the process as required in order to redirect additional profile folders.

4. Configure the optional **Files and Folders excluded from Folder Redirection** setting to exclude the specified subfolders of redirected folders on the local system from being redirected. Files and folder names are specified using paths relative to the root of the local user profile. The following is an example of how this setting can be configured:

    ❑ The `Desktop\DoNotRedirect` text will exclude the `DoNotRedirect` folder from being redirected

5. Configure the optional **Files and Folders excluded from Folder Redirection (exceptions)** setting to enable the folder redirection for folders located within folders that were marked excluded by the **Folders excluded from Folder Redirection** policy. The following is an example of how this setting can be configured:

    ❑ Using the previous example, a sample exception would be `Desktop\DoNotRedirect\DoRedirect`, which will enable redirection for the `DoRedirect` folder

6. Configure the optional **Add the administrators group to redirected folders** setting to grant permission to the administrators group on the file server or NAS for each redirected profile folder. If this setting is not enabled, only the user who created the folder will have permissions to access it.

To redirect a profile folder, a UNC path to an alternate location must be provided. In this example, we will redirect the `Desktop` folder to the `\\dc-01.vjason.local\$profiles\%username%\Desktop` location.

The following figure shows us a Persona Management folder that contains both the user profile and a redirected `Desktop` folder. By configuring our policies to place each of these folders within another dedicated folder—in this case, named after the user's AD logon—they will remain together, which should simplify the backup and restore operations.

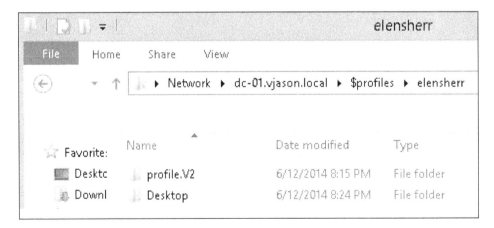

Desktop UI

The Desktop UI node provides control over various settings related to Horizon View Persona Management user notifications and file icons. The following steps outline how to configure the Desktop UI policies:

1. Enable the optional **Hide local offline file icon** setting to configure the Windows file icons to display their status. Note the following details regarding the use of this feature:

    ❏ By default, the setting is enabled, the offline icon is hidden, and all file icons in the user profile appear as normal icons

    ❏ When disabled, files that have not been copied from the remote Persona Management repository will appear with the offline symbol

    ❏ This setting is commonly disabled when troubleshooting Horizon View Persona Management, as it helps identify if and when files have been copied from the Persona Management repository

2. Enable the optional **Show progress when downloading large files** setting to enable a progress window on the desktop when downloading files that are 50 MB or larger from the Persona Management repository. Note the following details regarding the use of this feature:

    ❏ By default, this setting is disabled.

    ❏ The minimum file size that shows us progress window (MB) is an option of the **Show progress when downloading large files** setting and is used to specify the smallest file size that will display a download progress window. The default value is 50 MB, and values ranging from 0 to 4294967295 MB are supported.

3. Enable the optional **Show critical errors to users via tray icon alerts** setting to display critical errors using alert icons in the Windows tray. Note the following details regarding the use of this feature:

    ❏ By default, this setting is disabled

    ❏ This setting is commonly enabled when troubleshooting Persona Management, as it will display errors as and when they happen

In most cases, the default settings for the Desktop UI policies are suggested, as they provide an experience that closely matches what a user would see if they were using all local profiles.

Logging

The Logging node controls how and where information about Horizon View Persona Management is logged. Logging is enabled for error and informational messages by default, placing the log data in the `ProgramData\VMware\VDM\logs` folder. The Persona Management logfiles start with the `VMWVvp` characters. The following steps outline how to configure and customize the Persona Management logging settings:

1. Configure the optional **Logging filename** setting in order to specify the name and location of the Persona Management logfile. UNC paths are not supported when using this feature.

2. Configure the optional **Logging destination** setting to specify where the Persona Management log messages will be sent. Note the following details regarding the use of this feature:

   ❏ By default, all messages are sent to the Persona Management logfile

   ❏ Log messages can also be sent to the computer debug port

3. Configure the optional Logging flags setting in order to specify what types of data are recorded in the Persona Management logfiles. Note the following details regarding the use of this feature:

   ❏ By default, the **Log error messages and Log information messages** options are turned off

   ❏ The **Log debug messages** option can also be enabled, which provides the highest level of detail into Persona Management operations

4. Configure the optional Debug flags setting in order to enable the additional debug logging of Persona Management. Note the following details regarding the use of this feature:

   ❏ By default, this setting is disabled

   ❏ The debug flags options include the **error**, **information**, and **port** messages

In most cases, the Persona Management logging settings will only need to be changed in order to perform advanced troubleshooting, often while working with VMware technical support.

How it Works...

VMware Horizon View Persona Management expands upon the concept of Microsoft Windows roaming profiles and other native Windows group policies by introducing additional features as well as expanding existing ones, using a more optimized approach toward profile data management, and providing the ability to enable it based solely on which computer a user is working on.

In this section, we will review some of the ways in which Horizon View Persona Management expands upon the ideas first introduced in Windows roaming profiles and Windows group policies.

Folder Redirection

Horizon View Persona Management's expanded profile folder redirection capabilities enable it to redirect more folders than is possible with native AD group policies. The folder redirection is the use of a network folder in place of a local profile folder bypassing the use of the local profile folder entirely.

There are a number of cases where using folder redirection to compliment Horizon View Persona Management might the ideal solution for managing user profile data. Some of the reasons why folder redirection might be used include the following:

- In addition to Horizon View desktops that have Persona Management enabled, the user is required to use physical desktops with Windows roaming profiles, Windows RDSH servers, or Citrix XenApp. In this scenario, the different platforms should not share the same profile repository.

- The user will be using both Windows 7 or 8 and Windows XP desktops, which cannot share the same profile.

- The Persona Management repository is located in close proximity (from an infrastructure perspective) to the virtual desktops, enabling folder redirection to be used while still maintaining similar performance when we access the data locally.

6

Delivering Applications Using VMware ThinApp

In this chapter, we will cover the following recipes:

- ▶ Deploying VMware ThinApp
- ▶ Capturing an application using VMware ThinApp
- ▶ Updating an application captured with VMware ThinApp
- ▶ Distributing ThinApp packages using VMware Horizon View
- ▶ Removing applications distributed using VMware Horizon View

Introduction

VMware ThinApp is a component of the Horizon Suite that can be used to virtualize an application. ThinApp accomplishes this by capturing all the changes that occur when an application is installed, and then packaging the files and configuration data into a self-contained package. This process is described in more detail in the *Capturing an application with ThinApp* recipe found in this chapter. The following are some of the advantages we can realize using ThinApp to package and deliver applications:

- ▶ Applications packaged using ThinApp run within their own virtualization layer, eliminating the possibility of conflict with other applications as well as the host operating system.
- ▶ By deploying applications using ThinApp rather than installing them on the virtual desktop master image, we can reduce the size of that image. Additionally, we can now maintain these applications independently of the master image.

▶ Using ThinApp, our users can use different versions of the same application concurrently, which is a useful benefit when legacy applications, websites, or files require these older versions in order to function.

▶ Applications packaged using ThinApp are portable, require no additional application software, and are not required to be installed. Once packaged, application packages using ThinApp can be used anywhere including physical desktops; they can be streamed from a remote file share or even run from a portable USB drive. The only requirement is a supported OS, a current list of which is available in the VMware's *ThinApp User's Guide* (`https://www.vmware.com/pdf/thinapp51_manual.pdf`).

ThinApp has some restrictions that impact how it can be used and the type of applications it can capture. The following are some of these restrictions:

▶ The ThinApp capture computer as well as the computer executing the captured ThinApp should use an OS that is supported for the applications that it will capture. While this will not guarantee that the vendor will support the application once it is captured, it ensures that any issues related to the OS compatibility will not impact the capture process or the functionality of the application.

 When working with ThinApp, remember that nothing other than an explicit need for support prevents us from using unsupported configurations. The *VMware ThinApp: Application Notes and Recipes* forum (`https://communities.vmware.com/thinap.jspa`) is a good resource for learning how to successfully capture applications.

▶ ThinApp does not alter application-licensing requirements or their operation. Due to the way some applications handle licensing tasks, such as the activation methods used by companies such as Microsoft and Adobe, it is possible that additional procedures might be required to handle the licensing process. Many applications that are used in a corporate environment support some sort of alternative volume licensing method that might use different activation methods that are more suitable when using ThinApp. Consult application vendors for information on which software license or activation methods are suitable for virtualized applications. In many cases, the same methods that are used to preserve activation in nonpersistent desktop environments might also be suitable for use with ThinApp.

▶ Many application vendors do not support the use of ThinApp with their applications, regardless of whether or not the application appears to work. One example is Google Chrome, which can be captured using ThinApp but requires a number of potentially undesirable modifications in order to function.

If ThinApp addresses an otherwise difficult-to-address business need, the lack of formal support might be worth the risk. For example, with legacy apps, ThinApp might end up being the only option available to keep the application functioning.

▸ ThinApp cannot be used to virtualize applications that include Windows kernel-mode drivers. To support these applications, the drivers can be installed directly in the desktop. Some examples of applications that these drivers include are antivirus software, firewall software, and some VPN clients that will need to start their services at boot time.

Deploying VMware ThinApp

This recipe will go through the steps required to prepare a desktop for capturing applications using ThinApp.

Getting ready

VMware ThinApp requires a computer with the ThinApp application installed in order to capture applications. The ThinApp-captured computer should have a clean installation of Microsoft Windows that only has the base operating system installed. To ensure that the captured applications will be compatible, the ThinApp desktop should be representative of the master virtual desktop image that will be used with Horizon View, with similar core applications and tools installed.

The ThinApp-captured computer should also have the same Windows components installed as the computers on which the application will run. If components such as the Microsoft .NET Framework are required by the application and installed on the capture computer but not installed on the computers where ThinApp will be used, the applications will not work. In cases such as these, ThinApp should be used to capture the installation of both the .NET Framework and the application within the same ThinApp package, as this ensures that the application dependencies are met.

The ThinApp desktop works best when deployed as a virtual machine, as this enables us to use virtual machine snapshots to quickly roll back any changes that occur during the application capture process. To facilitate this and to remove the need to deploy a dedicated virtual machine on vSphere, ThinApp includes a license for VMware Workstation (`http://www.vmware.com/products/workstation/`), which will allow us to run the ThinApp desktop as a virtual machine on top of an existing Windows host while also allowing us to use virtual machine snapshots.

The ThinApp capture process generates not only the virtualized application, but also a collection of files and folders referred to as a **ThinApp Project**. Using the ThinApp Project files, the administrator can customize or update the ThinApp package as required.

Choosing an operating system version

In the event that the ThinApp packages will be executed on multiple versions of Windows, it is recommended that you capture the application on the earliest version of Windows that will be used, as this provides the greatest chance that the application will work on all OS's that are in use. For example, if our environment has both Windows XP and Windows 8.1 desktops, we will capture the application as it is installed on Windows XP.

 Regardless of which Windows OS version we use when capturing an application using ThinApp, once we have packaged it, we should test it on all of the OS versions where it will be run in order to ensure that it works as expected.

How to do it...

To install VMware ThinApp, first obtain the ThinApp license key and ThinApp installer, and complete the following steps to install the software on the dedicated ThinApp desktop:

1. Double-click on the ThinApp installer.
2. In the **Patent Lists** dialog box, click on **Next**.
3. Accept the ThinApp license, enter the serial number, and type a license display name. The license display name is displayed when we launch ThinApp applications.
4. Click on **Install** to complete the installation process.

The ThinApp software has now been installed and is ready for use.

Capturing an application with ThinApp

This recipe will guide us through the process of capturing the installation of an application using ThinApp and then building the ThinApp package.

Getting ready

The following is a list of key terms commonly seen when capturing and building applications using ThinApp:

Term	Definition
`build.bat`	The `build.bat` file is used to rebuild a ThinApp package to integrate any changes or updates.
The deployed execution mode	A ThinApp configured in the deployed execution mode is copied to and executed from the local desktop hard disk. This mode should not be used with linked clone desktops, as it will cause them to increase in size by the amount of space required to host the entire ThinApp package, potentially eliminating any space savings unique to the linked clone desktops.
The entry point	These are the points of entry into a ThinApp application that are typically an `.exe` or `.com` file. The entry points are specified when building the ThinApp.
The merged isolation mode	This grants a ThinApp permission to read and write from local nonsystem directories on the desktop. All other filesystem changes will be stored in the ThinApp sandbox. This option is recommended for Windows Logo Certified applications, one example being Microsoft Office.
`Package.ini`	A `Package.ini` file is created for every ThinApp project and is used to edit the configuration of the ThinApp package.
Sandbox	This is a component of a ThinApp where changes or other customizations are stored. The sandbox location is selected during the creation of the ThinApp and can reside either in the user's Windows profile, on a remote file share, or in the same directory as the ThinApp.
`Sbmerge.exe`	This is a command-line utility that performs the maintenance of ThinApp projects and is most often used after the installation of application updates in order to incorporate changed files or configuration data.
The streaming execution mode	A ThinApp configured in the streaming execution mode is typically run from a remote file share. ThinApps work by streaming application data to the desktop only when it is needed, on a block-by-block basis directly into the local memory. The streaming execution mode is typically used with linked clone desktops to reduce the amount of per-desktop storage required.
The ThinApp registration	The ThinApp registration is used to add common shortcuts and other traditional application features to the local desktop, making it appear similar to a traditionally installed application.

Term	Definition
The ThinDirect plugin	The VMware ThinDirect Internet Explorer plugin is installed on the virtual desktop master image and redirects the specified URLs to use a browser that has been packaged with ThinApp.
ThinReg.exe	ThinReg.exe is a command-line utility that is used to associate file extensions with specific applications. It is typically used to customize file associations in scenarios where a given file could be opened by multiple applications, including those packaged using ThinApp.
The WriteCopy isolation mode	The WriteCopy isolation mode prevents a ThinApp from writing to all but the users' My Documents and Desktop folders on the desktop. This setting is commonly used with applications that would otherwise modify files or registry keys that could impact the functionality of the OS itself or other applications on the desktop. This setting can be updated to allow write access to folders other than those allowed by default.

This chapter will focus on common ThinApp use cases and administrative tasks that even the smallest Horizon View environment might find useful. To learn about the full capabilities of the ThinApp suite, refer to the documents available on the *VMware ThinApp Documentation* page (http://www.vmware.com/support/pubs/thinapp_pubs.html).

> The ThinApp Packaging Community on the VMware Communities website is a great resource for learning about what is required to "ThinApp" a specific software package. The ThinApp Packaging Community is located at http://communities.vmware.com/thinap.jspa.

How to do it...

The following steps outline the process used to capture the installation of an application and package it using ThinApp. In this example, we will be capturing Adobe Acrobat Reader:

1. Take a snapshot of the ThinApp capture computer, power it on, and then log in.

2. From the Windows **Start** menu, navigate to **All Programs | VMware | ThinApp Setup Capture**.

3. In the **Setup Capture – Welcome** window, click on **Next**.

4. In the **Setup Capture – Ready to Prescan** window, click on **Prescan** to scan and then record the current configuration of the ThinApp desktop. Click on the **Advanced Scan Locations** button, if required, to open the **Advanced Scan Locations** window.

The **Advanced Scan Locations** window shown in the following screenshot is an optional feature that provides the ability to exclude certain directories or registry hives from the ThinApp prescan. Changes to these settings are not usually required.

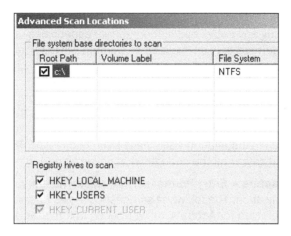

5. Once the ThinApp prescan has finished, the **Setup Capture – Install Application** window will be displayed, indicating that ThinApp is ready for the installation of the target application. If you want to add the ability to launch a virtualized instance of Microsoft Internet Explorer to the captured application, click on the **Internet Explorer** button to open the **Internet Explorer Entry Points** window. Once all options have been selected, minimize the **Setup Capture – Install Application** window during the installation process to ensure that it does not obscure any important dialog windows.

The **Internet Explorer Entry Points** window shown in the following screenshot is an optional feature that can be used to add an additional entry point to the ThinApp package. This entry point is for the locally installed instance of Internet Explorer and enables it to be launched within the ThinApp virtual environment. This allows us to use ThinApp virtualization with the locally installed version of IE even though we didn't capture it using ThinApp.

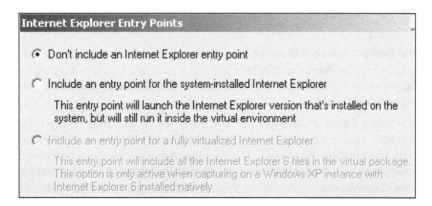

6. Install the target application and complete any additional configuration tasks such as:

   ❑ Accepting any license agreements

   ❑ Entering the software license information and performing any software activation tasks

   ❑ Disabling any native application update capabilities, as these tasks should be performed only on the master ThinApp project itself

   ❑ Installing additional required components such as web browser plugins

7. Once the application has been fully configured, close any open application windows to ensure that all files have been written to disk, restore the **Setup Capture – Install Application** window, and then click on the **Postscan** button. When prompted, confirm that the application installation tasks have been completed. ThinApp will now scan the desktop and gather all the changes that occurred during the installation process.

8. In the **Setup Capture – Entry Points** window, select the entry points that we wish to use for the application. The following screenshot shows us some of the entry points that ThinApp detected for Adobe Acrobat Reader. In this example, we only want users to have access to the primary Adobe Reader executable, so we have unchecked all others. Click on **Next** when the desired entry points have been selected.

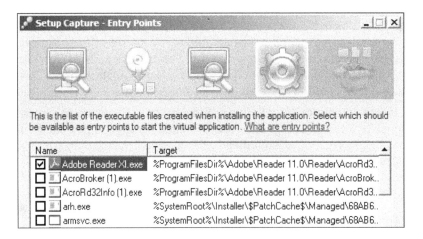

9. In the **Setup Capture – Manage with Horizon** window, make any required changes, and then click on **Next**. No changes are required if this ThinApp is going to be used only with Horizon View, and this step is optional even when using VMware Horizon Workspace.

10. In the **Setup Capture – Groups** window, apply any required application restrictions. By default, all users can use ThinApp; if restrictions are required, AD security groups can be used to limit the access. The ThinApp desktop must be a member of the domain in order to use this feature. AD groups that have been assigned permissions at this step will be able to execute the application regardless of their access rights to the Horizon View desktop. Click on **Next** when finished.

11. In the **Setup Capture – Isolation** window, choose the filesystem isolation mode from one of two options as described in the *Getting ready* section of this recipe. Click on either the **Merged isolation mode** or the **WriteCopy isolation mode** radio button, as shown in the following screenshot, and then click on **Next**:

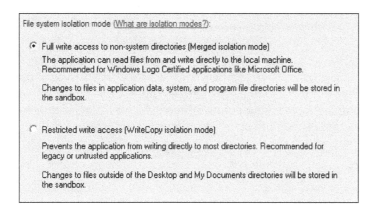

12. In the **Setup Capture – Sandbox** window, choose the Sandbox location from one of three options shown, and then click on **Next**. The description of each is described in the *Getting ready* section of this recipe as well as the following screenshot.

    The **User profile** option is the default and is the preferred choice for most common use cases.

> If we plan to use Horizon View Persona Management, described in *Chapter 5, Implementation of Horizon View Persona Management*, the **Thinstall** directory should be set to background-download rather than download on demand. The default Persona Management setting will only download this data as required, which can lead to performance issues with applications delivered using ThinApp. This setting is configured in the group policy setting by navigating to **VMware View Agent Configuration | Persona Management | Roaming & Synchronization | Folders to background download**. This recommendation also applies to other profile management platforms that include similar functionalities.

13. In the **Setup Capture – Quality Assurance Statistics** window, select whether or not to share ThinApp statistics with VMware, and then click on **Next**.

 If the machines that will use the ThinApp do not have Internet access, select the **No – Do not send any information to VMware** radio checkbox.

14. If a web browser is being captured, the **Setup Capture – Native Browser Redirection** window shown will now be displayed. This feature works alongside the VMware ThinDirect Internet Explorer plugin, and the URL specified here will load only through the ThinApp packaged browser rather than the local instance of Internet Explorer. Make changes as required and click on **Next**.

The ThinDirect plugin and associated group policy template can be found in the `Program Files\VMware\VMware ThinApp` directory on the ThinApp computer.

The `ThinDirect.adm` group policy template can also be used to configure the browser redirection settings, specified as individual URLs.

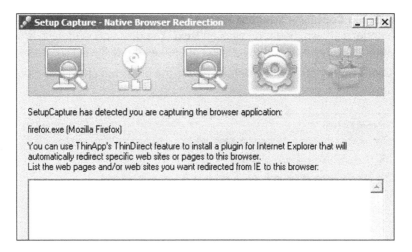

15. In the **Setup Capture – Project Settings** window, edit **Inventory name** and specify **Project location**, as shown in the following screenshot, and then click on **Next**:

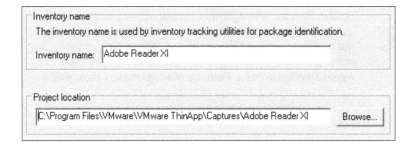

We might want to remove any software version or build numbers from **Inventory name**, as shown in the previous screenshot. This ensures that, when the ThinApp is updated, any changes to the software version number will not be displayed in the ThinApp name, eliminating any confusion that might occur should the application name suddenly change. However, if we intend to supply multiple versions of the same application, we might want to keep the version number intact.

16. In the **Setup Capture – Package Settings** window, make changes to the default settings as required. To enable the ThinApp registration, we must enable MSI package generation by selecting the **Generate MSI package** checkbox as shown in the following screenshot. We can also select the **Compress virtual package** checkbox to compress the resulting ThinApp package, although this will lead to a slight increase in the desktop CPU usage each time the ThinApp is launched. Click on **Save** when finished to create the ThinApp Project directory.

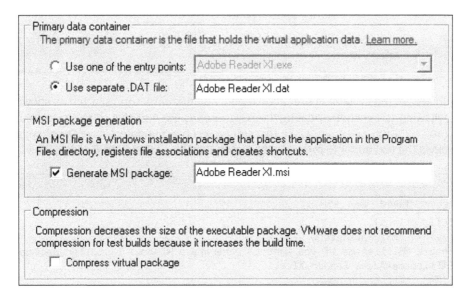

 The default options for the primary data container are usually the optimal choice, as the ThinApp will choose the preferred option based on the application configuration. Any changes at this point might affect the display of the application icon.

17. In the **Setup Capture – Ready to Build** window, make changes as required. In this example, we will click on the **Edit Package.ini** button shown in the following screenshot in order to enable **Streaming Execution Mode**, disabled by default:

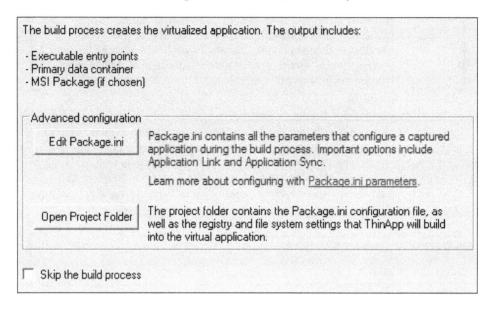

The build process creates the virtualized application. The output includes:

- Executable entry points
- Primary data container
- MSI Package (if chosen)

Advanced configuration

| Edit Package.ini | Package.ini contains all the parameters that configure a captured application during the build process. Important options include Application Link and Application Sync.

Learn more about configuring with Package.ini parameters. |
| Open Project Folder | The project folder contains the Package.ini configuration file, as well as the registry and file system settings that ThinApp will build into the virtual application. |

☐ Skip the build process

18. To enable the streaming execution mode, edit the `package.ini` file as shown in the following screenshot, updating the `MSIStreaming=0` configuration parameter to read `MSIStreaming=1`. Once this setting has been updated, save the changes and close the text editor to return to the **Setup Capture – Ready to Build** window.

```
Package.ini - Notepad
File  Edit  Format  View  Help
[BuildOptions]
;-------- MSI Parameters ----------
;Enable MSIFilename if you want to generate a Windows Installer package.
MSIFilename=Adobe Reader XI.msi
MSIManufacturer=Unknown
MSIProductVersion=1.0
MSIDefaultInstallAllUsers=1
MSIRequireElevatedPrivileges=1
MSIInstallDirectory=Adobe Reader XI (VMware ThinApp)
;MSIProductCode={14020D69-9B43-0D77-3ACA-811EAEDBA72A}
MSIUpgradeCode={F86868B8-F5A6-889F-9D87-1807263094FC}
MSIStreaming=1
MSICompressionType=Fast
MSIArpProductIcon=%SystemRoot%\Installer\{AC76BA86-7AD7-1033-7B44-AB00000
MSIIs64Bit=0
```

One additional configuration parameter that we might wish to change is `RemoveSandboxOnExit=1`. This setting instructs the ThinApp to retain the sandbox contents when the application is closed. By default, this setting is disabled; to enable it, remove `;` in front of the parameter and save the changes. When enabled, any changes to the ThinApp will be discarded when the ThinApp is closed. Enabling this feature allows us to tightly control the configuration of the application, as no changes will be retained between sessions. We might also want to use it with nonpersistent desktops, which typically discard any application changes upon logoff anyway.

Refer to the VMware document *ThinApp Package.ini Parameters Reference Guide* (`https://www.vmware.com/pdf/thinapp50_packageini._reference.pdf`) for a full description of all the parameters within the `Package.ini` file.

19. In the **Setup Capture – Ready to Build** window, click on **Save** to extract and save the files and configuration settings required to create the ThinApp package. The **Setup Capture – Save Project** window will be displayed while the files and settings are being saved; once the process is completed, we will be returned to the **Setup Capture – Ready to Build** window.

20. In the **Setup Capture – Ready to Build** window, click on **Build** to move to the **Setup Capture – Build Project** window, and create the ThinApp package.

21. In the **Setup Capture – Build Project** window, once the ThinApp build process has completed, uncheck the **Open folder containing project executables after clicking Finish** checkbox, and then click on **Finish**.

22. Verify in the operation of the new ThinApp package that any expected updates were applied and that the configuration settings performed after the installation were retained.

23. If the ThinApp project directory was saved on the ThinApp desktop, we must copy it to an alternate location, as it includes the files needed to repackage the application if required and also because it would otherwise be lost when the ThinApp capture computer is reverted to a previous snapshot in the next step.

24. Revert the ThinApp desktop to the saved snapshot to discard the changes that were made during the ThinApp capture process.

The completed ThinApp package will be placed in the `bin` folder within the ThinApp project directory. The following screenshot shows the contents of a sample ThinApp project `bin` folder for Adobe Acrobat, which includes both the `.exe`, `.dat`, and `.msi` files:

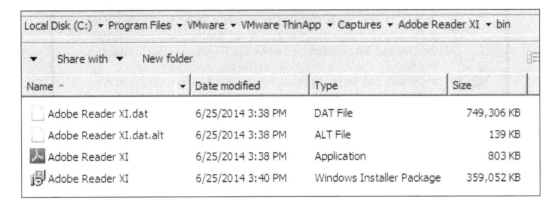

These files are what is required for the end user to be able to use the ThinApp package. To make them available for use, copy them to a file share with read-only permissions in order to prevent unauthorized changes. The only reason a ThinApp would ever need to be installed in a directory with write permissions is if the sandbox is configured to be stored alongside the ThinApp; this is typically only used when delivering the application in a portable storage device such as a USB drive or a portable hard drive.

 The `Package.ini` file's `OutDir` variable can be used to specify an alternate location for ThinApp to place the package files when the build process is completed. This value is set to `bin` by default, which places the application files in a folder with that name within the ThinApp project folder.

The ThinApp project folders should be retained and backed up for later use when updating the application files or settings. If the ThinApp project folders are discarded, the application will need to be captured again in order to make any changes or apply software updates.

How it works...

The following figure shows you the relationship between ThinApp applications and the host desktop where they are run:

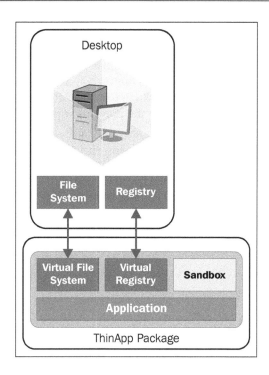

The ThinApp application runs self-contained using its own virtualized filesystem and Windows registry. This isolation is what prevents ThinApp applications from interfering with other applications or the host OS, as changes to the ThinApp application occur only within the dedicated application virtualization layer.

It is also possible to link together two or more ThinApp applications using a ThinApp feature called **Application Link** that can be used to address application dependencies without the need to install additional software in the master desktop image. One example of why this is important would be the Microsoft .NET Framework. If the capture computer has the .NET Framework installed and the application requires it, the resulting captured application will only work on computers that have it installed as well. The ThinApp Application Link feature is discussed in detail in *VMware ThinApp User's Guide* at `http://www.vmware.com/support/pubs/thinapp_pubs.html`.

Updating ThinApp packages

This recipe will focus on using the native features of ThinApp to update existing ThinApp projects and repackage them, which preserves any previous application customization and prevents the need to repeat the entire capture process.

Getting ready

There are multiple ways to update applications that have been packaged using ThinApp. The simplest of these ways is to repackage the updated application and redeploy it using whichever method we wish. This can even include using Horizon View to assign the newer version of the application and decommission the previous version.

 Do not attempt to update ThinApp packages when performing a major version upgrade of an application. It is best to capture a clean installation of the newer version of the application rather than attempt an in-place upgrade. By performing a clean installation of the target application, we eliminate the possibility that any settings or files associated with the previous version will affect the behavior of the newer version.

How to do it...

In this section, we will review two different options for updating a ThinApp package.

Using built-in application updaters

Applications such as Mozilla Firefox and many others include the ability to download and install updates using native features. This section will outline how we use these features to apply software updates, and then integrate these changes into our master ThinApp project. Firefox is used as an example for this section, although the process is similar for other applications with native update capabilities. The following steps outline how to repackage the Firefox application after updates have been applied:

1. Create a backup of the ThinApp project folder that will be updated.
2. Using the ThinApp desktop, attach the file share that contains the target ThinApp project folder.
3. For Windows 7 and newer Windows OS's, verify that the `AppData\Roaming\Thinstall` directory within the logged-on users Windows profile on the ThinApp desktop is empty. If it is not, delete the contents of the folder.

 For Windows XP, the directory is located in `Application Data\Thinapp\SANDBOXNAME`, where `SANDBOXNAME` is the value specified in the ThinApp's `Package.ini` file.

When updating a ThinApp, it is important to discard any existing sandbox data to prevent it from being included in the rebuilt application. Emptying the `Thinstall` folder deletes any existing sandbox data on the ThinApp desktop and ensures that only data that is critical to the update is merged into the ThinApp project folder.

4. Launch the ThinApp from the `bin` folder of the ThinApp project, and update the application using the native update features.

 For applications where this native update process fails or does not exist, or where patches must be installed outside the application runtime, we must use an alternate entry point to execute the update. In the next section, we will enable a Windows command prompt that can be used as an alternate endpoint into the ThinApp package.

5. Once the update has been applied, relaunch the application, verify that the update was applied, and configure the application as desired. When finished, close the application.

6. From the command prompt of the ThinApp desktop, navigate to the `Program Files\VMware\VMware ThinApp` directory.

7. Execute the following command to merge the application updates into the ThinApp project folder. In this example, the Firefox ThinApp project is located at `T:\Mozilla Firefox`:

   Sbmerge apply -ProjectDir "t:\Mozilla Firefox"

8. The `sbmerge` utility will update the ThinApp project folder to include any files and configuration changes that occurred when the application was updated. Once `sbmerge` has completed, execute the `build.bat` file from within the ThinApp project directory to rebuild the ThinApp and overwrite the existing contents of the `bin` folder. In our example, the `build.bat` file is located at `T:\Mozilla Firefox\build.bat`.

9. Test the operation of the updated ThinApp package, verifying that the expected updates were applied and that any changes to the application configuration settings were retained.

Once the ThinApp has been tested and the configuration verified, it can be deployed in place of the existing ThinApp.

Using alternate entry points

As mentioned in the previous section, it is not always possible to update an application using the native update features. Additionally, updates that are installed outside of the ThinApp application runtime, such as a patch for Microsoft Office, have no ThinApp entry point themselves, so they cannot be executed within the context of the ThinApp. If we were to update applications outside the ThinApp application runtime, the changes would not be captured in the ThinApp sandbox and would not be incorporated into the updated ThinApp when it is rebuilt.

To update these applications, we will create an alternate entry point into the application, in this case, a Windows command prompt that executes in the context of the ThinApp. Once we enable the Windows command prompt entry point, we can then install those updates that cannot be applied using native update features. The following steps outline how to enable the alternate endpoints, apply the required patches, and repackage the application. Adobe Reader XI is just used as the example in this section; the process is the same for other applications:

1. Create a backup of the ThinApp project that will be updated.

2. Using the ThinApp desktop, attach the file share that contains the target ThinApp project folder.

3. For Windows 7 and newer Windows OS's, verify that the `AppData\Roaming\Thinstall` directory within the logged-on users' Windows profile on the ThinApp capture computer is empty. If it is not, delete the contents.

 For Windows XP, the directory is located in `Application Data\Thinapp\SANDBOXNAME`, where `SANDBOXNAME` is the value specified in the ThinApp `Package.ini` file.

4. Open the `Package.ini` file located in the target ThinApp project folder.

5. Scroll down to the bottom of the `Package.ini` file and, under the `[cmd.exe]` section, update the `Disabled=1` setting to `Disabled=0`, as shown in the following screenshot. This setting enables `cmd.exe` as an additional entry point into the ThinApp. Save the `Package.ini` file and close the text editor.

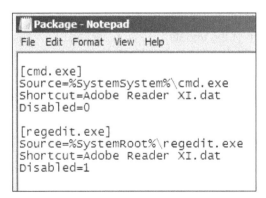

 In addition to the `cmd.exe` entry point, we can also enable the `regedit` Windows registry editing tool by making a similar change to the `[regedit.exe]` section of the `Package.ini` file.

6. Execute the `build.bat` file from within the ThinApp project directory. In our example, the `build.bat` file is located at `T:\Adobe Reader XI`. The `build.bat` file will rebuild the ThinApp package and overwrite the existing ThinApp in the `bin` directory. Once the rebuilt is completed, the `bin` folder will now contain a ThinApp entry point for `cmd.exe`, which we can use to install our patches. The following screenshot shows us the updated `bin` folder with the additional `cmd.exe` entry point:

Name	Date modified	Type	Size
Adobe Reader XI.dat	6/25/2014 5:22 PM	DAT File	749,626 KB
Adobe Reader XI.dat.alt	6/25/2014 5:22 PM	ALT File	139 KB
Adobe Reader XI.exe	6/25/2014 5:22 PM	Application	803 KB
Adobe Reader XI.msi	6/25/2014 5:24 PM	Windows Installer ...	359,103 KB
cmd.exe	6/25/2014 5:22 PM	Application	149 KB

7. Launch the `cmd.exe` ThinApp application from the ThinApp `bin` folder and use the command window to launch the software patches executables. If multiple software patches are required, simply install them in succession, closing and reopening the `cmd.exe` ThinApp entry point if required to satisfy any requests from the patch to perform a reboot. There is no need to reboot the ThinApp computer itself.

8. Verify that the updated application is functioning as expected, and reconfigure any applications settings as required.

9. Undo the previous changes to the `Package.ini` file so that the `cmd.exe` entry point will be removed when the application is repackaged using the `sbmerge` utility. This is accomplished by reverting the `Disabled=0` setting to `Disabled=1` under the `[cmd.exe]` section of `Package.ini`.

10. Execute the `sbmerge` utility to merge the application updates into the ThinApp project folder. In this example, the Adobe Reader XI ThinApp project is located at `T:\Adobe Reader XI`:

    Sbmerge apply -ProjectDir "t:\Adobe Reader XI"

11. The `sbmerge` utility will update the ThinApp project folder to include any files and configuration changes that occurred when Adobe Acrobat was updated. Once `sbmerge` has completed, execute the `build.bat` file from within the ThinApp project directory. In our example, the `build.bat` file is located at `T:\Adobe Reader XI`. The `build.bat` file will rebuild the ThinApp package and overwrite the existing contents of the `bin` folder. In addition, the `cmd.exe` ThinApp entry point will be removed during the execution of the `build.bat` script.

12. Test the operation of the updated ThinApp package, verifying that the expected updates were applied and that any configuration settings were retained.

Once the ThinApp has been tested and the configuration verified, it can be deployed in place of the existing ThinApp.

Configuring a Horizon View ThinApp repository

One of the benefits of using ThinApp with Horizon View is that Horizon View can automatically publish ThinApp packages to individual desktops or even desktop pools. This recipe will show you how to configure a Horizon View ThinApp repository, and then discover and publish ThinApp packages.

Getting ready

To create a ThinApp repository, Horizon View requires a Windows file share with read access granted to both Horizon View entitled AD users and computer accounts. The individual ThinApp packages should be copied to this folder using a dedicated subfolder for each.

How to do it...

In this section, we will configure the Horizon View ThinApp repository, and then perform an immediate ThinApp scan to recognize the ThinApp packages contained within.

Configuring a Horizon View ThinApp repository

The ThinApp repository is configured using the Horizon View Manager Admin console. The following steps outline how to add a ThinApp repository:

1. Navigate to **View Configuration | ThinApp Configuration** in the Horizon View Manager Admin console. Click on the **Add Repository** button in the **ThinApp Configuration** page to open the **Add Application Repository** window.

2. Provide **Display name** for the repository as well as the **Share path** to the Window file share that will host the ThinApp packages. A sample configuration is shown in the following screenshot. Click on **Save** when finished to add the ThinApp repository and close the window.

Add Application Repository	
	Repository
Display name:	ThinApp Repo 1
Share path:	\\vc-01.vjason.local\ThinApp
	(Example: \\host.vmware.com\fileshare) Note: IP addresses are not supported.
Description:		

The ThinApp repository should now be displayed in the Horizon View Manager Admin console's **ThinApp Configuration** page. In the next section, we will perform an immediate scan of the repository to identify our ThinApp packages.

Scanning for ThinApp packages

Once we have added our ThinApp repository in the Horizon View Manager Admin console, we must scan it so that we can indicate which applications we wish to assign. The following steps outline how to perform a scan of the ThinApp repository:

1. Navigate to **Catalog | ThinApps** in the Horizon View Manager Admin console. Click on the **Scan New ThinApps** button in the **ThinApps** page to open the **Scan New ThinApps** window.

2. In the **ThinApp repository** drop-down menu, select the repository we wish to scan. By default, the scan will begin in the root of the repository, which will reveal all ThinApp packages contained within it. If we wish to restrict which folders are scanned, expand the repository folder structure in the **Folder to scan** window and select the desired folder to start the scan from. An example of this window is shown in the following screenshot. Click on **Next** to begin the scan.

Only ThinApp packages that have MSI files will be detected during the scan. If we did not select the checkbox during the capture process to generate a MSI package with the ThinApp, we will need to enable this option in the ThinApp project's `Package.ini` file, rebuild the ThinApp, copy the updated ThinApp to the repository, and then perform the scan again.

3. In the results window, select the ThinApp MSI files we wish to scan. In the following example, we have highlighted both of the MSI files that were found. Click on **Scan** to begin the MSI scan.

Scan New ThinApps	
Select the MSI files to scan	
Select the MSI files to scan and add to View Administrator:	
MSI File	Path
Adobe Reader XI.msi	\\vc-01.vjason.local\ThinApp\Adobe Reader XI
Mozilla Firefox.msi	\\vc-01.vjason.local\ThinApp\Mozilla Firefox

4. Once the scan is completed, the results will be displayed in the window, as shown in the following screenshot. Click on **Finish** to close the window.

Scan New ThinApps			
Scanning: Scanning completed. 2 ThinApps added.			
Name	Path	MSI File	Status
Mozilla Firefox	\Mozilla Firefox	Mozilla Firefox.msi	Added
Adobe Reader XI	\Adobe Reader XI	Adobe Reader XI.msi	Added

The Horizon View Manager Admin console's **ThinApps** page will now display the ThinApp packages that were detected during the scan. These ThinApp packages can now be individually assigned to a desktop or desktop pool or added to a template that enables the assignment of multiple applications at once. The next recipe outlines how to assign individual ThinApp packages or how to create templates to assign multiple ThinApp packages at once.

Assigning ThinApp applications in Horizon View

In this recipe, we will review how to assign ThinApp packages in Horizon View desktops. Two options are covered: assigning individual ThinApp packages and creating templates that allow us to assign multiple ThinApp packages at a time.

Getting ready

To assign a ThinApp, we need two things: a Horizon View desktop pool and at least one ThinApp application registered with Horizon View using the techniques outlined in the previous recipe. Once these requirements are met, we can assign a ThinApp using the Horizon View Manager Admin console.

 ThinApp cannot place shortcuts on the desktop if that folder is being directed using folder redirection. If folder redirection is being used, the application shortcuts must be copied to the folder manually.

How to do it...

In this section, we will assign applications to a desktop pool. The same process is used to assign applications to an individual desktop, so only one example will be shown.

 VMware Horizon View does not verify ThinApp group restrictions when assigning a ThinApp package to a Horizon View desktop pool or individual desktop. If ThinApp restrictions prohibit a user from executing the application, they will not be able to use it even if it is assigned in the Horizon View Manager Admin console.

Assigning an individual ThinApp package

The following steps outline how to assign an individual application to a desktop or desktop pool:

1. Navigate to **Catalog | ThinApps** in the Horizon View Manager Admin console. Highlight the ThinApp we wish to assign, click on the **Add Assignment** drop-down menu, and select **Assign Desktop Pools...**, as shown in the following screenshot:

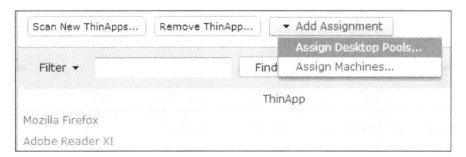

2. In the **Add Pool Assignment** window shown in the following screenshot, select the Horizon View desktop pool we wish to assign the ThinApp to and click on **Add**. Click on either the **Streaming** (execute the ThinApp from the remote repository—optimal for linked clone desktops) or **Full** (copied to and executed directly on the Horizon View desktop—optimal for full clone desktops) button to set the ThinApp installation method. Click on **OK** to complete the application assignment.

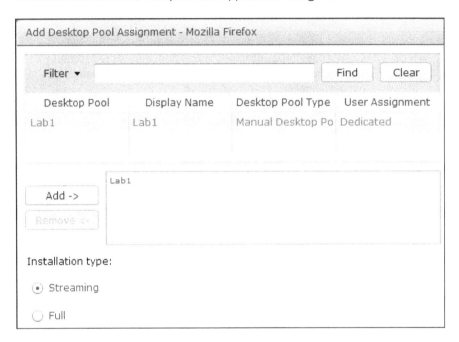

The ThinApp is now assigned to the Horizon View desktop pool. If the **Full** application type was selected, the ThinApp will be copied to the desktop during the user logon process. Since an MSI file was used to deploy the ThinApp, the default application shortcuts will be placed in the user's desktop and in the **Start** menu.

 Remember that, if we are redirecting the user's `Desktop` folder, ThinApp will not be able to create an application shortcut on the desktop. If a shortcut is required, we must manually copy it to the `Desktop` folder.

To assign applications to an individual desktop, select the target machine from the Horizon View Manager Admin console by navigating to **Resources | Machines** and use the **Add Assignment** button found on the target machine's **Summary** page.

By default, the ThinApp installation type will be set to **Streaming**. If the ThinApp was not configured to support streaming, the ThinApp installation type will revert to **Full**. As described in the *Capturing an application with ThinApp* recipe, the streaming mode must be enabled during the application build process, as it is not enabled by default. It can be enabled after editing the ThinApp `Package.ini` file and rebuilding the ThinApp.

Assigning applications using a ThinApp template

A ThinApp template can be used to assign multiple ThinApp packages to a desktop or desktop pool all at once. If large numbers of desktops require an identical collection of ThinApp packages, a template can be used to simpify the ThinApp deployment process. The following steps outline how to create and assign a ThinApp template:

1. Navigate to **Catalog | ThinApps** in the Horizon View Manager Admin console. Click on the **New Template** button to open the **New ThinApp Template** window.

2. In the **Template name** field, provide a name for the ThinApp template as shown in the following screenshot. Click on the **Add** button to select the ThinApp packages we wish to assign to the template.

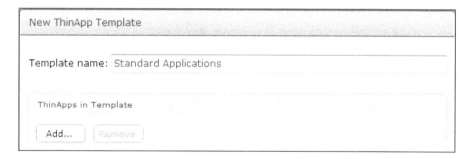

3. Highlight the applications we wish add to the template, click on the **Add** button, and click on **OK** to return to the previous window.

4. Click on **OK** to close the **New ThinApp Template** window, create the ThinApp template, and return to the **ThinApps** page in the Horizon View Manager Admin console.

The ThinApp template and the ThinApp packages it contains will now be displayed in the **ThinApps** page as shown in the following screenshot:

The template is assigned using the same steps used to assign a single ThinApp, including selecting the ThinApp installation type. Refer to the *Assigning an individual ThinApp package* section for the steps used to assign the template.

Removing ThinApp assignments

In this recipe, we will review how to remove ThinApp assignments from individual desktops as well as Horizon View desktop pools.

Getting ready

There are multiple reasons why we might need to remove a ThinApp assignment from an individual desktop or Horizon View desktop pool.

How to do it...

The process used to remove a ThinApp assignment is similar for both desktops and desktop pools.

Removing a ThinApp assignment from a Horizon View desktop

The following steps outline how to remove a ThinApp assignment from an individual Horizon View desktop:

1. Navigate to **Resources** | **Machines** in the Horizon View Manager Admin console and search for the target desktop.

2. Double-click on the target desktop to bring up the desktop **Summary** page.

3. In the **ThinApps** window of the desktop **Summary** page, highlight the target ThinApp to be removed, and click on the **Remove Assignment** button as shown in the following screenshot:

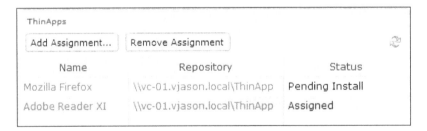

The ThinApp has now been unassigned from the desktop and will automatically be removed by the desktop Horizon View agent software.

Removing a ThinApp assignment from a desktop pool

The following steps outline how to remove a ThinApp assignment from a Horizon View desktop pool:

1. Navigate to **Catalog | Desktop Pools** in the Horizon View Manager Admin console, and double-click on the target Horizon View desktop pool.

2. Click on the **Inventory** tab, and then click on **ThinApps** (highlighted in red) as shown in the following screenshot:

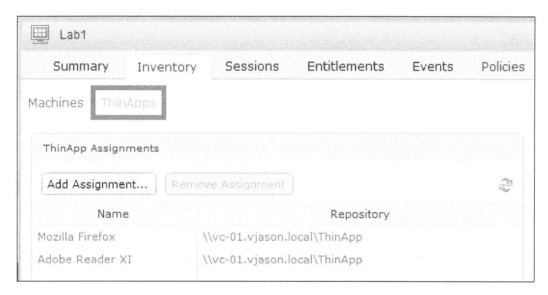

3. Click on the target ThinApp to be removed, and then click on the **Remove Assignment** button.

The ThinApp has now been unassigned from the desktop pool and will automatically be removed by the Horizon View agent software installed on each desktop in the pool.

7
Deploying Horizon View Clients in Kiosk Mode

In this chapter, we will cover the following recipes:

- Preparing your VMware Horizon View and Microsoft AD infrastructures for Kiosk Mode Clients
- Configuring the default values for Kiosk Mode Clients
- Adding AD accounts for Kiosk Mode Clients
- Verifying the configuration of Kiosk Mode Clients
- Configuring Kiosk Mode Client devices

Introduction

VMware Horizon View Kiosk Mode Clients are a type of client whose authentication has been previously configured using the **media access control (MAC)** address of the client device. Once properly configured, Kiosk Mode Clients can log in to Horizon View using nothing more than the name of a Connection Server.

Kiosk Mode Clients can be useful in a number of situations, including the following:

- Providing individuals who do not have **Active Directory** (**AD**) user accounts with access to a desktop so that they can perform a task
- Providing access to a general-use desktop in areas where user authentication might not be required, such as a lunch room, fitness centre, or reception area

Using Kiosk Mode Clients, the technology staff can provide an authentication-free desktop environment while still leveraging the benefits of virtual desktop computing.

It is important to note that VMware Horizon View does not offer the ability to secure Kiosk Mode Client devices as well as the Horizon View desktops that they will access. This must be accomplished using the Client device's native features or customization, AD group policies, or even third-party software packages. This chapter will provide us with an overview of some of these techniques within the context of various recipes but, due to the unique requirements of each organization, additional research might be required.

Preparing your VMware Horizon View and Microsoft AD infrastructures for Kiosk Mode Clients

There are multiple prerequisites that must be met prior to enabling and deploying Horizon View Kiosk Mode Clients. This recipe will review these prerequisites and provide examples.

Getting ready

To enable our Horizon View infrastructure in order to support Kiosk Mode Clients, we will need access to the following resources:

- ▶ The **Active Directory Users and Computers** (**ADUC**) console and the ability to create new AD OUs and security groups.

- ▶ **Active Directory Group Policy Management Console** (**GPMC**) and the ability to create and apply new group policy templates.

- ▶ The Horizon View Manager Admin console and the ability to create and entitle Horizon View desktop pools.

- ▶ The VMware vCenter console and the ability to create and modify a VM. The `TPVMGPoACmap.dll` file is used to enable the configuration of location-based printing and is available on any Connection Server at `Program Files\VMware\VMware View\Server\extras\GroupPolicyFiles\ThinPrint\x64`.

Once these tools and their required levels of access have been obtained, we are ready to make the necessary changes to our environment.

How to do it...

The following steps outline the procedure for preparing our infrastructure for the configuration of Kiosk Mode Clients:

1. Using the ADUC console, create an AD **organizational unit** (**OU**) that will be used to host the Kiosk Mode AD user accounts. Horizon View will automatically create the required AD user accounts when provisioning the clients, so we should not attempt to create them ourselves. Additionally, record the **distinguished name** (**DN**) of this OU for use in a later chapter. For this chapter, we will create an OU named **KioskClients**, as shown in the following screenshot. Based on our AD configuration, the DN of this OU will be `OU=KioskClients,OU=Kiosk,OU=View,DC=vjason,DC=local`. This is demonstrated in the following screenshot:

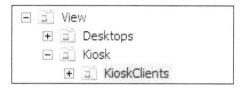

2. In this chapter, our AD OU structure uses a dedicated hierarchy of OUs that are dedicated to our Horizon View infrastructure. This is not an explicit requirement but merely a possible design. One reason why this design was selected was that it allows us to isolate our Horizon View environment from the rest of the AD domain, which simplifies the process.

3. When planning on using dedicated AD group policies for the desktops used by Kiosk Mode Clients or even Windows-based Horizon View clients themselves, we should create dedicated OUs for them as well. For this chapter, we have created an OU for each: **Desktops** for the Horizon View desktops used by Kiosk Mode Clients and **KioskClientComputers** for our Windows-based Kiosk clients. These OUs are also shown in the following screenshot:

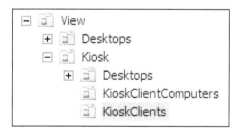

4. Using the ADUC console, create an AD security group that will be used with the Kiosk Mode AD user accounts. This security group will be entitled to use the desktop pool that contains the desktops used by Kiosk Mode Clients. In this example, we have created a security group named `KioskClients`. This security group must also have the **pre-Windows 2000** name specified, as shown in the following screenshot. The security group should have been given this by default when it was created. In our example, we have placed the `KioskClients` OU group created in step 1.

Group name:

KioskClients

Group name (pre-Windows 2000):

KioskClients

5. Using the VMware vCenter client, create a virtual desktop master image or template with the desired configuration. This is the desktop that our Kiosk Mode Clients will access, so it should be configured with the applications required and locked down where necessary. Additionally, Kiosk Mode users will not know the AD user account passwords used to establish their session, so the guest OS should be configured so that it does not lock itself after periods of inactivity or allow itself to be manually locked.

VMware's *Optimization Guide for Windows 7 and Windows 8 Virtual Desktops in Horizon with View* (`http://www.vmware.com/resources/techresources/10157`) provides information on how to optimize a master image in order to minimize the resources it requires and potentially, improve the performance.

Local group policies or domain-based group policies can be used to prevent a guest OS from locking itself after periods of inactivity. While the end results of either method are the same, local group policies are sometimes preferred, as they can be configured without needing to change or create any existing domain-based group policies. If using local group policies, we must verify that they will not be overwritten by domain-based policies, which can potentially change settings to something different from what we want. Microsoft TechNet's article, *Group Policy processing and precedence* (`http://technet.microsoft.com/en-us/library/cc785665`, explains if and when group policies will be overridden.

6. Using the **Horizon View Manager Admin** console, create a desktop pool using the image or template created in the previous step. The desktop pool requirements might vary from one organization to the other, so select the optimal pool choice based on our needs. In this chapter, we will use a floating assignment linked-clone pool, configured to refresh the desktops upon logoff. For this chapter, we have created a pool named **Kiosk-Win7**.

7. Using the **Horizon View Manager Admin** console, entitle the AD security group previously created in step 4 (**KioskClients**) in order to use the desktop pool created in step 6 (**Kiosk-Win7**). To ensure that Kiosk Mode Clients are assigned desktops from the desired desktop pool, this AD security group should not be entitled to use more than one desktop pool at a time.

8. Optional for Windows-based Kiosk Mode clients that require automatic printer configuration; to enable the configuration of a location-based printing group policy, register the `TPVMGPoACmap.dll` DLL file on a computer with the **Group Policy Management** console installed using the procedure outlined in the VMware document *Register the Location-Based Printing Group Policy DLL File* (`https://pubs.vmware.com/horizon-view-60/topic/com.vmware.horizon-view.desktops.doc/GUID-2B187B8A-30D2-47B2-BC6F-32DD2A0B8DDE.html#GUID-2B187B8A-30D2-47B2-BC6F-32DD2A0B8DDE`).

9. Optional for Windows-based Kiosk Mode Clients that require automatic printer configuration, also known as **ThinPrint** or **location-based** printing; use the Microsoft GPMC to enable the **AutoConnect Map Additional Printers for VMware View** setting. This computer-specific group policy is applied to the Windows-based computers that will be used as Kiosk Mode Clients and is described in greater detail in the VMware document *Setting Up Location-Based Printing* (`https://pubs.vmware.com/horizon-view-60/topic/com.vmware.horizon-view.desktops.doc/GUID-1EB46B6D-EBF7-499E-9AE1-D8253C9FB241.html`).

 The configuration of location-based printing from a Horizon View client perspective is discussed later in this chapter in the recipe titled *Configuring Kiosk Mode Horizon View Client devices*.

With these steps, we are now able to enable Kiosk Mode Clients in our Horizon View infrastructure.

How it works...

In this section, we will take a deeper look into some of the configuration steps described in the previous section.

Location-based printing

The optional VMware Horizon View ThinPrint feature allows us to assign and automatically map printers based on the client subnet, client name, username or security group membership, or the MAC address. In scenarios where we are using floating assignment desktops for our Kiosk clients and the kiosk client user's Windows profile settings are not retained between client sessions, location-based printing enables us to automatically assign printers.

The location-based printing setting is applied using AD group policies applied to Windows-based client computers and not the Horizon View desktops themselves. The following screenshot shows us the **AutoConnect Map Additional Printers for VMware View** group policy object that was enabled by registering the TPVMGPoACmap.dll DLL file as well as an example of how the ThinPrint feature might be configured:

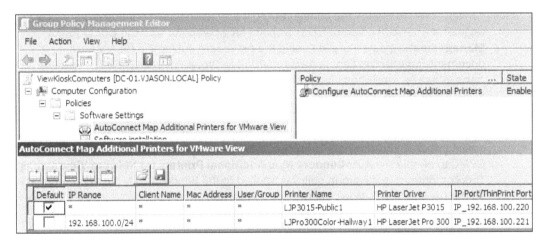

In this example, the first printer on the list is set as the default printer using the **Default** checkbox. Since the **IP Range**, **Client Name**, **Mac Address**, and **User/Group** fields are all filled with a wildcard (*****), this printer will be mapped to all the Horizon View clients to whom the policy applies. The second printer on the list will be mapped only to these clients in the **192.168.100.0/24** subnet. The **Printer Driver** field must match the driver name as it appears on each Horizon View desktop; if the driver is not available or the name does not match, the printer will not be mapped. The **IP Port/ThinPrint Port** field must contain the IP address of the printer network interface; it cannot be used with print servers.

Additional information on the VMware ThinPrint feature is available in the VMware document *Configure the Location-Based Printing Group Policy* (https://pubs.vmware.com/horizon-view-60/topic/com.vmware.horizon-view.desktops.doc/GUID-E1BF0A7A-CF5D-4E67-B347-E41274A9801F.html).

Configuring the default values for Kiosk Mode Clients

This recipe will review the procedures required to enable Kiosk Mode Clients in our VMware Horizon View pod.

Getting ready

The following items are required in order to prepare our Horizon View pod for use with Kiosk Mode Clients:

- Console and local administrator access to one of the Horizon View Connection Servers in our pod.

- The DN of the OU we created in the previous recipe in this chapter. For this example, we will be using OU=KioskClients,OU=Kiosk,OU=View,DC=vjason,DC=local.

- The **pre-Windows 2000** name of the security group we created in the previous recipe in this chapter. For this example, we will be using KioskClients.

Once the required information and access have been obtained, we can proceed with enabling Kiosk Mode Clients in our pod.

How to do it...

The following steps outline how to enable Kiosk Mode Clients in our pod. In this example, we will be setting the KioskClients OU as the default location for our Kiosk Mode Client accounts, adding the clients to the KioskClients group, and setting the passwords of these accounts to **Never Expire**. Perform the following steps:

1. From a command prompt on one of the Connection Servers in our pod, navigate to **Program Files** | **VMware** | **VMware View** | **Server** | **bin**.

2. Execute the following command and insert the information referenced earlier in this chapter for the OU and group names. The command and resulting output are shown in the following screenshot:

   vdmadmin -Q -clientauth -setdefaults -ou "OU=KioskClients,OU=Kiosk ,OU=View,DC=vjason,DC=local" –noexpirepassword -group KioskClients

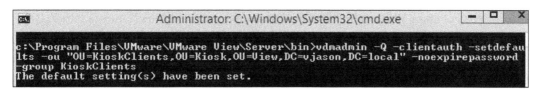

Our Horizon View pod is now ready to create Kiosk Mode Client accounts.

How it works...

The `vdmadmin -Q -clientauth` command includes several options that can be used to customize the client creation and authorization settings or retrieve the current settings. Unless otherwise specified, the following options are appended to the `vdmadmin -Q -clientauth` command:

- ▶ `-setdefaults`: This specifies the default settings for the client authentication user
- ▶ `-ou organizational_unit`: This specifies the AD DN of the organizational unit for client authentication users; this value should be contained within quotes
- ▶ `-noexpirepassword`: This means that there is no expiring password for the new Kiosk Mode Client authentication user
- ▶ `-expirepassword`: This sets the expiring password for the new Kiosk Mode Client authentication user
- ▶ `-group group_name`: This specifies the group to which the Kiosk Mode Client authentication user will be added
- ▶ `-nogroup`: This means that you should not add the Kiosk Mode Client authentication user to any group
- ▶ `-getdefaults`: This shows us the default settings for the client authentication user

Adding AD accounts for Kiosk Mode Clients

This recipe will review the procedures required to add AD accounts for Kiosk Mode Clients in our VMware Horizon View pod.

Getting ready

The following items are required in order to create accounts for Kiosk Mode Clients:

- ▶ Console and local administrator access to one of the Connection Servers in our pod.
- ▶ Console access to the Horizon View clients that will be used in the Kiosk Mode. The Horizon View client should have already been installed using the process described in the VMware document *Using VMware Horizon Client for Windows* (`https://www.vmware.com/pdf/horizon-view/horizon-client-windows-document.pdf`) or *Using VMware Horizon Client for Linux* (`https://www.vmware.com/pdf/horizon-view/horizon-client-linux-document.pdf`).

Once the required resources and access have been obtained, we can proceed with creating AD user accounts for our Kiosk Mode Clients.

How to do it...

The following steps outline how to create AD accounts for our Kiosk Mode Clients:

1. For Windows-based clients, execute the following command in order to display the client information, as shown in the following screenshot, using a console on the client computer in order to obtain the MAC address:

   ```
   vmware-view.exe --printEnvironmentInfo
   ```

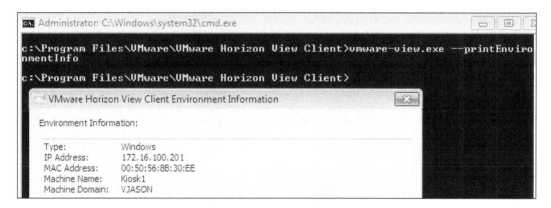

2. For Linux-based clients, execute the following command in order to display the client information, as shown in the following screenshot, using a console on the client computer in order to obtain the MAC address. Supply the FQDN or IP address of a Horizon View Connection Server with the −s switch:

   ```
   vmware-view --printEnvironmentInfo -s viewcs01.vjason.local
   ```

```
kiosk@Kiosk2: ~
kiosk@Kiosk2:~$ vmware-view --printEnvironmentInfo -s viewcs01.vjason.local
Using log file /tmp/vmware-kiosk/vmware-view.bin-2598.log
IP Address: 172.16.100.204
MAC Address: 00:50:56:8B:01:F5
Machine Name: Kiosk2
Machine Domain: (none)
Logged On Username: kiosk
Time Zone: America/New_York
```

3. From the command prompt on one of the Connection Servers in our pod, navigate to **Program Files** | **VMware** | **VMware View** | **Server** | **bin**.

4. Execute the following command in order to create an AD user account for the supplied Horizon View client, which is identified by the MAC address using the client ID switch. The command should be repeated for each client to be added. The command and resulting output are shown in the following screenshot. The group option is optional in this case, as we had already configured the default group in the previous recipe:

```
vdmadmin -Q -clientauth -add -domain VJASON -clientid
00:50:56:8b:30:ee -group KioskClients
```

5. Verify that the Kiosk Mode Client accounts have been successfully created in Horizon View using the following command. The command and resulting output are shown in the following screenshot:

```
vdmadmin -Q -clientauth -list
```

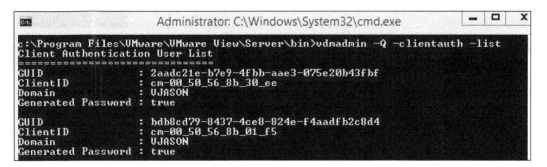

6. Verify that the Kiosk Mode accounts have been successfully created and added to the appropriate group in the ADUC console, as shown in the following screenshot. Note that the **ClientID** fields shown in the previous screenshot match the AD user account names. This is shown in the following screenshot:

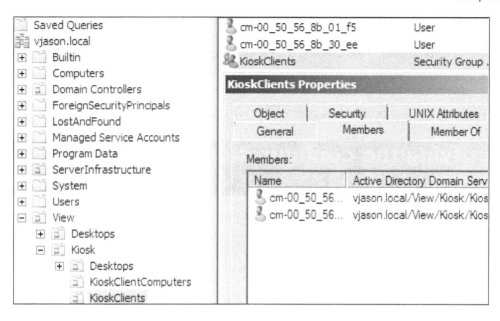

Our Kiosk Mode AD user accounts have been created and are ready for use.

How it works...

The vdmadmin -Q -clientauth command includes several options that can be used to create Kiosk Mode Clients and modify or retrieve the existing settings. Unless otherwise specified, the following options are appended to the vdmadmin -Q -clientauth command. An | operator is used to separate options when more than one option exists in order to complete the command. Note that options referenced in the earlier recipe titled *Configuring the default values for Kiosk Mode Clients* are still available but are not listed here:

- -add: This adds an item or entry.

- -domain name: This specifies the AD domain.

- -clientid ID: This specifies a client ID for the client authentication.

- -update: This updates an existing Kiosk Mode Client authentication user.

- -list: This requires no other command line options; it outputs a list of current client accounts. -r | -remove: This removes an item or entry.

- -removeall: This requires no other command line options; it remove all items/entries.

- -xml: This, when used with a -list option, produces output in the XML format.

- -description text: This is optional; it is the description for the Kiosk Mode Client authentication AD user.

▶ `-password`: This is optional; the password is to be stored for the client authentication or in conjunction with the username parameter. Use * in order to be prompted; it will override the default settings.

▶ `-genpassword`: This is optional; generate and remember a password for the Kiosk Mode Client authentication; it will override the default settings.

▶ `-force`: This performs an operation unconditionally.

Verifying the configuration of Kiosk Mode Clients

This recipe will review the procedure used to enable the Kiosk Mode Client authentication for individual Connection Servers.

Getting ready

To enable authentication for Kiosk Mode Clients, we need console and local administrator access to one of the Connection Servers in our pod and a list of all Connection Servers in the pod that we wish to enable access to. Once the required information and access has been obtained, we can proceed with enabling the Kiosk Mode authentication on our target Connection Servers.

How to do it...

The following steps outline how to enable the authentication for Kiosk Mode Clients on our Horizon View Connection Servers:

1. From the command prompt on one of the Connection Servers in our pod, navigate to `Program Files\VMware\VMware View\Server\bin`.

2. Execute the following command in order to enable Kiosk Mode Client authentication on the specified Connection Server (`viewcs01`). The command and resulting output are shown in the following screenshot. Repeat the process in order to enable authentication on additional Connection Servers, as required:

    `vdmadmin -Q -enable -s viewcs01`

3. Verify that the Kiosk Mode Client authentication has been enabled on the target Connection Servers using the following command. The command and resulting output are shown in the following screenshot. In the example provided, only one of the two Connection Servers has Client Authentication Enabled set to `true`, so only the enabled server will be able to authenticate Kiosk Mode Clients:

```
vdmadmin -Q -clientauth -list
```

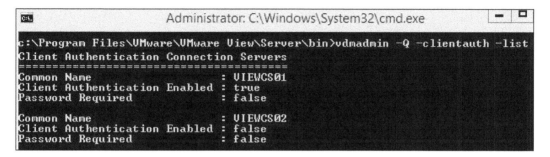

Our Connection Server's name, **VIEWCS01**, is now configured to accept Kiosk Mode Client connections.

How it works...

The `vdmadmin -Q -enable` command includes several options that can be used to enable the Kiosk Mode Client authentication. Unless otherwise specified, the following options are appended to the `vdmadmin -Q -enable` command. An | operator is used to separate options when more than one option exists in order to complete the command:

- ▶ `-e | -enable`: This enables the kiosk client authentication mode
- ▶ `-requirepassword`: If this is set, the Connection Server will require a password for the Kiosk Mode Client authentication
- ▶ `-s | -server name`: This is the computer name of a Horizon View Connection Server
- ▶ `-disable`: This is used instead of the `-e | -enable` command in order to disable the kiosk client authentication mode

 Note that, when the Kiosk Mode authentication is enabled, the Kiosk Mode Client accounts will not need to provide a username or password when logging in to unless the **requirepassword** option is specified. We must be careful when entitling access to our Horizon View desktop pools to ensure that the Kiosk Mode Client accounts are only granted access to the desktop pools that we intend them to use.

Configuring Kiosk Mode Horizon View Client devices

This recipe will review the procedure used to establish a client connection for Horizon View clients configured for the Kiosk Mode authentication.

Getting ready

The following items are required for the test Kiosk Mode authentication:

▸ A Horizon View desktop pool with desktops available for use.

▸ Our Kiosk Clients AD security group (**KioskClients**) that has been entitled to use the desktop pool configured for this test (**Kiosk-Win7**).

▸ Console access to the Horizon View clients that we wish to test. For this example, we will be testing a Windows client named **Kiosk1** and a Linux client named **Kiosk2**. Kiosk Mode authentication has already been configured for both of these clients using previous recipes in this chapter.

▸ The Horizon View clients should trust the SSL certificates used by Connection Servers. In this example, the internal Microsoft **Certificate Authority (CA)** certificate chain has already been imported to all of the client computers and is trusted.

 Horizon View SSL certificates are discussed in greater detail in the VMware document *Scenarios for Setting Up SSL Connections to View* (https://pubs.vmware.com/horizon-view-60/topic/com.vmware.horizon-view.certificates.doc/GUID-47B2EA38-E319-4DC2-9AA4-881AED3DBB58.html).

▸ Console access to the Horizon View clients that will be used in the Kiosk Mode. The client should have already been installed using the process described in the VMware documents *Using VMware Horizon Client for Windows* (https://www.vmware.com/pdf/horizon-view/horizon-client-windows-document.pdf) or *Using VMware Horizon Client for Linux* (https://www.vmware.com/pdf/horizon-view/horizon-client-linux-document.pdf).

▸ The VMware Horizon View 6 GPO bundle that is available for download from the VMware Horizon View download page (www.vmware.com/go/download-horizon). This is optional.

▸ The TPVMGPoACmap.dll file that is used to enable the configuration of location-based printing and is available on any Connection Server by navigating to **Program Files** | **VMware** | **VMware View** | **Server** | **extras** | **GroupPolicyFiles** | **ThinPrint** | **x64**.

Regardless of what OS you intend to use for your Horizon View clients, we must take steps to secure it against unauthorized use. Several options exist, including the following:

- The Windows 8.1 Assigned Access mode enables Windows to be configured to use a single application. The specified application is launched automatically at login and cannot be closed (`http://blogs.msdn.com/b/hyperyash/archive/2013/10/25/enable-kiosk-mode-in-windows-8-1.aspx`).

- Linux can also be configured in the Kiosk Mode, securing the endpoint yet simplifying the user interface and automatically launching applications as required (`http://www.instructables.com/id/Setting-Up-Ubuntu-as-a-Kiosk-Web-Appliance/`).

 Of all the AD group policies that can be configured on Horizon View clients, those that restrict which USB devices can be connected to Horizon View desktops are among the most important. Consult the VMware document *Using Policies to Control USB Redirection* (`https://pubs.vmware.com/horizon-view-60/topic/com.vmware.horizon-view.desktops.doc/GUID-A43F5E8E-2A15-4B2E-A1CE-FAB002FEEF8D.html`) for information on how to restrict the client's USB access to the Horizon View desktops.

Once the required resources and access have been obtained, we can proceed with testing the authentication of our Kiosk Mode Clients.

How to do it...

The following steps outline how to test Kiosk Mode authentication on our Horizon View clients. Assuming that a Kiosk Mode Client account was created using the correct client host computer MAC address, the desktop pool has sufficient available desktops, the clients trust the Connection Server SSL certificates, and that the DNS resolution and the network connection are working properly, the Clients should not prompt for any authentication information when connecting. If errors are displayed and the clients cannot connect, troubleshoot the client connection using the information provided.

Connecting to Horizon View using Windows-based clients

Perform the following steps:

1. From a command prompt in one of our Windows-based clients, navigate to **Program Files | VMware | VMware Horizon View Client**.

2. Execute the following command in order to launch the client and establish a connection without prompting for a username, domain, or password:

```
vmware-view -unattended -serverURL viewcs01.vjason.local
```

3. Once the command has been verified to work as expected, we can create a Windows batch file that contains the sample command referenced in the previous step. This batch file can be set to launch automatically upon login using group policies, Windows login scripts, in the local Windows startup folder. The following script assumes that the client was installed on the C drive:

```
C:\Program Files\VMware\VMware Horizon View Client vmware-view
-unattended -serverURL viewcs01.vjason.local
```

 We can set the script to launch automatically using group policies, login scripts, or even by placing it in the Windows startup folder.

Connecting to Horizon View using Linux-based clients

1. From a terminal session on our Linux-based client, execute the following command. The command should launch the client and establish a connection without prompting for a username, domain, or password:

```
vmware-view --kioskLogin --nonInteractive -s viewcs01.vjason.local
```

2. Once the command has been verified as working as expected, we can create a Linux shell script that we can manually or automatically launch from our client. The following is a sample shell script that will execute the command referenced in this section:

```
#!/bin/bash

vmware-view --kioskLogin --nonInteractive -s viewcs01.vjason.local
&
```

3. Save the script as a plain text file, and set it as executable using the chmod 755 scriptName command, where scriptName is the name of the file. Once the script is set as executable, it can be executed using the ./scriptName command, or it can be set to launch automatically when the client's host OS is booted.

How it works...

The clients are able to authenticate without providing credentials because their MAC address has been preregistered with Horizon View and has been granted access to log on to the desktop pool based on that specific piece of identifying information. Were the MAC address of the client device to change due to a hardware replacement or other similar event, the client would no longer be able to log in automatically. The new client will need to be registered using the techniques described earlier in this chapter in the recipe titled *Adding AD Accounts for Kiosk Mode Clients*.

The Windows and Linux `vmware-view` executables include several options that can be used to customize the client connection. The options listed in this section are limited to those that are useful to Kiosk Mode Clients; for a full list of current client options, execute the `vmware-view -help` command from either a Windows command prompt or a Linux Terminal window.

For Windows View clients, these and other settings can be configured using the Client's `vdm_client.adm` group policy template contained in the Horizon 6 GPO bundle. A description of the settings available in this group policy template is available in the VMware document *View Security* (`https://pubs.vmware.com/horizon-view-60/topic/com.vmware.horizon-view.security.doc/GUID-602C6F45-D758-410E-B552-E5A770773E8C.html`).

In the following command line examples, a | operator is used in order to separate options when more than one option exists in order to complete the command. Additionally, { } is used to enclose multiple command options. When specifying the desired option, only one option should be provided and neither | or { } should be included in the final command.

Windows Horizon View clients options

The following options are available for use when launching the Windows Horizon View client from the command line:

- `--nonInteractive`: This suppresses error message boxes for fully scripted startup, preventing them from being displayed to the client

- `--unattended`: This starts in an unattended mode that connects to the entitled desktop without user interaction

- `--printEnvironmentInfo`: This prints out information about the client system

- `--serverURL`: This is the URL for the Connection Server

- `--desktopProtocol`: This is the desktop display protocol to be used (if available)

- `--desktopLayout`: This specifies the desktop screen size (for example, `fullscreen`, `multi-monitor`, `windowLarge`, `windowSmall`, or `800x600`)

- `--file`: This is the file with additional command line parameters

- `--connectUSBOnStartup`: This connects all USB devices to a desktop when it is launched (`true` or `false`)

- `--connectUSBOnInsert`: This connects a USB device to the foreground desktop when the device is plugged in (`true` or `false`)

- `--noVMwareAddins`: This prevents the loading of VMware-specific virtual channels, such as ThinPrint

- `--appName`: This is the application that autostarts upon login

Linux Horizon View client options

The following options are available for use when launching the Linux client from the command line:

▶ `-q | --nonInteractive`: This suppresses error message boxes for a fully scripted startup, preventing them from being displayed to the client.

▶ `--kioskLogin`: This enable the kiosk login mode.

▶ `-s | --serverURL`: This is the URL for the Connection Server.

▶ `--printEnvironmentInfo`: This prints out information about the client system.

▶ `--Protocol={RDP | PCOIP}`: This is the desktop display protocol to be used (if available). This setting cannot override any protocol restrictions that were configured in the desktop pool.

▶ `--nomenubar`: This feature disables the fullscreen drop-down menu bar.

▶ `--fullscreen`: This feature enables the fullscreen mode in the single monitor mode.

▶ `--allmonitors`: This feature enables the fullscreen mode across all monitors.

▶ `--connectUSBOnInsert`: This connects a USB device to the foreground desktop when the device is plugged in (`true` or `false`).

▶ `--noVMwareAddins`: This feature prevents the loading of VMware-specific virtual channels, such as ThinPrint.

▶ `--appName`: This feature causes the application to autostart upon login.

8
vRealize Operations for Horizon

In this chapter, we will cover the following recipes:

- ► Implementing vRealize Operations for Horizon
- ► Monitoring the Horizon View infrastructure using vRealize Operations for Horizon
- ► Using vRealize Operations for Horizon to troubleshoot client sessions

Introduction

vRealize Operations for Horizon, also known as **V4V**, is a component of the VMware Horizon Enterprise suite of products. V4V simplifies the management of the Horizon View infrastructure by providing centralized, end-to-end visibility into its performance and level of health. V4V is also available as a standalone product.

This chapter assumes that the reader is familiar with the key concepts surrounding compute, network, and storage resources. The reader should also be familiar with the metrics that can be used to measure the current status and performance of resources such as utilization, latency, bandwidth, IOPS, and so on. Information on some of these topics is discussed in the VMware document, vSphere Resource Management (`http://pubs.vmware.com/vsphere-55/topic/com.vmware.ICbase/PDF/vsphere-esxi-vcenter-server-55-resource-management-guide.pdf`).

V4V provides organizations with the following capabilities:

- **Horizon View infrastructure monitoring and event correlation**: V4V monitors the status of all the components of the Horizon View infrastructure using information from clients (agents within each Horizon View desktop and Microsoft Windows RDS server), VMware vCenter, as well as Connection Servers. The data from these sources is recorded and analyzed to assist with monitoring and troubleshooting the Horizon View infrastructure.

- **Perform an extensive analysis of the monitoring data**: V4V analyzes all the monitoring data so that it can establish a custom baseline for the performance of the Horizon View infrastructure. This enables V4V to identify performance anomalies without the need to establish hard thresholds for alerting.

- **Quickly identify the root cause of issues**: V4V uses all the available sources of monitoring data to analyze alerts and determine their root cause. When multiple possible items are judged to be at fault, V4V ranks them according to which is most likely to be the primary issue.

- **Identify Horizon View infrastructure resource utilization**: Using historical monitoring data, V4V can identify infrastructure components that are under or over utilized. This includes resources that are constrained or are otherwise acting as a bottleneck in some way. This data can be used to adjust the configuration of the infrastructure as needed in order to optimize how it is used.

V4V can only monitor data obtained from the Horizon View software components and the accompanying vSphere infrastructure. While V4V can use this data to gain insight into the status of the physical hardware the Horizon View infrastructure resides on; it is not a replacement for monitoring tools specifically created for monitoring those hardware platforms.

Some vendors provide vRealize Operations adapters that can be used to monitor their equipment using vRealize Operations; however, V4V only includes the licenses required to monitor the Horizon View software components and vSphere infrastructure (`https://www.vmware.com/support/vcops-view/doc/vcops-horizon-17-release-notes.html#license`). If you want to use the adapters provided by these vendors or monitor non-Horizon View related vSphere infrastructure components, additional vRealize Operations licenses will be required. Consult the VMware vRealize Operations home page (`http://www.vmware.com/products/vrealize-operations/`) for information about license requirements and their associated costs.

If you require a comprehensive understanding of the status of this hardware, you should consider implementing additional tools as needed based on your infrastructure's configuration.

This recipe will provide you with an overview of how to implement, configure, and use V4V for monitoring our Horizon View infrastructure. It is not meant to cover all the different features of V4V, nor cover additional ways to use these features beyond the recipes provided in this chapter. To learn more about all the features of V4V and vRealize Operations, including how to construct custom V4V dashboards that display only the items of interest to us, consult the following VMware documentation:

▶ *VMware vCenter Operations Manager for Horizon View 1.5 Documentation Center* at `http://pubs.vmware.com/VCOPS-view-15/index.jsp`

▶ *vCenter Operations Manager for Horizon Supplement* at `https://www.vmware.com/pdf/vcops-horizon17-supplement.pdf`

▶ *vCenter Operations Manager 5.8.2 vApp Deployment and Configuration Guide* at `https://www.vmware.com/pdf/VCOPS-vapp-582-deploy-guide.pdf`

Implementing vRealize Operations for Horizon

This recipe will review the steps that are required to implement vRealize Operations for Horizon.

Getting ready

The following items are required to implement V4V:

- vSphere hosts and storage resources with sufficient capacity to host the V4V platform. These requirements are described in detail in this section.

- The vCenter IP pool is an IP pool required during the V4V virtual application's (vApp) installation process. Consult the *VMware vCenter Operations Manager (VCOPS) vApp Deployment and Configuration Guide* (https://www.vmware.com/pdf/VCOPS-vapp-582-deploy-guide.pdf) for instructions on how to configure an IP pool. The IP pool does not need to be enabled, but it must be created.

- Two IP addresses for use by the V4V appliance virtual machines.

- A V4V license key.

- A vRealize Operations OVA file to deploy the base vRealize Operations vApp.

- A V4V vCenter Operations Manager PAK file in order to install the software required to enable vRealize Operations to monitor VMware Horizon View.

- A V4V broker agent installer should be installed on one Connection Server in the pod to enable monitoring using V4V.

- V4V desktop agent installers are optional; starting with Horizon View 5.2, the V4V agent was added as a component of the Horizon View agent and is installed by default.

- The Virtual desktop master image, which is the V4V agent that is installed by default as part of the Horizon View agent; if it was deselected during the installation process, it can be enabled later.

If V4V was included as a part of the VMware Horizon Enterprise suite, the files will be available from the same location where the VMware Horizon View files were downloaded (http://www.vmware.com/go/download-horizon). If V4V was purchased as a standalone product, the files will be available on the V4V product page (http://www.vmware.com/go/download-VCOPS-view).

V4V is deployed as a vSphere vApp, a prepackaged collection of virtual machines that include a UI virtual appliance and an Analytics virtual appliance. The appliance virtual machines have specific hardware requirements, depending on how many desktops will be monitored. These requirements are outlined in the following table:

Number of desktops (up to)	Infrastructure resources required
1,000	UI appliance requirements: 2 vCPU, 7 GB RAM, and 100 GB hard disk space.
	Analytics appliance requirements: 2 vCPU, 9 GB RAM, 800 GB hard disk space, and 1,500 IOPS.
2,000	UI appliance requirements: 4 vCPU, 11 GB RAM, and 200 GB hard disk space.
	Analytics appliance requirements: 4 vCPU, 14 GB RAM, 1.6 TB hard disk space, and 3,000 IOPS.
4,000	UI appliance requirements: 8 vCPU, 13 GB RAM, and 400 GB hard disk space.
	Analytics appliance requirements: 8 vCPU, 21 GB RAM, 3.2 TB hard disk space, and 6,000 IOPS.
8,000	UI appliance requirements: 16 vCPU, 26 GB RAM, and 800 GB hard disk space.
	Analytics appliance requirements: 24 vCPU, 63 GB RAM, 6.4 TB hard disk space, and 12,000 IOPS.

The resources should be set automatically for all but the 8,000 desktop configuration; if this configuration is required, the CPU and RAM settings for each V4V appliance must be set manually after it has been deployed. The disk space required for the Analytics appliance assumes that the **full set** metrics set will be used when capturing infrastructure statistics and that the data will be retained for a 6-month period. If the **Reduced set** metric set, which records less monitoring data, is used, the disk space required is reduced by approximately 50 percent.

How to do it...

In this section, we will review the steps required to deploy and configure all the components required by the V4V platform. If a specific instruction mentions the vSphere client, here it means the vSphere web client. In each case, the procedures mentioned are similar for both the vSphere web client and the legacy vSphere C Sharp (C#) client. The installation process is broken down into the following sections:

1. Install the vRealize Operations vApp.
2. Install and configure the V4V PAK file, V4V license, and the V4V vRealize Operations adapter instance.
3. Install and configure the V4V broker agent.
4. Verify the installation of the V4V desktop agent, enabling it if required.

Install the vRealize Operations vApp

The following steps outline the procedure used to deploy and configure the vRealize Operations vApp:

1. In the VMware vSphere client, click on **vCenter**, select **Hosts and Clusters**, and then go to **Actions | Deploy OVF Template**.

2. Navigate to the **Deploy OVF Template | Select Source** window, click on the **Local file** radio checkbox, and then click on **Browse**. Select the V4V OVA file, click on **Open**, and then click on **Next**.

3. Navigate to the **Deploy OVF Template | Review Details** window, review the template details and then click on **Next**.

4. Navigate to the **Deploy OVF Template | Accept EULAs** window, review the license agreement, click on **Accept**, and then click on **Next**.

5. Go to the **Deploy OVF Template | Select Name and Folder** window, provide a **Name** for the vApp, select a folder for the vApp appliance virtual machines, and then click on **Next**.

6. Go to the **Deploy OVF Template | Select configuration** window; use the **Configuration** drop-down menu to select **Small** (1,000 desktops), **Medium** (2,000 desktops), or **Large** (4,000 desktops); and then click on **Next**.

7. Go to the **Deploy OVF Template | Select resource** window, select a vSphere cluster, host, vApp, or resource pool to host the vApp and then click on **Next**.

> DRS must be enabled on the selected cluster in order to install the vApp. If our vSphere license does not include DRS, VMware KB's article 2013695 (http://kb.vmware.com/selfservice/microsites/search.do?language=en_US&cmd=displayKC&externalId=2013695) provides instructions on how to install vRealize Operations using a standalone vSphere server.

8. Go to **Deploy OVF Template | Select storage**; select a datastore, virtual disk format, and **VM Storage Policy** (if required) for the vApp; and then click on **Next**. If thin provisioning is used, ensure that the destination datastore has sufficient available space based on the requirements of the vApp, as outlined earlier in this recipe.

9. Go to the **Deploy OVF Template | Setup networks** window and select a **Destination** virtual machine network for the vApp. For the **IP allocation** method, select **Static-Manual**, verify that the **Protocol** settings are correct for the destination network, and then click on **Next**.

10. Go to the **Deploy OVF Template | Customize template** window, select a **Timezone** setting, expand the **Networking Properties** section, provide IP addresses for the vApp appliance UI and Analytics virtual machines, and then click on **Next**.

11. Go to the **Deploy OVF Template | Ready to complete** window, review the vApp configuration, make changes as needed, and then click on **Finish**.

12. If you are monitoring more than 4,000 virtual desktops, make the required changes to the vApp appliance virtual machines once the vApp deployment has been completed, as outlined in the *Getting ready* section of this recipe.

13. In the VMware vSphere Client, power on the V4V vApp. This automatically powers on the virtual machines.

14. Using a web browser, navigate to `https://UI_IP_or_FQDN/admin` and log in using the username `admin` and password `admin`. Replace `UI_IP_or_FQDN` with either the IP address or with the **Fully Qualified Domain Name** (**FQDN**) of the V4V UI VM. This will load the vRealize Operation's **Initial Setup Wizard** dialog box.

15. Navigate to the **Initial Setup Wizard | Virtual Appliance Details** window, provide the name of the vCenter Server used with VMware Horizon View, a vCenter user account that has at minimum read access in vCenter (this account is used to read the properties of the vRealize Operations vApp), the password for this user account, and then click on **Next**. In the following screenshot, we are using an active directory account that we have appended with the domain name:

Provide the details of the vCenter Operations Manager virtual appliance.

☑ Use hosting vCenter Server details

Deselect this check box if the virtual appliance cannot reach the hosting vCenter

Hosting vCenter Server address:	vc-01.vjason.local
Hosting vCenter Server user:	administrator@vjason.local
Hosting vCenter Server password:	••••••••••••

While we used an administrator account for the purpose of this exercise, a dedicated account with the minimum required permissions is the ideal choice. VMware KB's article 2018670 (`http://kb.vmware.com/selfservice/microsites/search.do?language=en_US&cmd=displayKC&externalId=2018670`) provides instructions on how to create custom roles in vCenter for use with vRealize Operations administrative and user-level accounts. The vCenter **Global | vCenter Operations Manager User** privilege set will be acceptable for this step.

16. If you are prompted by the **Security Alert** window, verify the vCenter Server SSL certificate by clicking on **Yes**.

17. Navigate to the **Initial Setup Wizard | Change Passwords** window, provide the current passwords, select new passwords for the vRealize Operations **root** and **admin** accounts, and then click on **Next**. The default password for the admin account is `admin` and for the root account is `vmware`. The new passwords require a minimum of eight characters and must include at least one upper case letter and one lower case letter, as well as one digit and one special character.

18. Navigate to the **Initial Setup Wizard | Specify a vCenter Server** window, provide a display name for the vCenter Server, the vCenter Server FQDN or IP address, an account with administrative access in vCenter to be used as the **Registration user**, the password for this account, an account with read permissions in vCenter to be used as the **Collector user**, and the password for this account, and then click on **Next**:

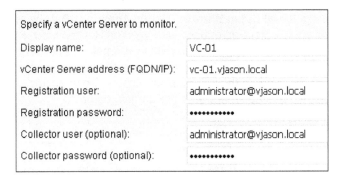

> As mentioned previously, use an account with the minimum required privileges, which is easily achieved by navigating to the vCenter **Global | vCenter Operations Manager Admin** privilege set described in VMware KB's article 2018670 (`http://kb.vmware.com/selfservice/microsites/search.do?language=en_US&cmd=displayKC&externalId=2018670`).

19. Go to **Initial Setup Wizard | Import Data** and click on **Next**. This option is generally not required for new vRealize Operations installations.

20. Go to **Initial Setup Wizard | Linked VC Registration** and click on **Finish** to complete the initial vRealize Operations configuration. This option is only required if vRealize Operations will monitor two vCenter Servers.

21. Using a web browser, again navigate to the vRealize Operations admin console located at `https://UI_IP_or_FQDN/admin` and log in using the username `admin` and the password specified in step 20. Replace `UI_IP_or_FQDN` with either the IP address or the FQDN of the V4V UI VM.

22. Verify that the vCenter Server appears in the **Registration** tab of the **vCenter Operations Manager Administration** portal, as shown in the following screenshot:

---

vCenter Server Registration

New Registration

vCenter: VDI-VC-01

vCenter Server Address:	https://vc-01.vjason.local/sdk
Connection Status:	Connected
Registration Status:	Registered
Registration User:	administrator@vjason.local
Collection User:	administrator@vjason.local

---

23. Log off and log on again to the vSphere Client and verify that the **vCenter Operations Manager** icon is displayed on the **Home** screen. This icon enables us to access the vRealize Operations web interface from within the vSphere client.

This completes the setup of the vRealize Operations platform.

Installing and configuring the V4V PAK file, license, and vRealize Operations adapter instance

The following steps outline the procedure used to deploy the vRealize Operations V4V PAK file and to apply the V4V license:

1. Using a web browser, navigate to the vRealize Operations admin console located at `https://UI_IP_or_FQDN/admin` and log in using the username `admin` and the password specified in step 17 of the *Install the vRealize Operations vApp* section of the *Implementing vRealize Operations for Horizon* recipe. Replace `UI_IP_or_FQDN` with either the IP address or the FQDN of the V4V UI VM.

2. Navigate to the **Update** tab of the vRealize Operations administrative console, click on **Browse**, and select the vRealize Operations for Horizon Adapter PAK file, as shown in the following screenshot. This file is named in a format similar to `VMware-VCOPS-viewadapter-x.x.x-yyyyyyy.pak`. Click on **Update** to begin the installation of the PAK file:

Update package

Download the update bundle from the vCenter Operations Manager support page to your loca

| C:\fakepath\VMware-vcops-viewadapter-1.6.0-1867839.pak | Browse... |

Update

---

3. In the **Confirm Update** window, click on **OK**.

> During this step, you will be prompted to backup your vRealize Operations environment prior to applying the update. While this is optional, if the installation of the PAK file were to fail for some reason, we could restore vRealize Operations using a backup rather than redeploy from scratch. The easiest way to satisfy this recommendation is to take a snapshot of both vRealize Operations VMs and delete the snapshot later, once we have confirmed that vRealize Operations is working properly.

4. Review the V4V license agreement, check the **I accept the terms of this agreement** checkbox, and then click on **OK**.

5. In the second **Confirm Update** window, click on **OK**.

6. The **Update** tab of the vRealize Operations administrative console will now change to display a status bar for the PAK file installation. Once the installation is complete, the tab will revert to the previous format and the message **Last update completed successfully** will be displayed, as shown in the following screenshot:

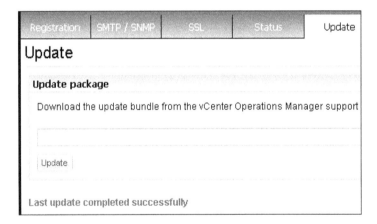

7. Using the vSphere client, navigate to **Home | Licensing | Licenses** and click on the green **+** symbol in the **Licenses** window to open the **Add License Keys** window.

8. Go to **Add License Keys | Enter license keys**, type the V4V license key including the dashes (as shown in the following screenshot), and then click on **Next**. Please note that the license key is partially obscured; it will be displayed in full when it is entered in this window:

9. Go to **Add License Keys** | **Ready to complete**, review the license key, and then click on **Finish**.

10. In the vSphere client, go to **Home** | **Licensing** | **Licenses** | **Solutions**, as shown in the following screenshot, click on the **vCenter Operations Manager-x.x.x.x** solution, and click on **Assign License Key** to open the **Assign License Key** window. Note that the actual solution name will include the IP address of the UI virtual appliance in place of x.x.x.x:

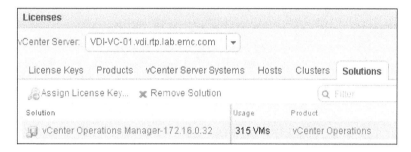

 Note that the license key has already been applied in this step; the screenshot is just for reference.

11. In the **Assign License Key** window (shown in the following screenshot), select the radio checkbox of the license to apply the key and click on **OK**. Please note that the license key is partially obscured:

12. Navigate to the **Status** tab of the vRealize Operations administrative console and click on **Restart** to immediately apply the license key.

13. Open the vRealize Operations V4V console located at `https://UI_IP_or_FQDN/VCOPS-custom`, and log in using the username `admin` and the password specified in step 17 of the *Install the vRealize Operations vApp* section of the *Implementing vRealize Operations for Horizon* recipe. Replace `UI_IP_or_FQDN` with either the IP address or the FQDN of the V4V UI VM.

14. Navigate to **ENVIRONMENT | CONFIGURATION** (shown in the following screenshot) and click on **ADAPTER INSTANCES...** to open the **Manage Adapter Instances** window:

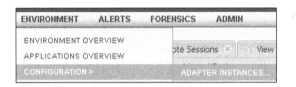

15. In the **Manage Adapter Instances** window (shown in the following screenshot), select **vCenter Operations Standard Server** from the **Collector** drop-down menu, then select **V4H Adapter** from the **Adapter Kind** drop-down menu, and then click on the green **+** symbol under **Adapter Instances** to open the **Add Adapter Instance** window:

16. In the following **Add Adapter Instance** window, provide an **Adapter Instance Name**, change the **Metric Set** if desired, and then click on **Add** next to **Credential** in order to open the **Add Credential** window:

17. In the **Add Credential** window shown in the following screenshot, select **V4H Adapter** from the **Adapter Kind** drop-down menu and select **Pairing Credential** from the **Credential kind** drop-down menu. Then, provide a numeric **Server Key** and select either the **Full Set** or **Reduced Set Metric Set**. Then, provide an **Instance name**, and then click on **OK** to return to the **Add Adapter Instance** window:

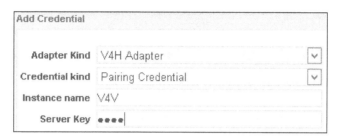

18. Click on **OK** to close the **Add Adapter Instance** window and then on **OK** again to close the **Manage Adapter Instances** window.

19. If a snapshot of the vRealize Operations vApp VMs was taken to act as a backup, remember to delete the snapshot once we verify that V4V is working properly.

This completes the setup of the V4V platform.

Installing and configuring the V4V broker agent

The following steps outline the procedure used to deploy and configure the V4V broker agent:

1. Log on to the Windows console of one of the Connection Servers in the pod that will be monitored and launch the V4V broker agent installer. The installer will have a name similar to `VMware-v4vbrokeragent-x86_64-x.x.x-yyyyyyy.exe`.

2. On the **Welcome to the VMware vCenter Operations Manager View Broker Agent Setup Wizard** screen, click on **Next**.

3. On the **End-User License Agreement** screen, check the **I accept the terms in the License Agreement** checkbox and click on **Next**.

4. On the **Ready to install the Broker Agent** screen, click on **Install**.

5. On the **Completed the VMware vCenter Operations Manager View Broker Agent Setup Wizard** screen, click on **Finish**.

6. If the broker agent is being installed on a system running Windows Server 2012 R2, install Microsoft .NET 3.5 if it is not already installed.

7. From the Windows Start menu on the Connection Server, navigate to **Programs |
   VMware | vCenter Operations Manage View Broker Agent Settings** in order to
   open the **vCenter Operations Manager View Broker Agent Configuration** utility.

8. Navigate to the **vCenter Operations Manager View Broker Agent Configuration
   | vCenter Operations Manager View Adapter** screen (shown in the following
   screenshot), specify the IP address of the V4V analytics virtual machine in the
   Address field and then click on **Next**:

9. Go to **vCenter Operations Manager View Broker Agent Configuration | View
   Pod**, provide the **Username**, **Password**, and **Domain** of a user with administrative
   credentials in the Horizon View pod, and then click on **Next**.

10. Go to **vCenter Operations Manager View Broker Agent Configuration | View Event
    Database**, provide the **View Event DB username** and **Event DB password**, and then
    click on **Next**.

11. Go to **vCenter Operations Manager View Broker Agent Configuration | View Pool
    Filter** and select **Specify desktop pools** if required (optional) to monitor or exclude
    from monitoring. We can also deselect the option to **Monitor application pools and
    hosted applications (View 6 only)**. Once done, click on **Next**. Both these settings
    are optional.

12. Navigate to the **vCenter Operations Manager View Broker Agent Configuration |
    Summary** window, review the settings, and then click on **Finish** to open the **vCenter
    Operations Manager View Broker Agent Settings** window.

13. Navigate to the **vCenter Operations Manager View Broker Agent Settings** window
    and click on **Pair Adapter...** to open the **View Adapter Server Key** window, shown in
    the following screenshot:

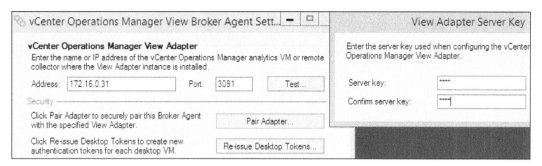

14. Navigate to the **View Adapter Server Key** window, provide the key specified in step 17 of the *Installing and configuring the V4V PAK file, license, and vRealize Operations adapter instance* section of this recipe and then click on **OK** to complete the pairing process. A **Pair View Adapter** window will be displayed to confirm that the pairing was successful.

15. Navigate to the **vCenter Operations Manager View Broker Agent Settings** window, click on the **Test...**, **Validate Credentials...**, and **Validate DB Credentials...** option in turn to verify communication between the broker agent and V4V.

16. Navigate to the **vCenter Operations Manager View Broker Agent Settings** window and click on **Apply** to save the changes. An **Applying Configuration Settings** window will be displayed to confirm that the settings were applied. Click on **Close** to close the window.

This completes the setup of the V4V broker agent.

Verifying that the V4V virtual desktop agent is installed

The following steps outline the procedure used to verify that the V4V agent is installed on the virtual desktop master image and, if it is not, how to enable it. The procedure assumes that the Horizon View agent is already installed; if it is not, simply install it using the default options as this will automatically install the V4V agent:

1. Log on to the Windows console of one of the virtual desktop master images and launch the VMware Horizon View Agent installer. This installer will have a name similar to `VMware-viewagent-x.x.x-xxxxxxx.exe` or `VMware-viewagent-x86_64-x.x.x-xxxxxxx.exe`, depending on the version of Windows being used.

2. In the **Welcome to the installer for VMware Horizon View Agent** window, click on **Next**.

3. In the **Program Maintenance** window, click on the **Modify** radio checkbox and then click on **Next**.

4. In the **Custom Setup** window, verify that the **vCenter Operations Manager Agent** is installed, as shown in the following screenshot; if it is, click on **Cancel** and shut down the virtual machine. If the agent is not installed, use the drop-down menu to the left of the option to enable it and then click on **Next**:

5. Complete the modification of the Horizon View agent configuration and then shut down the virtual machine.

This completes the setup of the V4V desktop agent.

Monitoring Horizon View client sessions using V4V

This recipe will review the steps that are required to use V4V to review monitoring data related to Horizon View client sessions.

Getting ready

Once all the individual components have been deployed and configured and Horizon View desktops made available for use, we can use V4V to monitor the client sessions.

The exercises used in this recipe will be performed using the V4V console located at `https://UI_IP_or_FQDN/VCOPS-custom`. Log in using the V4V admin account. Replace `UI_IP_or_FQDN` with either the IP address or the FQDN of the V4V UI VM.

How to do it...

In this section, we will review how to monitor Horizon View client connections using the V4V platform. The **View Users** dashboard used in this section is specifically designed to quickly locate and investigate the status of individual client connections:

1. On logging in, the V4V console will display the **View Overview** tab, as shown in the following screenshot. If there are any current issues with the client connections, this information will be displayed in the **VIEW ALERTS** column, in the upper-left hand corner of the display. For information about prior issues, go to **ALERTS | ALERTS OVERVIEW** found along the menu bar at the top of the console. Note the different tabs across the top of the console that enable rapid access to the various V4V monitoring dashboards. When any objects in this screen appear red, this will indicate a problem that needs further investigation. Since all the objects are green, V4V has determined that the infrastructure is currently working within acceptable levels of utilization and is experiencing no issues:

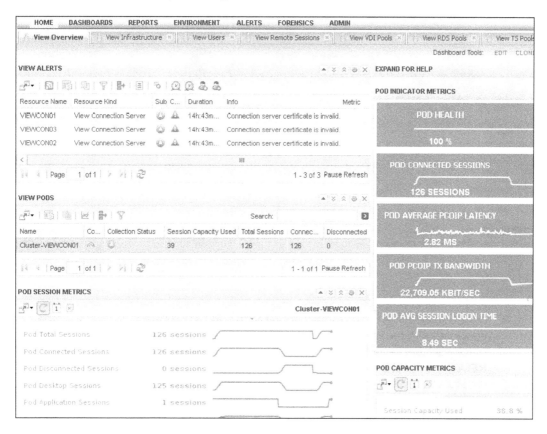

2. Select the **View Users** tab to view information about the current client connections. From there, select an individual user from the **VIEW SESSIONS** window identified with a red colored **1** as shown in the following screenshot. The user sessions can be sorted by the **Health** column if desired:

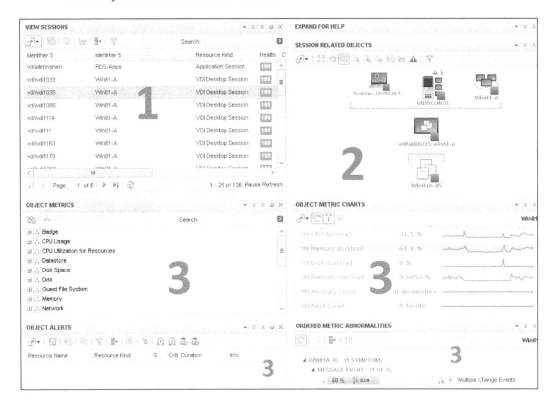

3. Once a session has been selected, the **SESSION RELATED OBJECTS** window will be populated with the Horizon View infrastructure objects that the session is using. This window is identified with a red colored **2** in the preceding screenshot. In the **SESSION RELATED OBJECTS** window, select an object to view all the available monitoring data for this object, which will be displayed in the **OBJECT METRICS**, **OBJECT METRICS CHARTS**, **OBJECTS ALERTS** (if any alerts exist), and **ORDERED METRIC ABNORMALITIES** (if any abnormalities exist) windows, marked with a red colored **3** in the preceding screenshot. Selecting a different object in the **SESSION RELATED OBJECTS** window will refresh the remaining windows with information about this object.

4. Expand a metric object in the **OBJECT METRICS** window, and select an individual metric to display the current data about this metric in the **OBJECT METRIC CHARTS** window, as shown in the following screenshot:

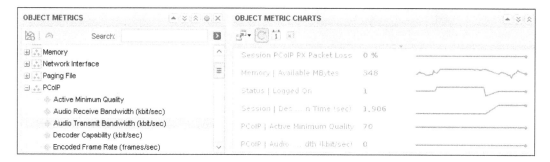

5. Expand the object in the **ORDERED METRIC ABNORMALITIES** window and double-click on the blue bar to open the event window, as shown in the following screenshot. From here, we can review events related to the desktop we selected:

Monitoring the Horizon View infrastructure using V4V

This recipe will review the steps that are required to use V4V to review monitoring data related to the Horizon View infrastructure.

Getting ready

Once all the individual components of V4V have been deployed and configured, we can use V4V to monitor the Horizon View infrastructure.

The exercises used in this recipe will be performed using the V4V console located at `https://UI_IP_or_FQDN/VCOPS-custom`. Log in using the V4V admin account. Replace `UI_IP_or_FQDN` with either the IP address or the FQDN of the V4V UI VM. This recipe assumes that you have the knowledge of how to navigate the V4V console using the information provided in the previous recipe.

How to do it

In this section, we will review how to monitor the Horizon View infrastructure using the V4V platform:

1. Select the **View Infrastructure** tab to view information about the **VIEW INFRASTRUCTURE HOSTS (vSphere servers)**, **VIEW VDI DESKTOP VMS**, **VIEW DATASTORES**, and **VIEW RDS HOSTS (VIEW 6)** windows as shown in the following screenshot:

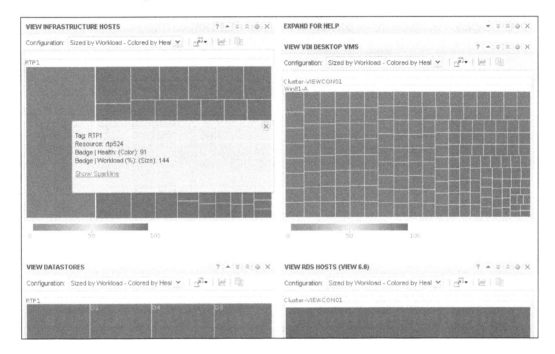

2. The green objects in the different windows under the **VIEW INFRASTRUCTURE** tab represent individual objects. The size of the objects reflects their overall infrastructure resource utilization in relation to their peers. In the previous screenshot, we single-clicked on an object in the **VIEW INFRASTRUCTURE HOSTS** window as it is much larger than all of the others. We can see that **Workload (%): (Size)** is **144**, whereas it averages less than 20 for the other objects. Since the object is still green and not red, V4V feels that this level of utilization is not causing problems with the Horizon View infrastructure.

3. Single-click on the object from step 2 and click on the **Resource Detail** button highlighted in black in the following screenshot to open the **V4V RESOURCE DETAIL** page for this object:

4. Using the **RESOURCE DETAIL** page shown in the following screenshot, we can quickly identify that the constraint is CPU-related and that this server is currently bound by the CPU. The messages concerning these conclusions have been highlighted in black. We can also see that, based on the 3D historical graph labeled **Last 6 Hours** (also highlighted in black), this server has been experiencing this load for an extended period of time:

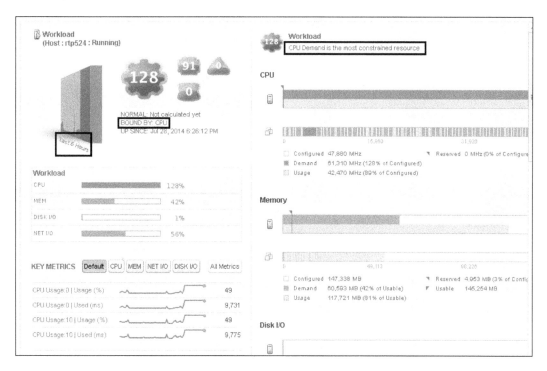

5. Go to **RESOURCE DETAIL | All Metrics** in order to display the available metrics for the Horizon View infrastructure host. This includes the health of the desktops that run on this host (**HEALTH TREE**), the events related to these desktops ranked according to their impact on the host (**ROOT CASE RANKING**), and all of the metrics available concerning the host (**METRIC SELECTOR** and **METRIC GRAPH**):

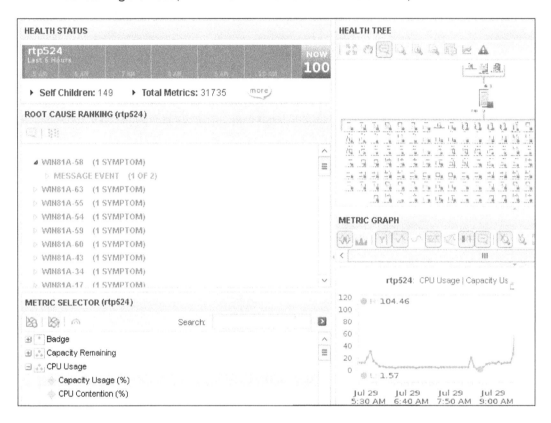

Using the V4V Horizon View Dashboards

This recipe will review the different V4V dashboards and describe how each can be used to monitor the Horizon View infrastructure.

Getting ready

Once all the individual components of V4V have been deployed and configured, we can use the V4V dashboards to monitor the Horizon View infrastructure.

The exercises used in this recipe will be performed using the V4V console located at `https://UI_IP_or_FQDN/VCOPS-custom`. Log in using the V4V admin account. Replace `UI_IP_or_FQDN` with either the IP address or the FQDN of the V4V UI virtual machine. This recipe assumes that you have the knowledge of how to navigate the V4V console using the information provided in the previous recipes.

How to do it...

In this section, we will review each of the remaining dashboards of the V4V platform. The **View TS Pools** dashboard will not be reviewed, as it is only used with earlier versions of VMware Horizon View and this book focuses on VMware Horizon View 6. The dashboards are accessed using the following bar located below the V4V menus, as shown in the following screenshot:

Horizon View Remote Sessions

The **View Remote Sessions** dashboard in the V4V console is shown in the following screenshot and can be used to quickly identify clients who are experiencing problems. The dashboard shows the top sessions for several key metrics, including desktop resource utilization within each cluster (**VDI DESKTOP SESSIONS**), Windows RDS resource utilization by the application (**APPLICATION SESSIONS**), the Horizon View client application and desktop session bandwidth, latency, and packet loss. We can click on any resource on the page to learn more about the information it displays, and where applicable, double-click to load the monitoring page for that specific object:

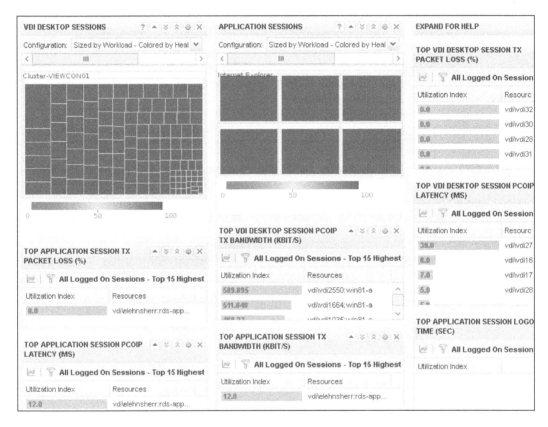

Horizon View VDI Pools

The **View VDI Pools** dashboard in the V4V console is shown in the following screenshot, and it can be used to quickly review the status of desktop pools and the metrics concerning them, the desktops they contain, and any current client sessions for up to one desktop pool at a time. Select another desktop pool in the **VDI DESKTOP POOLS** window to display the statistics for that pool. We can highlight individual objects in this dashboard to learn more about their status:

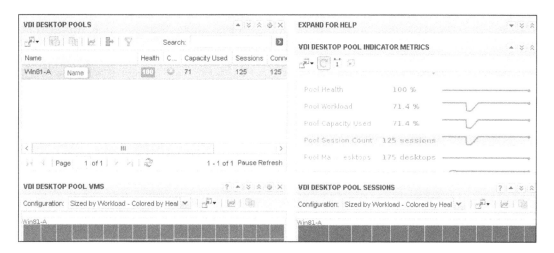

Horizon View RDS Pools

The **View RDS Pools** dashboard in the V4V console is shown in the following screenshot, and it can be used to quickly review the status of and the metrics concerning Windows RDS Server pools used for both applications and desktop sessions, including the pool status, server resource utilization, and client connection statistics.

We can click on any resource on the page to learn more about the information it displays, and where applicable, double-click to load the monitoring page for that specific object:

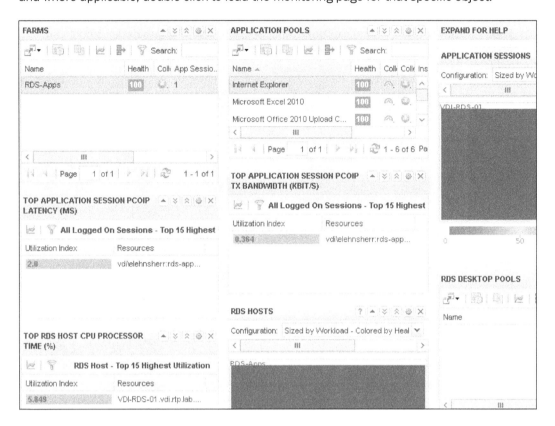

Horizon View VDI Topology

The **View VDI Topology** dashboard in the V4V console is shown in the following screenshot, and it can be used to quickly review the status and metrics of various components of the Horizon View infrastructure. This dashboard displays similar information as the **View Infrastructure** dashboard but in a different format that is more suitable as an ongoing status display.

We can click on any resource on the page to learn more about the information it displays, and where applicable, double-click to load the monitoring page for that specific object. In the example shown, the current metrics for one of the Connection Servers is displayed in the **OBJECT METRICS** window:

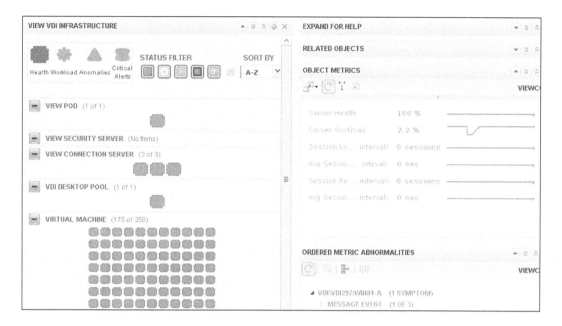

Horizon View RDS Topology

The **View RDS Topology** dashboard in the V4V console is shown in the following screenshot, and it can be used to quickly review the status and metrics of the various components of the Windows RDS server components of the Horizon View infrastructure. This dashboard displays similar information as the **View Infrastructure** dashboard but in a format that is more suitable as an active status display.

We can click on any resource on the page to learn more about the information it displays, and where applicable, double-click to load the monitoring page for that specific object. In the example shown, we have clicked on a **RDS HOST** option, which populated the **OBJECT METRICS** window with the current statistics:

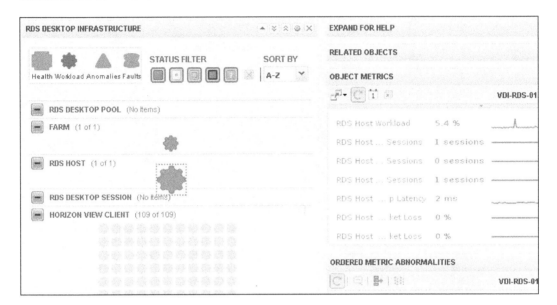

Horizon View Application Topology

The **View RDS Topology** dashboard in the V4V console is shown in the following screenshot; it can be used to quickly review the status and metrics of various components of the Windows RDS server components of the Horizon View infrastructure. This dashboard displays similar information as the **View RDS Pools** dashboard but includes more information about the Horizon View infrastructure as a whole, which may make it a more ideal ongoing status display.

We can click on any resource on the page to learn more about the information it displays, and where applicable, double-click to load the monitoring page for that specific object. In the example shown, we have clicked on a **HOSTED APPLICATION** option, which populated the **OBJECT METRICS** window with the current statistics:

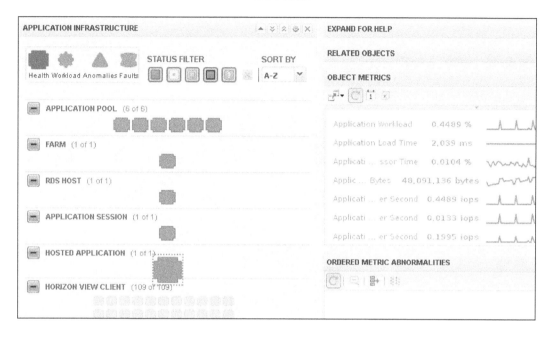

vSphere Topology

The **vSphere Topology** dashboard in the V4V console is shown in the following screenshot; it can be used to quickly review the status and metrics of the various components of the vSphere infrastructure. This dashboard does not display information about the Horizon View itself, just the underlying infrastructure that hosts and manages the virtual machines.

We can click on any resource on the page to learn more about the information it displays, and where applicable, double-click to load the monitoring page for that specific object. In the example shown, the statuses of the objects that comprise the vSphere clusters are displayed in the **RELATED OBJECTS** window:

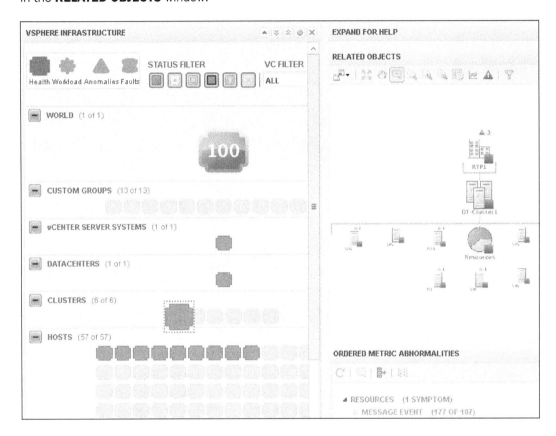

Horizon View Adapter Status

The **View Adapter Status** dashboard in the V4V console is shown in the following screenshot, and it can be used to quickly review the status of the vRealize Operations adapter used to collect data related to our Horizon View infrastructure, as well as view license usage statistics. This dashboard is commonly used to verify that the adapter is functioning correctly, gathering the information needed for V4V:

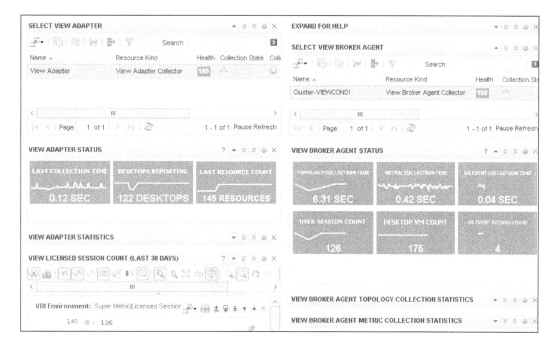

9
Using VMware Mirage with Horizon View

In this chapter, we will cover the following recipes:

- ▸ Specifying the Mirage server name in Horizon View
- ▸ Installing the Mirage client
- ▸ Capturing a Mirage base layer
- ▸ Capturing an application using Mirage
- ▸ Centralizing Horizon View desktops using Mirage
- ▸ Creating Mirage collections
- ▸ Installing applications using Mirage
- ▸ Upgrading the Horizon View desktop OS using Mirage

Introduction

The VMware Horizon Mirage license is included with the VMware Horizon View Advanced and Enterprise editions and adds a number of different capabilities to the VMware Horizon platform. In this chapter, we will focus primarily on those features of Mirage that benefit and enhance VMware Horizon View; however, as you learn about these features, you will come to realize that Horizon View is but one of the many potential use cases for Mirage.

The following are some of the ways in which Mirage can enhance an organization's end user computing offerings:

- **Dynamic layering for endpoints and applications**: Mirage enables organizations to manage their desktop image as a set of logical layers, enabling them to add, remove, or upgrade individual layers as required. With Mirage, we can update individual layers, irrespective of whether they are application layers or the underlying system layer itself, while maintaining end user files and personalization. The following screenshot is a graphical representation of an image that is managed by Mirage; it shows the individual layers that are assembled to create a fully configured computer and differentiates between those managed by IT and those managed by the end user:

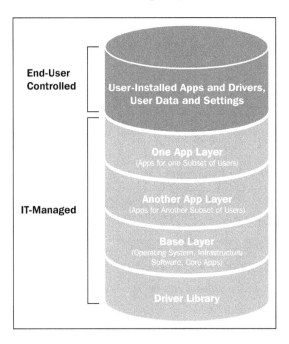

- Additionally, we can restore the system layers to resolve any OS corruption issues, still without overwriting the user layers.

- With layers, we can also migrate users from an old PC to a new one without losing their data, Windows profiles, or even user-installed applications.

 It is important to note that this functionality is not available until after Mirage has been configured to manage the target machine and the assigned Mirage driver, base, and application layers have been downloaded and implemented.

- **Unified image management for our desktops**: Mirage enables us to manage the OS on physical, **Bring Your Own Device** (BYOD), or Horizon full-clone persistent virtual desktops at scale. With layering, user-installed applications and data remain intact during our image updates.

- **Automated backup and system recovery**: Mirage provides desktop recovery, with the ability to perform full endpoint snapshots as well as to synchronize smaller deltas in applications and data within the layers whenever is a change in the data center. This includes both changes to the endpoint as well as updates to the centralized OS and application layers upon which the desktop is built.

- **Self-service user file access and recovery**: With Mirage, our users can access or restore any file from their desktop using any web browser, even from another device.

- Mirage can significantly reduce the time required and complexity associated with migrating desktops to newer versions of Windows, while offering the ability to roll back those migrations with user data intact if any problems occur.

Common Mirage terms

The following terms are used throughout this chapter and are unique to the Mirage platform:

- **Application layer**: The application layer contains information and files required to install and run an application. Using application layers, Mirage can add and remove applications from Mirage desktops on demand, without requiring user assistance.

- **Base layer**: The base layer is a base Windows operating system image that forms the foundation of the endpoints managed with Mirage. While Horizon View can use a single image to deploy a large number of identical desktops, Mirage can migrate a large number of existing, unique desktops to all those who use the same base layer, even while running a different version of Windows, while also deploying new desktops using the same image.

- **CVD** (**Centralized Virtual Desktop**): An endpoint that has been centralized using Mirage has its unique data copied to the Mirage server and its base image migrated to match a selected Mirage base layer; it is now able to leverage all the different features of Mirage. Centralized desktops can benefit from Mirage data protection, Windows image (the base layer) management, and application (the application layer) management.

- **Collection**: This is a collection of Mirage CVDs, usually used as a point offer management of the base and application layers or application layer operations.

- **CVD policy**: This is a policy that controls how Mirage interacts with the devices that it manages. Mirage includes two policies by default, one optimized for VMware Horizon View desktops, and one for all other desktops.

▸ **Endpoint**: This is a device that is managed by Mirage. While this chapter focuses on using Mirage with VMware Horizon View, Mirage can be used with physical desktops and laptops as well (assuming that the required licenses have been purchased).

▸ **Pending device**: This is a device that has the Mirage client installed and has registered with the Mirage server but has not yet been centralized.

The installation and configuration of the individual VMware Mirage components, including additional ones not referenced in this chapter, are sufficiently detailed that they cannot be described in this chapter. For information on how to install and integrate Mirage into our environment, as well as more detailed information concerning Mirage administration, consult the VMware Mirage documentation at `https://www.vmware.com/support/pubs/mirage_pubs.html`.

Specifying the Mirage server name in Horizon View

This recipe will discuss the steps that need to be performed to specify the Mirage server name in VMware Horizon View. This step eliminates the need to specify the server name when the Mirage client is installed. Additionally, this enables an organization to specify Mirage servers on a per-View desktop per-desktop level, which is useful for those environments that contain multiple Mirage servers and need to distribute the load.

Getting ready

The Mirage server name can be configured in VMware Horizon View either as a global setting or as a configuration option in a Horizon View desktop pool. The setting is optional though, as it is possible to specify the server name during the client installation process.

To configure the setting at the global level in Horizon View, we require global administrative permissions. Alternatively, to set the Mirage server name in a Horizon View desktop pool, we require only administrative permissions to that pool.

When configuring this setting, we should provide the FQDN of the server running the Mirage server service and not of the Mirage management server or any other server role.

How to do it...

In this section, we will perform the steps required to set our Mirage server name in either the global or desktop pool layer in VMware Horizon View. As previously noted, changing this setting requires administrative access in Horizon View, either at the global or desktop pool level depending on where the change is being made. Separate sections are provided based on where the Mirage server name is being set.

Setting the Mirage server name at the global level in Horizon View

Perform the following steps to set the Mirage server name for all Horizon View desktops in the pod:

1. Log on to the Horizon View Manager Admin console.

2. Go to **View Configuration | Global Settings** and then click on the **Edit** button in the **General** section.

3. In the **General** settings window, provide the name of the Mirage server in the format `mirage://serverFQDN:8000`, as shown in the following screenshot, and then click on **OK**:

| Mirage Server configuration: | mirage://mirageserv01.vjason.local:8000 |

4. Verify that the Mirage server name is displayed correctly in the updated **Global Settings** window under **View Configuration**, as shown in the following screenshot. The Mirage server name is highlighted in red:

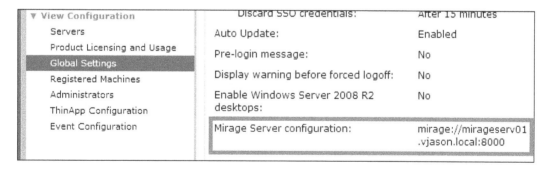

Setting the Mirage server name at the Horizon View desktop pool level

Perform the following steps to set the Mirage server name at the Horizon View desktop pool level. In this example, the Mirage server name was already set at the global level:

1. When creating a Horizon View desktop pool, in the **View Desktop Pool Settings** window (shown in the following screenshot), check the **Override global Mirage settings** check box and provide the Mirage server name in the format `mirage://serverFQDN:8000`. If the Mirage server name was not set at the global level, we would be able to provide the Mirage server name without having to check the check box:

Mirage Settings

☐ Override global Mirage settings

Mirage Server
configuration: mirage://mirageserv01.vjason.local:80

---

2. Click on **Next** and complete the steps required to create the Horizon View desktop pool.

Installing the Mirage client

This recipe will discuss the steps that are required to install the Mirage client. In the example provided, we will set the Mirage server name at the time of installation.

Getting ready

The Mirage client is available in both 32-bit and 64-bit versions and is currently supported for installation on Windows desktop OSs only. The client has the following requirements:

▶ Windows XP SP2 or a newer Windows desktop OS with Microsoft .NET Framework 3.5 SP1 installed

▶ A minimum of 512 MB RAM for Windows XP or 1 GB RAM for all other versions of the Windows desktop OSs

▶ At least 5 GB of free hard disk space is required

 It is important to note that, when it comes to VMware Horizon View, Mirage is only supported for use with full-clone persistent desktops. While nothing prevents it from being used with a linked clone for purposes such as data protection, this is not something that VMware currently supports.

How to do it...

In this section, we will perform the following steps to install the Mirage client:

1. Execute the Mirage client installer on the target desktop system. The client should have a name similar to `MirageClient.xyy.zzzzz.msi`, where the letters `yy` are replaced with either `32` or `64` and `zzzzz` is replaced with the current build number of the client installer.

2. In the **Welcome to the VMware Mirage Client Setup Wizard** screen, click on **Next**.

3. In the **End-User License Agreement** screen, check the **I accept the terms in the License Agreement** check box and then click on **Next**.

4. In the **VMware Mirage Client Configuration** screen, shown in the following screenshot, provide the FQDN of the server running the Mirage server service, check the **Use SSL to connect to the server** check box, and then click on **Next**:

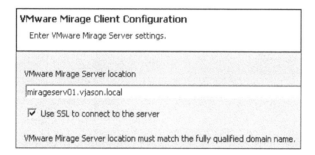

5. In the **Ready to install VMware Mirage Client** screen, click on **Next** to begin the installation.

6. In the **Completed the VMware Mirage Client Setup Wizard** screen, click on **Finish**. The Mirage client is now installed.

Capturing a Mirage base layer

This recipe will discuss the steps that are required to capture a Mirage base layer.

Getting ready

When working with VMware Horizon View, a common use for a base layer is to perform OS upgrades on our existing Horizon View full-clone desktops. As such, the target desktop for our base layer capture should be configured similar to the virtual desktop master image that we use with Horizon View.

The following services must be enabled on the target Windows endpoint to capture a Mirage base layer:

- ▶ Volume Shadow Copy Service
- ▶ Microsoft Software Shadow Copy Provider

In order to capture a Mirage base layer, the target desktop must be connected to our domain, have the Mirage client installed, and be registered with our Mirage server. The desktop should be displayed in the Mirage console's **Pending Devices** window by going to **VMware Mirage | VMware Mirage System | Inventory**, as shown in the following screenshot:

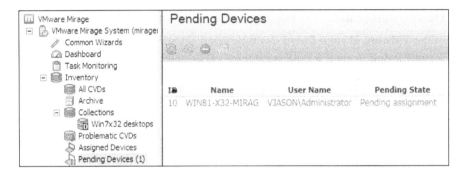

How to do it...

In this section, we will perform the steps required to capture a Mirage base layer:

1. In the Mirage console's **Common Wizards** window, click on **Capture Base Layer**.

2. Go to **Capture Base Layer | Select Capture Type**, click on the **Create a new reference CVD** radio checkbox, as shown in the following screenshot, and then click on **Next**:

3. Navigate to the **Capture Base Layer | Select a Pending Device** window, select the device that you wish to capture, as shown in the following screenshot, and then click on **Next**:

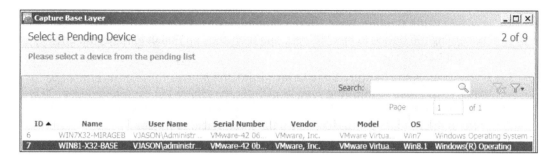

4. Go to **Capture Base Layer | Selected Pending Device**, review the information concerning the device we selected, and then click on **Next**.

5. Navigate to the **Capture Base Layer | Select CVD Policy** window, verify that the default CVD policy is selected (the VMware Mirage default CVD policy), and then click on **Next**.

6. Navigate to the **Capture Base Layer | Select Base Layer** window, select the **Don't use a Base Layer** radio checkbox, and then click on **Next**.

7. Go to **Capture Base Layer | Capture Base Layer**, select the **Create a new layer** radio checkbox, provide a **Name**, **Description**, and **Version** number for our base layer, as shown in the following screenshot, and then click on **Next**:

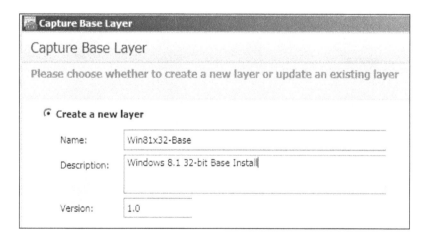

8. If Microsoft Office is installed on the image being captured, a **License Keys** window under the **Capture Base Layer** window will be displayed. We are required to enter the appropriate Office license keys, provide an optional description, and then click on **Next**.

9. Navigate to the **Capture Base Layer | Check Compatibility** window, verify that no compatibility issues exist, and then click on **Next**. If compatibility issues are detected, cancel the wizard, resolve the issues using the information provided, and restart the **Capture Base Layer** wizard.

10. Navigate to the **Capture Base Layer | Summary** window, review the information concerning the device to be captured, and then click on **Finish** to begin the base layer capture.

11. On completing the **Capture Base Layer** wizard, the Mirage console will prompt us to switch to the **Task Monitoring** window in order to monitor the capture process. Click on **Yes** to switch to the **Task Monitoring** window, shown in the following screenshot, or **No** to return to the Mirage console's **Common Wizards** window.

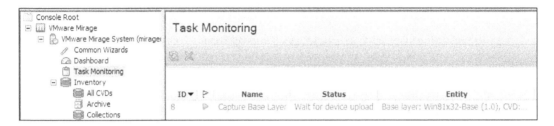

12. When the capture process is completed, the new base layer will be displayed in the Mirage console's **Base Layers** window under **Image Composer**, as shown in the following screenshot:

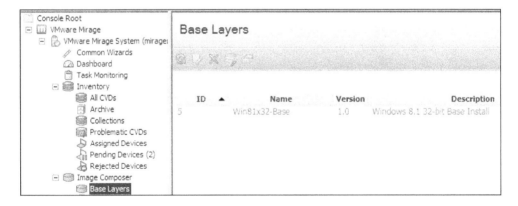

Capturing an application using Mirage

This recipe will discuss the steps that are required to capture an application base layer using Mirage. Once captured, the application base layer can be used to seamlessly install the applications on desktops running the Mirage client.

Mirage application layers can only be applied to desktops running the same base OS version, including 32-bit and 64-bit versions. If our environment includes different OS versions and we wish to leverage Mirage to deploy application base layers to each, we will need to repeat the capture process for each desktop type that we are running.

Getting ready

To capture an application base layer using Mirage, we require a desktop that has a similar application configuration to the desktops in which we plan to deploy the resulting application layer. Specifically, the capture desktop must not already have application dependencies installed that our target desktops do not have, unless we plan to install these dependencies separately using other Mirage application layers or other software installation methods.

In the example provided, the device that is used to capture the application layer consists of nothing more than a base installation of a Windows desktop OS and the required Mirage client. The device is successfully registered with the Mirage server and is listed in the Mirage console's **Pending Devices** window, under **Inventory**.

We cannot capture an application using the same application capture endpoint that we previously used to capture a base layer. We can, however, reuse the same application capture endpoint to capture multiple applications.

How to do it...

In this section, we will perform the steps required to capture a Mirage application layer. In the following example, we will be capturing the VMware Horizon View Agent:

1. Log in to the console session on the desktop where the application will be captured from.

2. Navigate to the Mirage console's **Common Wizards** window and click on **Capture App Layer**.

3. Go to **Activate Device | Select a Pending Device**, select the device on which we will perform the application capture, and then click on **Next**.

4. Navigate to the **Activate Device | Select CVD Policy** window, verify that the default CVD policy is selected (the VMware Mirage default CVD policy) and then click on **Next**.

5. Navigate to the **Activate Device | Select Target Volume** window, check the **Automatically choose a volume radio** checkbox, and then click on **Next**. If our Mirage server has multiple volumes and we wish to select a different volume for our captured application layer, we will do so here by selecting the **Manually choose a volume** radio checkbox and selecting the desired volume.

6. Navigate to the **Activate Device | Check Compatibility** window, verify that no compatibility issues exist and then click on **Next**. If compatibility issues are detected, cancel the wizard, resolve the issues using the information provided, and restart the **Capture App Layer** wizard.

7. Navigate to the **Activate Device | Summary** window, review the information concerning the device to be captured, and then click on **Finish** to begin the application capture process.

8. Mirage will now perform a prescan of the target desktop so that it can later identify the changes that occur during the application process. This process can be monitored either in the Mirage console's **Task Monitoring** screen or directly on the console of the target desktop itself, as shown in the following **Initializing App Layer Recording** notification window. When the prescan is completed, the notification window changes to **Recording App Layer** and instructs us to begin the application installation:

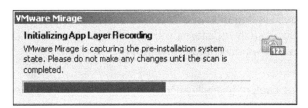

9. Install the target application, making any configuration changes as needed and installing patches if required. The desktop can be rebooted as needed to complete the installation or configuration process.

10. Once the application has been installed, right-click on the target device in the Mirage console's **Task Monitoring** window and click on **Finalize App Layer Capture**, as shown in the following screenshot. Mirage will now perform a postscan to determine which applications were installed:

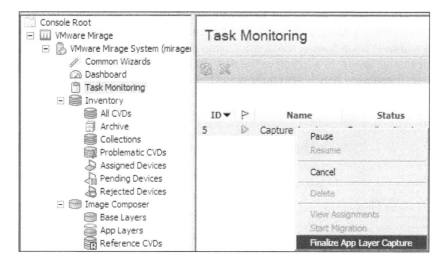

11. Go to **Capture App Layer | Review Recorded Applications**, shown in the following screenshot, review the results of the Mirage postscan, and then click on **Next**:

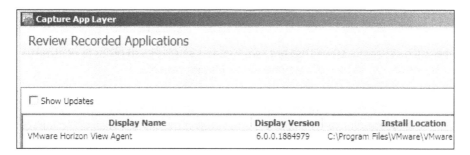

12. Navigate to the **Capture App Layer | Capture App Layer** window, select the **Create a new layer** radio checkbox, update the application layer's **Name**, **Description**, and **Version** number if required, and then click on **Next**.

13. Navigate to the **Capture App Layer | Check Compatibility** window, verify that no compatibility issues exist, and then click on **Next**. If any compatibility issues are detected, then cancel the wizard, resolve the issues using the information provided, and restart the capture process.

14. Navigate to the **Capture App Layer | Summary** window, review the information concerning the application to be captured, and then click on **Finish** to begin the base layer capture.

15. Click on the Mirage console's **Task Monitoring** window to monitor the capture process.

16. When the capture process has been completed, the new application layer will be displayed in the Mirage console's **App Layers** window under **Image Composer**, as shown in the following screenshot. Note that the screenshot shows additional application layers, in addition to the new **VMware Horizon View Agent (W7x32)** layer; these were previously captured as follows:

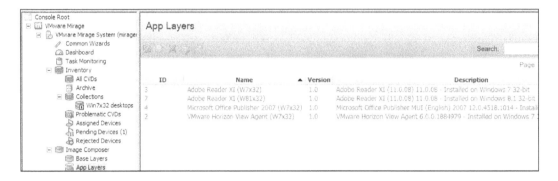

Centralizing Horizon View desktops using Mirage

This recipe will discuss the steps that are required to use Mirage in order to centralize desktops or endpoints, as they are named in the Mirage console.

> As with VMware Horizon View itself, ensure that any Mirage implementation includes redundant components that protect the configuration of the Mirage platform and the associated Horizon View desktop data in the event of an infrastructure outage or other failure.

Getting ready

Only the following two things are explicitly required to centralize endpoints using Mirage:

▸ The target endpoints must be listed in the Mirage console's **Pending Devices** window

▸ The Mirage server must have sufficient space, after deduplication, to host the data it imports from the devices being centralized

Determining Mirage server space requirements is difficult due to the fact that each organization is likely to generate different amounts of unique data. When deploying your Mirage server, follow recommended guidelines for space requirements and monitor the ongoing space utilization to see if additional space is required. Consult *VMware Mirage Administrator's Guide* (`http://pubs. vmware.com/mirage-51/index.jsp#com.vmware. mirage.admin.doc/GUID-9A6BE718-C8B7-426C-A164- 29E496CBAC7A.html`) for instructions on how to add additional Mirage storage volumes; alternatively, if your storage infrastructure supports it, you can also increase the size of the disk that underlies the existing Mirage storage volume.

How to do it...

In this section, we will perform the steps required to centralize an endpoint using Mirage:

1. In the Mirage console's **Common Wizards** window, click on **Centralize Endpoint**.

2. Go to **Activate Device | Select Device Filter**, create a filter that will include the endpoints to be centralized, and then click on **Next**. In the following screenshot, we filtered in the desktop's **Name**, using the **Contains** condition, and the value `win7-x32-`. Individual endpoints might also be selected using more restrictive filters.

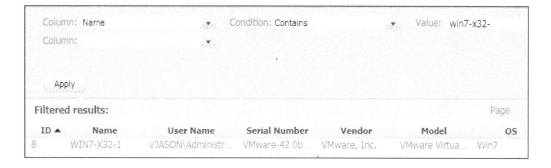

3. Since you are centralizing Horizon View desktops, go to **Activate Device | Select CVD Policy**, select **VMware Mirage CVD policy optimized for Horizon View**, and then click on **Next**. This policy ensures optimal performance when using Mirage to centralize Horizon View desktops.

4. Navigate to the **Activate Device | Select a Base Layer** window, select the base layer that matches the endpoint being centralized, as shown in the following screenshot, and then click on **Next**:

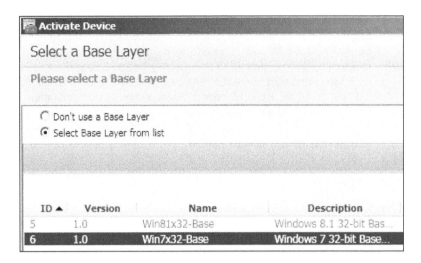

5. Navigate to the **Activate Device | Select Layers** window, shown in the following screenshot; we have the option of immediately assigning application layers to the device. For now, we will just click on **Next**:

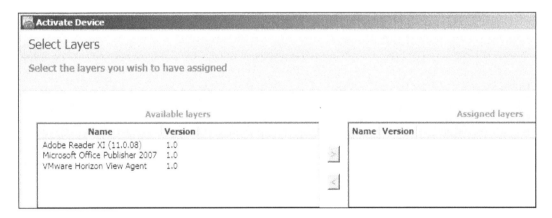

6. Navigate to the **Activate Device | Select Target Volume** window, check the **Automatically choose a volume** radio checkbox, and then click on **Next**. If our Mirage server has multiple volumes and we wish to select a different volume for our centralized device, we will do so here by selecting the **Manually choose a volume** radio checkbox and selecting the desired volume.

7. Navigate to the **Activate Device | Check Compatibility** window, verify that no compatibility issues exist, and then click on **Next**. If compatibility issues are detected, cancel the wizard, resolve the issues using the information provided, and restart the **Centralize Endpoint** wizard.

8. Navigate to the **Activate Device | Summary** window, review the information concerning the application to be captured, and then click on **Finish** to begin the centralization process.

9. The centralization process can be monitored from either the Mirage console's **Task Monitoring** page or from the Mirage status window on the endpoint being centralized. The status window can be accessed by right-clicking on the Mirage Windows tray icon (it appears as a blue square with a white letter M) and clicking on **Show Status**, which will display the window, as shown in the following screenshot:

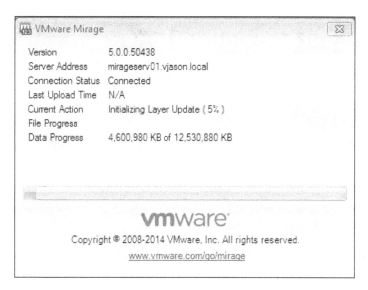

10. Since the endpoint we are centralizing was not deployed using a Mirage base layer, meaning that its configuration did not match that of the base layer we selected in a previous step, Mirage has made changes that require us to reboot the desktop. When prompted in the console of the desktop being centralized, click on either **Restart Now** or **Restart Later** as desired.

11. If additional updates are required, Mirage will display a pop-up notification in the desktop console, as shown in the following screenshot, and prompts for an additional restart if needed. Once the centralization process is completed, Mirage will begin protecting the data contained on the endpoint and is now able to deploy application and OS base layer updates as required, including OS version updates if required:

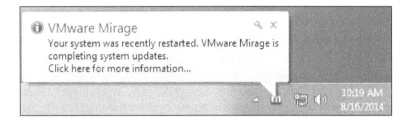

Creating Mirage collections

This recipe will discuss the steps that are required to create collections in Mirage.

Getting ready

To add an endpoint to a collection in Mirage, it must have been centralized using the process described in the previous recipe. Two types of collections can be created:

▸ **Static**: These endpoints are manually added or removed

▸ **Dynamic**: These endpoints are automatically added or removed based on the identifying parameters provided

This recipe will show you how collections are created using both console types, with one example provided for each.

 The Mirage Web Manager console is not explicitly required to be installed in a Mirage environment but is nice to have as it enables us to manage our Mirage environment using a web browser, instead of forcing us to use computers that have the Mirage console installed.

How to do it...

In this section, we will perform the steps required to create and populate a collection in Mirage. Separate sections are provided for the Mirage software console and the Web Manager console.

Creating a dynamic collection using the Mirage console

Perform the following steps to create and populate a collection using the Mirage console:

1. Navigate to the Mirage console, expand the **Inventory** menu, right-click on **Collections**, and then click on **Add a Collection...**.

2. Navigate to the **Add Collection | Add Collection** window, provide a **Name** and an optional **Description**, click on the **Dynamic Collection** radio checkbox, use the **Column**, **Condition**, and **Value** drop-down menus to specify the parameters that are used to populate the collection, click on **Apply**, and then click on **OK** to create the collection. In the example provided, we added all the desktops with OS equal to **Win7**, which will add all the desktops running the 32-bit version of Windows 7. A number of additional filtering parameters are available in the Column drop-down menu:

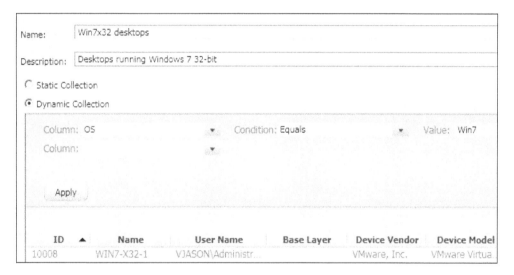

3. The new collection can be found in the Mirage console's **Collections** menu under **Inventory**; since it is dynamic, the accompanying icon will also include a white letter D.

Creating a static collection using the Mirage Web Manager

Perform the following steps to create and populate a collection using the Mirage Web Manager console:

1. Log on to the Mirage Web Manager console using an account with administrative permissions in Mirage and using the URL `https://WebManagerServer:7443/VmwareMirage`, where `WebManagerServer` is the FQDN of the server that has the Mirage Web Manager component installed.

2. Click on **Collections** to load the **Collections** window and then go to **Create New |
Static Collection**, as shown in the following window:

3. Navigate to the **Add Static Collection** window, provide a Name for the collection, and
double-click on any CVDs listed in **Available CVDs** that you wish to add to the static
collection. Once selected, the CVDs should appear in the **Selected CVDs** pane:

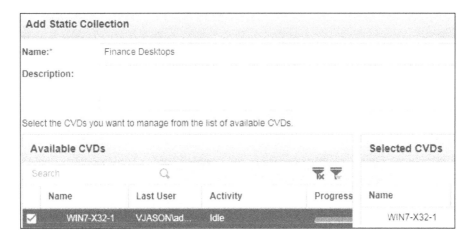

4. Click on **Save** to save the new collection; it will now be displayed in the **Collections**
window alongside any previously created collections.

The *VMware Mirage Administrator's* guide (`http://pubs.vmware.
com/mirage-51/index.jsp#com.vmware.mirage.admin.
doc/GUID-A94065A2-5C7E-49C2-B225-B8A938FBFD97.html`)
provides instructions on how to create a static collection using the Mirage
console. The Mirage Web Manager console can also be used to create
dynamic collections by navigating to **Create New | Dynamic Collection**
in step 2, shown in this section, and providing conditions that determine
how the collection is populated.

Installing applications using Mirage

This recipe will discuss the steps that are required to deploy application layers using Mirage.

Getting ready

Mirage application layers can be deployed to either Mirage collections or individual CVDs. Desktops that have not been centralized cannot have application layers applied using Mirage.

How to do it...

In this section, we will perform the steps required to deploy an application layer using Mirage. In the following example, we will apply this layer directly to a Mirage collection:

1. In the Mirage console's **Common Wizards** window, click on **Update App Layers**.

2. Go to **Update App Layers | Select CVDs or Collections**, select one or more CVDs or collections that you wish to update the application layers on and then click on **Next**. Use the **CVDs and Collections** tabs to switch updates between the two objects that are displayed in the window.

3. Go to **Update App Layers | Select App Layer**, click on the application layer that you wish to deploy, and then click on the **>** button to add it. Repeat as needed if additional applications need to be deployed:

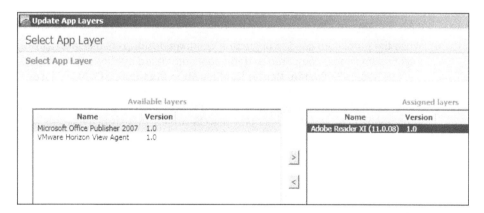

4. Navigate to the **Update App Layers | Image Validation** window, verify that no validation issues exist, and then click on **Next**. If validation issues are detected, cancel the wizard, resolve the issues using the information provided, and restart the **Update App Layers** wizard.

5. Navigate to the **Update App Layers | Summary** window, review the information concerning the device to be captured, and then click on **Finish** to assign the application layer.

6. In the console of systems where the application layer was assigned, the Mirage client will display a pop-up window with the message that the system is being updated, as shown in the following screenshot. As with other Mirage operations, you can also right-click on the Mirage Windows tray icon and click on **Show Status**, which will display a more detailed window relating to the operation being performed:

7. If prompted, reboot the desktop when the layer assignment completes. The application is now available for use and will appear and function exactly as it would if it was installed using traditional methods.

Upgrading the Horizon View desktop OS using Mirage

This recipe will discuss the steps that are required to upgrade a desktop OS using Mirage.

 While the procedure used to upgrade a Windows desktop OS using Mirage might seem simple compared to traditional automated methods using tools, such as Microsoft **System Center Configuration Manager** (**SCCM**), it does not mean that it doesn't require extensive testing prior to attempting large-scale upgrades. Even though desktop data is protected by Mirage and the endpoint can be restored to the previous OS version and state if needed, you need to make sure that you limit the number of upgrades you perform at first, and ensure that those that you do upgrade are thoroughly tested to ensure that they function as required.

Getting ready

Mirage requires endpoints to be centralized prior to performing an OS upgrade, which itself is actually a base layer upgrade. You are replacing one OS base layer with another that just happens to be a newer version of Windows.

The following resources are required to perform the upgrade:

-   The target endpoints must be centralized and must contain sufficient free space to host the new base image during the upgrade process.

-   A Microsoft **Key Management Server** (**KMS**) infrastructure is used to activate the desktops; if deploying Windows 8 or newer OSs, **Active Directory-Based Activation** (**ADBA**) can also be used.

-   A destination base layer that contains the new OS.

-   If the source OS currently has Mirage application layers assigned, we will need the same layers to be created for the new OS. As mentioned in the *Capturing an application using Mirage* recipe, these layers must have been captured on an endpoint running the same OS as the one you are migrating your endpoints to.

-   The Mirage server must have the Microsoft Windows **User State Migration Tools** (**USMT**) installed, using the procedure outlined in the *VMware Mirage Installation Guide* (`http://pubs.vmware.com/mirage-51/index.jsp#com.vmware.mirage.installation.doc/GUID-8F496DE3-573A-4FB2-80E7-F00C3CE08234.html`).

How to do it...

In this section, we will perform the steps required to upgrade a Windows desktop OS using Mirage. In the example provided, we will upgrade a single endpoint to Microsoft Windows 8.1:

1. Navigate to the Mirage console's **Common Wizards** window and click on **Windows OS Migration**.

2. Navigate to the **Windows OS Migration** window, click on **CVDs or Collections**, select one or more CVDs or collections that you wish to upgrade the OS on, and then click on **Next**. Use the **CVDs and Collections** tabs to switch updates between the two objects that are displayed in the window.

3. Navigate to the **Windows OS Migration | Select Base Layer** window, click on the **Download and Apply Base Layer** radio checkbox, click on the target OS base layer from **Base Layer List**, as shown in the following screenshot, and then click on **Next**:

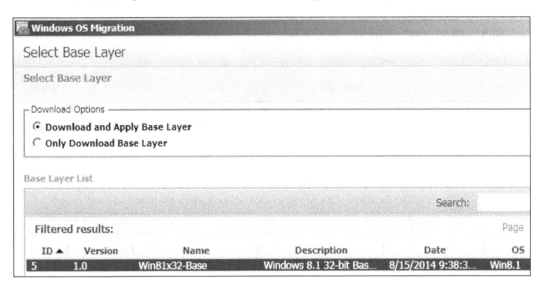

The **Only Download Base Layer** option can also be selected if you want to stage the Mirage base layer for later installation, such as a time when the computer will not be in use.

4. Navigate to the **Windows OS Migration | Select Layers** window, click on any of the Mirage application layers that you wish to assign to the upgraded desktop, and then click on the **>** button to assign it. Repeat as needed for any additional applications that are required and then click on **Next**.

5. Navigate to the **Windows OS Migration | Target Machine Name** window, provide the **User** name (in the format domain\userID) and **Password** of an account with permission to join Windows computers to the domain, as shown in the following screenshot, and then click on **Next**. The **Active Directory** (**AD**) domain might also be changed, but the destination **Organizational Unit** (**OU**) cannot be changed unless the AD domain is also changed:

6. Go to **Windows OS Migration | Image Validation**, verify that no validation issues exist, and then click on **Next**. If validation issues are detected, cancel the wizard, resolve the issues using the information provided, and restart the **Windows OS Migration** wizard.

7. Navigate to the **Windows OS Migration | Summary** window, review the information concerning the device to be migrated, and then click on **Finish** to begin the migration process.

8. In the console of systems where the application layer was assigned, the Mirage client will display a pop-up window with a message that the system is being migrated, as shown in the following screenshot. As with other Mirage operations, you can also right-click on the Mirage Windows tray icon and click on **Show Status**, which will display a more detailed window relating to the operation being performed:

9. When prompted, reboot the desktop when the migration completes. Multiple reboots will be required to complete the migration, which also includes migration of the Windows profile to ensure that it works with the upgraded OS. As shown in the following screenshot, Mirage will provide status updates during the migration process if the user logs in before it fully completes:

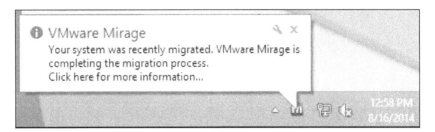

10. The workstation is now migrated to the new base image, has all the required application layers installed, and is ready for use.

10
Implementing VMware Virtual SAN for Horizon View

In this chapter, we will cover the following recipes:

▸ Sizing a Horizon View environment for Virtual SAN (VSAN)

▸ Enabling Virtual VSAN

▸ Using VSAN with Horizon View

Introduction

VMware **Virtual SAN** (**VSAN**) is an optional component of VMware vSphere that enables the use of local magnetic and flash-based storage devices that create a high-performing, replicated, software-defined storage platform that can be use to store Horizon View desktop virtual machines. VSAN is highly integrated with the vSphere hypervisor, vCenter Server, and many other VMware products while requiring minimal vSphere host overhead and offering simplified management yet detailed VSAN storage policies that can be applied at the individual **Virtual Machine Disk** (**VMDK**) level. Additionally, all aspects of VSAN are managed using the vSphere web client, further reducing the points of management for the VMware Horizon View infrastructure.

In this chapter, we will review how to size our vSphere hosts for use with VMware VSAN, understand what resources are available for building VSAN-compatible hosts, walk through the process of enabling VSAN, and review how to use VSAN when creating a Horizon View desktop pool.

At VMworld 2014 US, VMware announced the EVO:RAIL (`http://www.vmware.com/products/evorail`) and EVO:RACK (`http://blogs.vmware.com/cto/evo-rack-tech-preview-vmworld-2014/`) platforms that combine vSphere, VSAN, a purpose-built hardware platform, a customized and simplified setup, and an administration interface.

The VMware EVO platform is only available as a complete solution that includes a supported hardware configuration. Organizations that are implementing a new or replacement vSphere environment and are also considering using VSAN as their storage platform might find that a VMware EVO-based solution is an optimal choice for their virtualization infrastructure. At the time of writing this, only the EVO:RAIL platform has been launched; consult the product page (`http://www.vmware.com/products/evorail`) for additional information on availability, features, and other resources.

Common VSAN terms

The following terms will be used throughout this chapter when discussing the vSphere VSAN feature:

- **Storage Policy-Based Management** (**SPBM**): This is a component of the vSphere VSAN that is applied to individual virtual machine hard disks and influences how that data is written, replicated, cached, and striped within the VSAN cluster. SPBM provides a framework for all policies related to VSAN.

- **Components**: This term is used to refer to the virtual machine datafiles once they have been written to a VSAN datastore. The components include the virtual machine files, any replicas as defined by the vSphere VSAN SPBM, witness components, and metadata. Understanding the number of components required is important as this impacts the number of vSphere VSAN hosts that are required.

- **Datastore**: A VSAN datastore is similar in appearance to a traditional vSphere datastore but is created using VSAN disk groups rather than local or remote storage devices.

- **Disk group**: This is a collection of magnetic hard disks and a flash-based storage device within a VSAN cluster.

- **Network**: VSAN uses a vSphere VMkernel network adapter to replicate data between hosts in the VSAN cluster.

- **Objects**: These are the files that make up a virtual machine; when written to a VSAN datastore, these objects comprise multiple components.

Sizing a Horizon View environment for VMware Virtual SAN (VSAN)

This recipe will discuss how to properly size our VMware vSphere hosts so that they can accommodate VSAN in addition to the Horizon View desktops. This section assumes that you are already aware of the storage, networking, and CPU requirements of the Horizon View desktops themselves and are only looking to add VSAN as your virtual desktop storage platform.

Getting ready

Prior to determining vSphere's host, disk, or flash-based storage requirements, we must first ensure that our hosts have sufficient CPU resources available. VMware recommends that 10 percent of the vSphere host CPU capacity be set aside for VSAN, which is to say, once you have determined the number of Horizon View desktops the vSphere host will accommodate and reduce that figure by 10 percent in order to ensure that VSAN will not have to contend with the desktops for vSphere host CPU resources.

The following VMware documents provide additional information on VSAN's sizing and design:

- *VMware Virtual SAN Design and Sizing Guide* at `http://www.vmware.com/files/pdf/products/vsan/VSAN_Design_and_Sizing_Guide.pdf`
- *VMware Virtual SAN Design and Sizing Guide for Horizon View Virtual Desktop Infrastructures* at `http://www.vmware.com/files/pdf/products/vsan/VMW-TMD-Virt-SAN-Dsn-Szing-Guid-Horizon-View.pdf`

How to do it...

In this section, we will go over how to determine the number and capacity of magnetic and flash-based storage devices required to support our Horizon View infrastructure as well as the number of vSphere hosts our VSAN cluster will require.

Determining the total number of vSphere host disks required

The following are the sizing recommendations based on the type of Horizon View pool deployed in a Virtual SAN cluster.

Magnetic disk capacity sizing

The recommended total capacity of all magnetic disks in the VSAN cluster should be at least 130 percent of the total size of data to be stored, which will ensure that approximately 30 percent of free space is available for future growth. The following are recommendations concerning the number of magnetic disks that should be used once you have determined the overall capacity required:

▶ Linked-clone virtual desktops: It is recommended that you have at least three 10K or 15K RPM SAS disks within each VSAN disk group

▶ Dedicated full-clone virtual desktops: It is recommended that you have at least four 10K RPM SAS or 7.2K RPM NL-SAS disks within each VSAN disk group

▶ VSAN disk groups: Create additional VSAN disk groups to scale performance or for capacity reasons

Flash capacity sizing

In a VSAN cluster, flash-based storage devices are used as a read/write cache and are not part of the overall VSAN cluster storage capacity. 30 percent of each flash-based storage device in the VSAN cluster is used as a write-back buffer. In this configuration, all writes from virtual machines are written first to the local flash-based storage device and later written to magnetic disks for long term storage. Additionally, based on vSphere's VSAN SPBM settings, these writes are replicated to other flash-based storage devices in the cluster in order to ensure availability in the event of a failure. The data replication settings are discussed later on in the *Number of Failures to Tolerate* section of this recipe.

VSAN uses the remaining 70 percent of each flash-based storage device as a read cache. Since the VSAN read cache will only contain blocks of data that are already present in the magnetic disks in the cluster, which means that it is already protected in the event of a failure, the data contained within the flash-based read cache is not replicated between hosts. This has the added benefit of maximizing the amount of flash-based storage available for use as a VSAN read cache.

VMware recommends that, for all desktop pool types, the amount of flash-based storage used in the VSAN cluster be at least 10 percent of the projected virtual machine storage requirements. The additional 30 percent of storage added to support future virtual machine storage requirements does not need to be considered as part of this calculation. Additionally, we must account for the additional space required for the replicas that VSAN uses in order to provide data protection as well as the 100 percent space reservation used with full clone desktops and linked-clone persistent data disks, as both of these influence the actual amount of space the desktops will require.

10 percent of flash-based storage is just the minimum required by VMware and might not be applicable in all cases. If it is later determined that additional flash-based storage is required and your vSphere host has sufficient capacity, you can add it to VSAN at a later date by creating a new VSAN disk group. The VMware blog post *Virtual SAN: Scaling Storage Capacity* (`http://blogs.vmware.com/vsphere/2014/03/virtual-san-scaling-storage-capacity.html`) demonstrates the procedure for adding additional storage to a VSAN cluster.

The following table shows us the amount of storage required for two different Horizon View desktop configurations, including the additional amount of magnetic storage required to support the indicated replicas of the VSAN data. The virtual desktop storage requirements have already been adjusted so that they reflect the total space that will be reserved by VSAN when they are configured:

Item	Dedicated full clone example	Dedicated linked clones with persistent data disk example
Virtual desktop's storage requirements	32 GB	7 GB
The number of virtual desktops	750	1,500
The base amount of space required to store virtual desktops	24,000 GB (approximately 24 TB)	10,500 GB (approximately 10.5 TB)
The additional space added for future growth	30 percent	30 percent
The base amount of space required to store virtual desktops (with additional space for future growth)	31,200 GB (approximately 31.2 TB)	13,650 GB (approximately 13.65 TB)
The target flash-based storage capacity	10 percent	10 percent
The number of additional replicas	2	1
The total flash-based storage required in the VSAN cluster	2,400 GB (approximately 2.4 TB)	1,050 GB
The total magnetic storage required in the VSAN cluster (includes 30 percent additional capacity for future growth)	93,600 GB (approximately 93.6 TB)	27,300 GB (approximately 27.3 TB)

In the examples provided, the total magnetic storage required was determined using the following calculation:

▸ The base amount of space required to store virtual desktops is 1.3 times the number of replicas

▸ 1.3 represents the addition of 30 percent more space to the base figure that supports future storage growth

Calculating the total number of VSAN objects required

VMware VSAN supports a maximum of 3,000 components per host; this is important as the desktop pool configuration impacts the number of objects that are required, which might influence the number of vSphere hosts our cluster must contain.

The information contained in the following two tables was obtained from the *VMware Virtual SAN Design and Sizing Guide for Horizon View Virtual Desktop Infrastructures* guide and shows us the different objects created for each VMware Horizon View 6 virtual desktop type. The final line of the table shows us the number of objects created for each virtual desktop type. Using these values, we can determine the number of VSAN components that will be required after taking into account the creation of VSAN witnesses and replicas:

Virtual machine object	Dedicated linked clones with disposable data disks	Floating linked clones with disposable data disks	Floating linked clones	Floating full clones	Dedicated full clones
Namespace	Required for all Horizon View virtual desktops				
VMDK					
Swap					
Snapshot	Required for all Horizon View linked clone virtual desktops			Not applicable	
Internal					
Disposable	Required	Required	Not applicable		
Persistent	Required	Not applicable	Not applicable		
The total number of objects per desktop	7	6	5	3	3

The right-most column of the following table shows us the number of VSAN components that are created for each desktop type, based on the default Horizon View vSphere VSAN SPBM policies:

The user-assignment Method	The Horizon View desktop type	Will a desktop disposable data disk be used?	The number of objects per desktop VM	The total number of components per desktop VM with VSAN
Floating	Linked clone	No	5	9 replica disks 9 per desktop VM
		Yes	6	9 replica disks 10 per desktop VM
Dedicated		Yes	7	9 replica disks 21 per desktop VM
Floating	Full clone	Not applicable	3	7 per desktop VM
Dedicated		Not applicable	3	9 per desktop VM

For the linked-clone desktop pools, the replica disk components are counted only once per pool. The following calculations can be used to determine the number of components that will be created based on the desktop type:

▶ Total linked-clone desktop VSAN components = (Number of desktops * number of components per desktop type) + number of components required for replica disks

▶ Total full clone desktop VSAN components = Number of desktops * number of components per desktop type

Using the examples provided in the previous section of this recipe and the accompanying calculations, we can determine the total number of VSAN components our proposed Horizon View configuration will require:

Item	The dedicated full clone example	The dedicated linked-clone with persistent data disk example
The number of virtual desktops	750	1,500
The number of VSAN components for replica disks	Not applicable	9
The number of VSAN components for each virtual desktop	4	21
The total number of VSAN components required	3,000	31,509
The minimum number of hosts required in the VSAN cluster based on the 3,000 component per server limit	1	11

The values in the *Total number of VSAN components* row were reached using the following calculations:

▸ A dedicated full clone example is 750 * 4 = 3,000

▸ A dedicated linked clone with persistent data disk example is (1,500 * 21) + 9 = 31,509

Based on these results, we see that, while a single vSphere host can host the number of VSAN components required for the proposed number of desktops, due to the number of components required for the linked-clone configuration, we will require at least 11 vSphere servers in our VSAN cluster in order to host these 1,500 desktops.

 Since VSAN requires at least 3 vSphere hosts in a cluster, the full clone configuration will require at least that many hosts even if they aren't required based on the number of VSAN components the desktops require.

How it works...

In this section, we will discuss several topics that impact how VMware VSAN works with vSphere and VMware Horizon View.

VSAN limits and maximums

The following limits are strictly related to VSAN clusters as a whole, but by extension, they impact how they can be used with VMware Horizon View:

▸ The maximum number of vSphere hosts in a VSAN cluster is 32

▸ The maximum capacity of a fully provisioned VSAN cluster (35 magnetic disks multiplied by 32 vSphere hosts) is 4.4 PB

▸ The maximum number of virtual machines hosted on a VSAN cluster is 3,200

 Note that vSphere HA supports a maximum of 2,048 virtual machines per cluster, although this feature is not typically used with Horizon View desktops.

▸ The maximum IOPS of a VSAN cluster (fully provisioned) is 2 million

The following table outlines various limits related to the VSAN disk groups, magnetic disks and flash-based storage devices, and the overhead related to the disk-formatting method used by VSAN.

Object	Minimum	Maximum
VSAN disk group (per vSphere VSAN host)	One	Five
Flash-based storage devices (includes SAS, SATA, PCIe, and SSD) per VSAN disk group	One	
Magnetic disks per VSAN disk group	One	Seven
Disk formatting overhead (VMware VMFS-L file system) per magnetic disk	750 MB	

While not typically an issue with vSphere hosts that are used with VMware Horizon View, a minimum of 32 GB of RAM is required in a vSphere host that will support the upper limits of the VSAN platform, be it the number of disk groups, the number of supported magnetic disks, or a combination of both of those items.

VSAN and the vSphere VSAN SPBM framework

VMware VSAN uses the vSphere VSAN SPBM framework to control how Horizon View desktops utilize VSAN storage resources. When a Horizon View desktop pool is created on a VSAN datastore, a set of default policies is created based on the recommended VMware guidelines. The policies shown in the following screenshot can be viewed by clicking on the **VM Storage Policies** icon on the vSphere Web Client home page. Note that these policies will not be created until after you provision a Horizon View desktop pool that uses VSAN as a storage target.

In this figure, we see a collection of default policies that were created for a dedicated assignment linked-clone desktop pool. The policies are applied automatically to each individual Horizon View desktop when it is created, and they are applied directly to the desktop virtual hard disk to which they apply. To review or edit these policies, right-click on one of them under the **Objects** window and select **Edit VM Storage Policy** to open the **Edit VM Storage Policy** window. For the default Horizon View vSphere VSAN SPBM policies, the policy values are displayed in the **Rule-Set 1** tab, as shown in the following screenshot. As shown in the previous screenshot, additional policies were created for OS, replica, and persistent data disks.

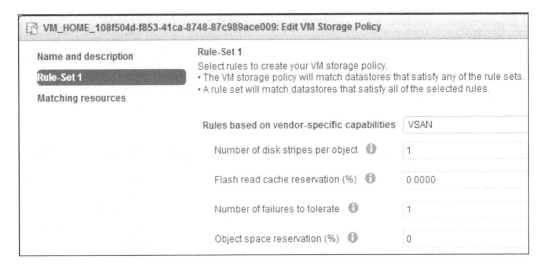

In this section, we will review the default Horizon View vSphere VSAN SPBM policies, their impact on VSAN storage utilization, and the default SPBM policies that Horizon View creates when configuring desktop pools.

For additional information on vSphere VSAN SPBM policies, consult the *VMware Virtual SAN Design and Sizing Guide*, referenced earlier in this chapter, as well as the *What's New in VMware Virtual SAN* paper at http://www.vmware.com/files/pdf/products/vsan/ VMware_Virtual_SAN_Whats_New.pdf.

Number of disk stripes per object

VSAN's **number of disk stripes per object** is the number of disks in a VSAN cluster across which each replica of a VSAN storage object will be distributed. Horizon View configures the recommended value of 1 for all desktop pool configurations.

Flash read cache reservation (%)

VSAN's **flash read cache reservation (%)** is the percentage of flash capacity reserved as the read cache for a VSAN storage object, specified as a percentage of the logical size of the object. When configuring linked-clone desktop pools, Horizon View configures the recommended value of 10 percent for the desktop replica disk object, as this will serve the majority of the read IO for the pool. All other linked-clone and full-clone disk objects are set to the recommended value of 0 percent.

Number of Failures to Tolerate

This vSphere VSAN SPBM **Number of Failures to Tolerate** (**FTT**) policy defines the number of vSphere hosts, disks, or network failures a VSAN storage object can tolerate. The policy states that, for *n* failures tolerated, *n+1* copies of the object are created, and *2n+1* vSphere hosts that contribute storage for VSAN are required.

For example, a VSAN cluster requires a minimum of three vSphere hosts with sufficient storage resources. Based on the *2n+1* calculation provided in this section, this configuration will support an FTT policy of either 1 (the default) or 0. If the FTT policy was increased to 2, a minimum of five vSphere hosts as well as the storage required to write an additional copy of each desktop object on the cluster will be required.

> An FTT value of 0 can conceivably be used for the desktop OS virtual hard disks in a linked-clone floating assignment or full-clone non-persistent desktop pools. Under these scenarios, if the VSAN cluster experiences the failure of the vSphere host, only the non-persistent data disks will be lost; they should not contain any data of value. However, ensure that additional Horizon View desktops are available for the affected clients while the vSphere host or VSAN is being repaired.

The FTT policy has the greatest impact on the capacity of a VSAN cluster due to, in part, the 3,000 VSAN component limit per vSphere host as well as the additional storage required for higher policy values. Higher FTT values can increase the storage required by each virtual desktop by up to a factor of four, which is why it is important to consider any changes to the policy beyond the Horizon View default of 1.

Object space reservation (%)

VSAN's **object space reservation (%)** is the percentage of the logical size of the virtual machine storage object that will be reserved using thick provisioning when it is created. The remainder of the virtual machine storage object will be thin-provisioned. Horizon View configures the following VSAN object space reservation policies by default:

- The linked-clone desktop persistent data disks are 100 percent
- The full-clone desktop disks are 100 percent
- The linked-clone desktop disks (other than the user-persistent data disks) are 0 percent

Object space reservation for the Horizon View linked-clone desktop persistent data disks and full-clone desktop disk VSAN components is set to 100 percent by default in order to ensure that they are evenly balanced across the VSAN cluster when they are deployed. This placement ensures that, as Horizon View's desktop storage capacity utilization increases over time, the VSAN datastore is more likely to provide consistent levels of performance.

Enabling VMware Virtual SAN

This recipe will discuss the steps that are required to enable VMware VSAN.

Getting ready

To ensure that the VSAN configuration is supported by VMware, it must either be built using hardware that is validated by VMware or selected from a list of validated VMware Virtual San Ready Nodes. The following resources can assist in selecting hardware that is known to be supported by VMware VSAN:

- *VMware Virtual SNA Ready Nodes* at `http://partnerweb.vmware.com/programs/vsan/Virtual%20SAN%20Ready%20Nodes.pdf`

- *VMware Compatibility Guide* at `http://www.vmware.com/resources/compatibility/search.php?deviceCategory=vsan`

- *Virtual SAN Hardware Quick Reference Guide* at `http://partnerweb.vmware.com/programs/vsan/Virtual%20SAN%20Hardware%20Quick%20Start%20Guide.pdf`

The following are additional items that are either required or recommended in order to enable VMware VSAN.

The required items are as follows:

- At least 3 vSphere hosts with sufficient available storage are required in order to create a VSAN cluster. VSAN can only be configured using the vSphere Web Client, a required component of vCenter Server.

- VMware VSAN requires a license key that is included by default with the Horizon Advanced and Horizon Enterprise editions. This license key should be installed prior to enabling VSAN using instructions provided in the VMware vSphere 5.5 documentation (`http://pubs.vmware.com/vsphere-55/index.jsp`).

- A dedicated IP address will be required for the VSAN VMkernel port on each vSphere server.

The recommended items are as follows:

▸ Consider using a dedicated VSAN VMkernel report rather than enabling the VSAN VMkernel option on an existing VMkernel port.

▸ Use a dedicated **Virtual LAN** (**VLAN**) or another private network for your VSAN network traffic. This is very important for production environments and will ensure that this critical network traffic is not impacted by other traffic on the network.

▸ The VSAN VMkernel port and the virtual switch it is created on will be configured with a **Maximum Transmission Unit** (**MTU**) value of 9,000, which is commonly referred to as jumbo frames. With jumbo frames enabled, fewer Ethernet frames will be required in order to transmit the VSAN network traffic, which reduces the CPU load on the vSphere server. Prior to changing the MTU value, verify that the networking infrastructure will support it.

> The instructions provided in the next section assume that the target vSphere vSwitch has already been configured with a MTU of 9,000; if not, consult *VMware vSphere 5.5 Documentation* for information on how to edit the vSwitch MTU configuration.

▸ If dedicated network connections are not being used with VSAN, utilize vSphere **Network I/O Control** (**NetIOC**) in order to ensure that it is guaranteed a minimum of 1GbE of bandwidth, which is the minimum required by VSAN. *VMware vSphere 5.5 Documentation* or *VMware Virtual SAN Design and Sizing Guide* provide information on how to configure the network I/O control feature. Whenever possible, use NetIOC to guarantee more than the 1 GbE minimum or even use 10 GbE links that are dedicated for use solely with VSAN.

How to do it...

In this section, we will perform the steps that are required to enable VMware VSAN. These instructions assume that at least 3 vSphere servers with a VSAN-compatible configuration have been deployed and added to a vSphere cluster in vCenter.

> Standard vSphere vSwitches and IPv4 were used for this recipe. When creating the VSAN VMkernel interfaces, we must avoid using IPv6 as it is not supported, as outlined in the VMware document *Working with Virtual SAN* (http://pubs.vmware.com/vsphere-55/topic/com.vmware.vsphere.storage.doc/GUID-8408319D-CA53-4241-A3E4-70057F70030F.html).

Configuring the VSAN VMkernel adapters

The following steps outline how to configure the VSAN VMkernel adapters required in order to enable VSAN:

1. Access the vSphere Web Client using the default URL `https://vSphere_Server_Name_` or `_FQDN:9443/vsphere-client`.

2. On the vSphere Web Client home page, click on the **Hosts and Clusters** icon.

3. On the vSphere Web Client **Hosts and Clusters** page, click on the triangle to the left of the vSphere cluster that contains your VSAN hosts in order to expand it, as shown in the following figure:

4. Click on one of the vSphere hosts in the cluster, then click on the **Manage** tab, then select the **Networking** entry, and finally, go to the **VMkernel adapters** page, as shown in the following screenshot:

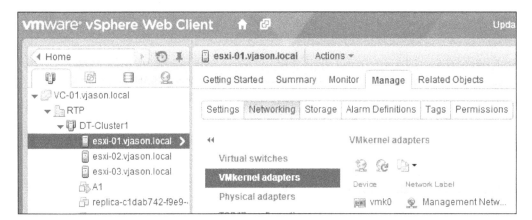

5. Click on the **Add host networking** button that appears as a globe with a green plus sign above the **Device** column, as shown in the previous figure. This opens the **Add Networking** window.

6. Navigate to **Add Networking | Select connection type**, select the **VMkernel Network Adapter** radio checkbox, and then click on **Next**.

7. Navigate to the **Add Networking | Select target** device window, select the **Select an existing standard switch** radio checkbox, click on **Browse**, click on the target switch in the **Select switch** window, and then click on **Next**.

 Optionally, configure a new standard switch for use with VSAN if desired, although, if you do, it will interrupt this task, and you will most likely be required to start the recipe from the beginning.

8. Navigate to **Add Networking | Port properties**, provide **Network label**, **VLAN ID**, select the **Virtual SAN traffic** checkbox as shown in the following screenshot, and then click on **Next**:

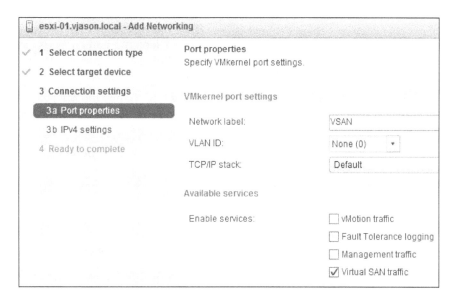

9. Navigate to **Add Networking | IPv4 settings**, select the **Use static IPv4 settings** radio checkbox, provide an unused IP address and subnet mask, and then click on **Next**.

10. Navigate to **Add Networking** | **Ready to complete**, review the settings, and then click on **Finish**. The new VMkernel adapter will now be displayed in the **VMkernel adapters** page, as shown in the following screenshot:

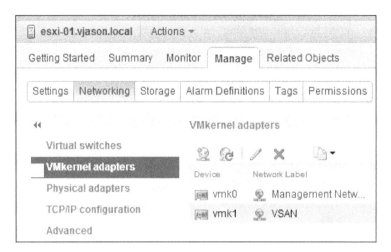

11. Highlight the **VSAN** VMkernel adapter, and then click on the **Edit settings** icon that appears as a yellow pencil above the **Network Label** column shown in the previous figure. This opens the **Edit Settings** window.

12. Go to **Edit Settings** and click on the **NIC settings** tab, change the MTU to `9000`, and then click on **OK**. This step is not explicitly required, but it is recommended if the network infrastructure supports it.

13. Repeat steps 4 through 12 for the other vSphere hosts in the VSAN cluster using a unique IP address for step 9.

The VMware vSphere hosts are now ready for VSAN to be enabled.

Enabling and configuring VSAN

The following steps outline how to enable and configure the VMware VSAN:

1. Access the vSphere Web Client using the default URL of `https://vSphere_ Server_Name_` or `_FQDN:9443/vsphere-client`.

2. On the **vSphere Web Client** home page, click on the **Hosts and Clusters** icon.

3. On the vSphere Web Client's **Hosts and Clusters** page, click on the vSphere cluster that contains the hosts configured for VSAN, and then click on the **Manage** tab; then, navigate to **Virtual SAN | General**, as shown in the following screenshot:

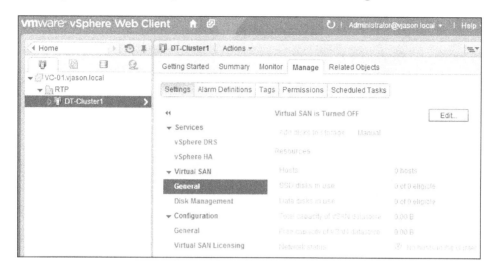

4. Click on the **Edit** button to open the **Edit Virtual SAN Settings** window, check the **Turn ON Virtual SAN** checkbox as shown in the following figure, and then click on **OK**. By default, the **Add disks to storage** setting is set to **Manual**, which prevents VSAN from automatically adding in new magnetic disks that it discovers in the vSphere VSAN hosts; to enable this feature, change the setting to **Automatic**.

5. VMware VSAN will now be configured, in this case automatically selecting the identical magnetic and flash-based storage devices from each of our vSphere hosts. The configuration process can be monitored using the **Recent Tasks** window of the vSphere Web Client. When the VSAN configuration is complete, the vSphere cluster's **General** page under **Virtual SAN** will get updated, as shown in the following screenshot. The values shown will vary based on the storage configuration of our vSphere VSAN hosts.

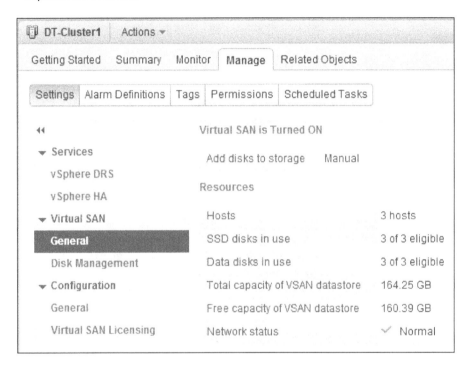

6. The vSphere cluster's **Disk Management** page under **Virtual SAN** now displays the **Disk group** information for each VSAN vSphere host. Select an individual host as shown in the following screenshot in order to show which disks from that host are currently being used by VSAN:

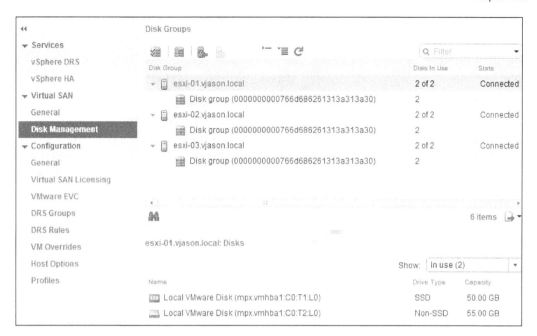

VMware VSAN is now ready for use with VMware Horizon View.

Using VSAN with VMware Horizon View

This recipe will discuss how to use VSAN with VMware Horizon View.

Getting ready

VMware Horizon View requires no additional configuration in order to use VSAN as a target datastore for Horizon View desktops. In the *How to do it...* section of this recipe, we will see how to select VSAN when creating a new Horizon View desktop pool. This recipe assumes that we are already familiar with how View desktop pools are created.

How to do it...

The following steps outline how to use a VSAN datastore to deploy VMware Horizon View desktops:

1. Use the Horizon View Manager Admin console to begin the process of creating a Horizon View desktop pool, stopping at the **Storage Optimization** window.

2. Navigate to **Add Desktop Pool | Storage Optimization**, select the **Use VMware Virtual SAN** radio checkbox as shown in the following screenshot, and then click on **Next**. This option will ensure that the vSphere VSAN SPBM policies are created and applied to the virtual machines.

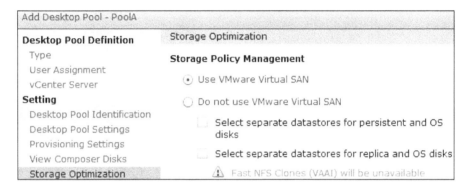

3. Navigate to **Add Desktop Pool | vCenter Settings**. Under the **Datastores** step, select the VSAN datastore as the target datastore for the desktops. This process is identical to selecting non-VSAN datastores. By default, the datastore will be named **vsanDatastore**, which can be changed prior to creating the Horizon View desktop pool using the vSphere Web Client, using the same process that was used to rename non-VSAN datastores.

4. Complete the Horizon View desktop's pool-creation process.

VMware Horizon View will now create the desktops as well as the default vSphere VSAN SPBM policies previously shown in the *How it works...* section of the *Sizing a Horizon View environment for VMware Virtual SAN (VSAN)* recipe earlier in this chapter.

11
Implementing Application Streaming Using Windows Remote Desktop Services

In this chapter, we will cover the following recipes:

- Configuring the Windows Remote Desktop Services (RDS) server for use with Horizon View
- Creating an RDS farm in Horizon View
- Creating an RDS application pool in Horizon View
- Using the Client to access RDS-streamed applications
- Monitoring the status of RDS hosts and sessions in Horizon View
- Modifying an RDS application pool in Horizon View
- Modifying an RDS farm or server in Horizon View

Introduction

VMware Horizon View 6 introduced the ability to stream individual applications to Clients, a valuable feature that enables even more potential use cases for the platform. While application streaming is not in itself a new feature, after all even ThinApp has a streaming mode, this is the first time that VMware has enabled individual applications to be accessed directly from Horizon View Client.

Application streaming has been made possible through the use of Microsoft Windows **Remote Desktop Services** (**RDS**), a feature formally known as **Terminal Services**. By installing the Horizon View Agent directly on a supported Windows server with the RDS feature installed, we can entitle applications to users, just as we would entitle desktops. An additional benefit is that on a per-client basis, for users that use a very small number of applications or for a small number of applications concurrently, fewer resources will be required to deploy streamed applications in many cases when compared to deploying individual desktops for each client.

 The Horizon View web client cannot be used to access streamed applications; you must use the full software-based client or a thin or zero client capable of either the RDP or PCoIP protocol.

In this chapter, we will review all the steps required to implement, configure, and administer RDS application streaming using Horizon View.

Configuring the Windows RDS server for use with Horizon View

This recipe will provide an introduction to the minimum steps required to configure Windows RDS and integrate it with our Horizon View pod. For a more in-depth discussion on Windows RDS optimization and management, consult the Microsoft TechNet page for Windows Server 2012 R2 (`http://technet.microsoft.com/en-us/library/hh801901.aspx`).

Getting ready

VMware Horizon View supports the following versions of Window server for use with RDS:

- ▶ Windows Server 2008 R2: Standard, Enterprise, or Datacenter, with SP1 or later installed
- ▶ Windows Server 2012: Standard or Datacenter
- ▶ Windows Server 2012 R2: Standard or Datacenter

The examples shown in this chapter were performed on Windows Server 2012 R2. Additionally, all of the applications required have already been installed on the server, which in this case included Microsoft Office 2010.

 Microsoft Office has specific licensing requirements when used with a Windows Server RDS. Consult Microsoft's *Licensing of Microsoft Desktop Application Software for Use with Windows Server Remote Desktop Services* document (`http://www.microsoft.com/licensing/about-licensing/briefs/remote-desktop-services.aspx`), for additional information.

The Windows RDS feature requires a licensing server component called the Remote Desktop Licensing role service. For reasons of availability, it is not recommended that you install it on the RDS host itself, but rather on an existing server that performs some other function or even on a dedicated server if possible. Ideally, the RDS licensing role should be installed on multiple servers for redundancy reasons. The Remote Desktop Licensing role service is different from the Microsoft Windows **Key Management System** (**KMS**), as it is used solely for Windows RDS hosts. Consult the Microsoft TechNet article, *RD Licensing Configuration on Windows Server 2012* (`http://blogs.technet.com/b/askperf/archive/2013/09/20/rd-licensing-configuration-on-windows-server-2012.aspx`), for the steps required to install the Remote Desktop Licensing role service. Additionally, consult *Microsoft document Licensing Windows Server 2012 R2 Remote Desktop Services* (`http://download.microsoft.com/download/3/D/4/3D42BDC2-6725-4B29-B75A-A5B04179958B/WindowsServerRDS_VLBrief.pdf`) for information about the licensing options for Windows RDS, which include both per-user and per-device options.

Windows RDS host – hardware recommendations

The following resources represent a starting point for assigning CPU and RAM resources to Windows RDS hosts. The actual resources required will vary based on the applications being used and the number of concurrent users; so, it is important to monitor server utilization and adjust the CPU and RAM specifications if required. The following are the requirements:

- One vCPU for each of the 15 concurrent RDS sessions
- 2 GB RAM, base RAM equal to 2 GB per vCPU, plus 64 MB of additional RAM for each concurrent RDS session
- An additional RAM equal to the application requirements, multiplied by the estimated number of concurrent users of the application
- Sufficient hard drive space to store RDS user profiles, which will vary based on the configuration of the Windows RDS host:

  - Windows RDS supports multiple options to control user profile configuration and growth, including a **RD user home directory**, **RD roaming user profiles**, and **mandatory profiles**. For information about these and other options, consult the Microsoft TechNet article, *Manage User Profiles for Remote Desktop Services*, at `http://technet.microsoft.com/en-us/library/cc742820.aspx`.

 This space is only required if you intend to store user profiles locally on the RDS hosts.

  - Horizon View Persona Management is not supported and will not work with Windows RDS hosts. Consider native Microsoft features such as those described previously in this recipe, or third-party tools such as AppSense Environment Manager (`http://www.appsense.com/products/desktop/desktopnow/environment-manager`).

Based on these values, a Windows Server 2012 R2 RDS host running Microsoft Office 2010 that will support 100 concurrent users will require the following resources:

- Seven vCPUs to support up to 105 concurrent RDS sessions
- 45.25 GB of RAM, based on the following calculations:
  - 20.25 GB of base RAM (2 GB for each vCPU, plus 64 MB for each of the 100 users)
  - A total of 25 GB additional RAM to support Microsoft Office 2010 (Office 2010 recommends 256 MB of RAM for each user)

While the vCPU and RAM requirements might seem excessive at first, remember that, to deploy a virtual desktop for each of these 100 users, we would need at least 100 vCPUs and 100 GB of RAM, which is much more than our Windows RDS host requires.

By default, Horizon View allows only 150 unique RDS user sessions for each available Windows RDS host; so, we need to deploy multiple RDS hosts if users need to stream two applications at once or if we anticipate having more than 150 connections. It is possible to change the number of supported sessions, but it is not recommended due to potential performance issues.

Importing the Horizon View RDS AD group policy templates

Some of the settings configured throughout this chapter are applied using AD group policy templates. Prior to using the RDS feature, these templates should be distributed to either the RDS hosts in order to be used with the Windows local group policy editor, or to an AD domain controller where they can be applied using the domain. Complete the following steps to install the RDS group policy templates:

 When referring to VMware Horizon View installation packages, `y.y.y` refers to the version number and `xxxxxx` refers to the build number. When you download packages, the actual version and build numbers will be in a numeric format. For example, the filename of the current Horizon View 6 GPO bundle is `VMware-Horizon-View-Extras-Bundle-3.1.0-2085634.zip`.

Obtain the `VMware-Horizon-View-GPO-Bundle-x.x.x-yyyyyyy.zip` file, unzip it, and copy the `en-US` folder, the `vmware_rdsh.admx` file, and the `vmware_rdsh_server.admx` file to the `C:\Windows\PolicyDefinitions` folder on either an AD domain controller or your target RDS host, based on how you wish to manage the policies. Make note of the following points while doing so:

- If you want to set the policies locally on each RDS host, you will need to copy the files to each server

▶ If you wish to set the policies using domain-based AD group policies, you will need to copy the files to the domain controllers, the group policy **Central Store** (`http://support.microsoft.com/kb/929841`), or to the workstation from which we manage these domain-based group policies

How to do it...

The following steps outline the procedure to enable RDS on a Windows Server 2012 R2 host. The host used in this recipe has already been connected to the domain and has logged in with an AD account that has administrative permissions on the server. Perform the following steps:

1. Open the **Windows Server Manager** utility and go to **Manage | Add Roles and Features** to open the **Add Roles and Features Wizard**.

2. On the **Before you Begin** page, click on **Next**.

3. On the **Installation Type** page, shown in the following screenshot, select **Remote Desktop Services installation** and click on **Next**. This is shown in the following screenshot:

4. On the **Deployment Type** page, select **Quick Start** and click on **Next**.

> You can also implement the required roles using the standard deployment method outlined in the *Deploy the Session Virtualization Standard deployment* section of the Microsoft TechNet article, *Test Lab Guide: Remote Desktop Services Session Virtualization Standard Deployment* (`http://technet.microsoft.com/en-us/library/hh831610.aspx`). If you use this method, you will complete the component installation and proceed to step 9 in this recipe.

5. On the **Deployment Scenario** page, select **Session-based desktop deployment** and click on **Next**.

6. On the **Server Selection** page, select a server from the list under **Server Pool**, click the red, highlighted button to add the server to the list of selected servers, and click on **Next**. This is shown in the following screenshot:

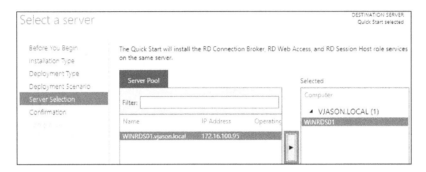

7. On the **Confirmation** page, check the box marked **Restart the destination server automatically if required** and click on **Deploy**.

8. On the **Completion** page, monitor the installation process and click on **Close** when finished in order to complete the installation. If a reboot is required, the server will reboot without the need to click on **Close**. Once the reboot completes, proceed with the remaining steps.

9. Set the RDS licensing server using the Set-RDLicenseConfiguration Windows PowerShell command. In this example, we are configuring the local RDS host to point to redundant license servers (RDS-LIC1 and RDS-LIC2) and setting the license mode to PerUser. This command must be executed on the target RDS host. After entering the command, confirm the values for the license mode and license server name by answering Y when prompted. Refer to the following code:

```
Set-RDLicenseConfiguration -LicenseServer @("RDS-LIC1.vjason.
local","RDS-LIC2.vjason.local") -Mode PerUser
```

   ❑   This setting might also be set using group policies applied either to the local computer or using **Active Directory (AD)**. The policies are shown in the following screenshot, and you can locate them by going to **Computer Configuration | Policies | Administrative Templates | Windows Components | Remote Desktop Services | Remote Desktop Session Host | Licensing** when using AD-based policies. If you are using local group policies, there will be no Policies folder in the path:

Setting	State
🗒 Use the specified Remote Desktop license servers	Not configured
🗒 Hide notifications about RD Licensing problems that ...	Not configured
🗒 Set the Remote Desktop licensing mode	Not configured

10. Use local computer or AD group policies to limit users to one session per RDS host using the **Restrict Remote Desktop Services users to a single Remote Desktop Services session** policy. The policy is shown in the following screenshot, and you can locate it by navigating to **Computer Configuration | Policies | Administrative Templates | Windows Components | Remote Desktop Services | Remote Desktop Session Host | Connections**:

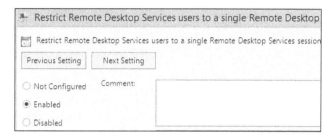

11. Use local computer or AD group policies to enable **Timezone redirection**. You can locate the policy by navigating to **Computer Configuration | Policies | Administrative Templates | Windows Components | Horizon View RDSH Services | Remote Desktop Session Host | Device and Resource Redirection** when using AD-based policies. If you are using local group policies, there will be no `Policies` folder in the path. To enable the setting, set **Allow time zone redirection** to **Enabled**.

12. Use local computer or AD group policies to enable **Windows Basic Aero-Styled Theme**. You can locate the policy by going to **User Configuration | Policies | Administrative Templates | Control Panel | Personalization** when using AD-based policies. If you are using local group policies, there will be no `Policies` folder in the path. To configure the theme, set **Force a specific visual style file or force Windows Classic** to **Enabled** and set **Path to Visual Style** to `%windir%\resources\Themes\Aero\aero.msstyles`.

13. Use local computer or AD group policies to start `Runonce.exe` when the RDS session starts. You can locate the policy by going to **User Configuration | Policies | Windows Settings | Scripts (Logon/Logoff)** when using AD-based policies. If you are using local group policies, there will be no `Policies` folder in the path. To configure the **logon** settings, double-click on **Logon**, click on **Add**, enter `runonce.exe` in the **Script Name** box, and enter `/AlternateShellStartup` in the **Script Parameters** box.

14. On the Windows RDS host, double-click on the 64-bit Horizon View Agent installer to begin the installation process. The installer should have a name similar to `VMware-viewagent-x86_64-y.y.y-xxxxxx.exe`. On the **Welcome to the Installation Wizard for VMware Horizon View Agent** page, click on **Next**.

15. On the **License Agreement** page, select the **I accept the terms in the license agreement** radio check box and click on **Next**.

16. On the **Custom Setup** page, either leave all the options set to default or, if you are not using vCenter Operations Manager, deselect this optional component of the agent and click on **Next**.

17. On the **Register with Horizon View Connection Server** page, shown in the following screenshot, enter the hostname or IP address of one of the Connection Servers in the pod where the RDS host will be used. If the user performing the installation of the agent software is an administrator in the Horizon View environment, leave the **Authentication** setting set to the default; otherwise, select the **Specify administrator credentials** radio check box and provide the username and password of an account that has administrative rights in Horizon View. Click on **Next** to continue:

```
┌─────────────────────────────────────────────────────────────────┐
│ Register with Horizon View Connection Server                      │
│   Enter the Horizon View Connection Server that this machine will connect to. │
│                                                                   │
│ Enter the server name of a Horizon View Connection Server (standard or replica instance) │
│ administrator login credentials to register this machine with the View Connection Server. │
│                                                                   │
│ Server:                                                           │
│ [viewcs01.vjason.local]                        (hostname or IP address) │
│                                                                   │
│ Authentication:    ● Authenticate as the currently logged on user │
│                    ○ Specify administrator credentials            │
│                                                                   │
│       Username:  [                    ]        (Domain\User)      │
│                                                                   │
│       Password:  [                    ]                           │
└─────────────────────────────────────────────────────────────────┘
```

18. On the **Ready to Install the Program** page, click on **Install** to begin the installation.

19. When the installation completes, reboot the server if prompted.

The Windows RDS service is now enabled and configured with the optimal settings for use with VMware Horizon View; it also has the necessary agent software installed. This process should be repeated on additional RDS hosts, as needed, to support the target number of concurrent RDS sessions.

How it works...

The following resources provide detailed information about the configuration options used in this recipe:

▸ Microsoft TechNet's *Set-RDLicenseConfiguration* article at `http://technet.microsoft.com/en-us/library/jj215465.aspx` provides the complete syntax of the PowerShell command used to configure the RDS licensing settings.

▸ Microsoft TechNet's *Remote Desktop Services Client Access Licenses (RDS CALs)* article at `http://technet.microsoft.com/en-us/library/cc753650.aspx` explains the different RDS license types and reveals that an RDS per-user **Client Access License** (**CAL**) allows our Horizon View clients to access the RDS servers from an unlimited number of endpoints while still consuming only one RDS license.

▸ The Microsoft TechNet article, *Remote Desktop Session Host, Licensing* (`http://technet.microsoft.com/en-us/library/ee791926(v=ws.10).aspx`) provides additional information on the group policies used to configure the RDS licensing options.

▸ The VMware document *Enable Windows Basic Theme for Applications in View* (`https://pubs.vmware.com/horizon-view-60/index.jsp?topic=%2Fcom.vmware.horizon-view.desktops.doc%2FGUID-931FF6F3-44C1-4102-94FE-3C9BFFF8E38D.html`) explains that the Windows Basic aero-styled theme is the only theme supported by Horizon View, and demonstrates how to implement it.

▸ The VMware document *Enable Time Zone Redirection for RDS Desktop and Application Sessions* (`https://pubs.vmware.com/horizon-view-60/topic/com.vmware.horizon-view.desktops.doc/GUID-443F9F6D-C9CB-4CD9-A783-7CC5243FBD51.html`) explains why time zone redirection is required, as it ensures that the Horizon View RDS client session will use the same time zone as the client device.

▸ The VMware document *Configure Group Policy to Start Runonce.exe* (`https://pubs.vmware.com/horizon-view-60/topic/com.vmware.horizon-view.desktops.doc/GUID-85E4EE7A-9371-483E-A0C8-515CF11EE51D.html`) explains why we need to add the `runonce.exe /AlternateShellStartup` command to the RDS logon script. This ensures that applications that require Windows Explorer will work properly when streamed using Horizon View.

Creating an RDS farm in Horizon View

This recipe will discuss the steps that are required to create an RDS farm in our Horizon View pod. An RDS farm is a collection of Windows RDS hosts and serves as the point of integration between the Connection Server and the individual applications installed on each RDS server. Additionally, key settings concerning client session handling and client connection protocols are set at the RDS farm level within Horizon View.

Getting ready

To create an RDS farm in Horizon View, we need to have at least one RDS host registered with our pod. Assuming that the Horizon View Agent installation completed successfully in the previous recipe, we should see the RDS hosts registered in the **Registered Machines** menu under **View Configuration** of our **View Manager Admin** console. Consult the *Monitoring the status of RDS hosts and sessions in Horizon View*, later in this chapter, for instructions on how to verify the status of our Windows RDS hosts. The tasks required to create the RDS pod are performed using the **Horizon View Manager Admin** console.

How to do it...

The following steps outline the procedure used to create a RDS farm. In this example, we have already created and registered two Window RDS hosts named **WINRDS01** and **WINRDS02**. Perform the following steps:

1. Navigate to **Resources | Farms** and click on **Add**, as shown in the following screenshot:

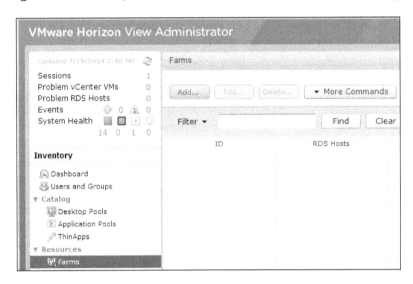

2. On the **Identification and Settings** page, shown in the following screenshot, provide a farm **ID**, enter a description if desired, make any desired changes to the default settings, and then click on **Next**. The settings can be changed to **On** if needed:

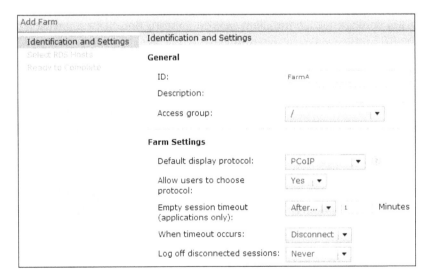

3. On the **Select RDS Hosts** page, shown in the following screenshot, click on the RDS hosts to be added to the farm and then click on **Next**:

4. On the **Ready to Complete** page, review the configuration and click on **Finish**.

The RDS farm has been created and allows us to create application pools using the techniques described in the next recipe.

How it works...

The following RDS farm settings can be changed at any time and are described in the following points:

▶ **Default display protocol**: **PCoIP** (the default) and **RDP** are available.

▶ **Allow users to choose protocol**: By default, Horizon View Clients can select their preferred protocol; we can change this setting to **No** in order to enforce the farm defaults.

▶ **Empty session timeout (applications only)**: This denotes the amount of time that must pass after a client closes all RDS applications before the RDS farm will take the action specified in the **When timeout occurs** setting. The default setting is 1 minute.

▶ **When timeout occurs**: This determines which action is taken by the RDS farm when the session's timeout deadline passes; the options are **Log off** or **Disconnect** (default).

▶ **Log off disconnected sessions**: This determines what happens when a RDS session is disconnected; the options are **Never** (default), **Immediate**, or **After**. If **After** is selected, a time in minutes must be provided.

Creating an RDS application pool in Horizon View

RDS application pools are used to publish and entitle RDS-streamed applications for Horizon View Clients. We must create an application pool for each application that we want to publish and, as in the case of desktop pools, we must entitle users to each application pool individually. Fortunately, we can create and entitle multiple applications at once, which simplifies the initial creation process. In this recipe, we will configure application pools for each of the core Microsoft Office applications installed on our Windows RDS hosts.

Getting ready

To create an application pool in Horizon View, we need to have at least one RDS farm configured in our pod. Assuming that the RDS farm creation process completed successfully in the previous recipe, we should see the farm in the **Farms** menu under **Resources** of our **Horizon View Manager Admin** console. The tasks required to create an application pool are performed using the **Horizon View Manager Admin** console.

How to do it...

The following steps outline the procedure for creating an RDS application pool. An RDS farm is required before you can create an application pool; in this example, we are using the farm created in the previous recipe:

1. Navigate to **Catalog** | **Application Pools** and click on **Add**. This is shown in the following screenshot:

2. On the **Add Application Pools** page, shown in the following screenshot, use the **Select an RDS farm** drop-down menu to specify the RDS farm to be used and then select the checkbox next to each application. Click on **Name** to add the application to the application pool and then click on **Next**:

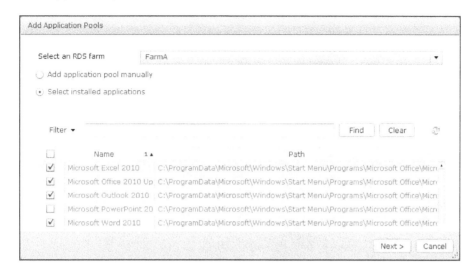

3. On the **Add Application Pools** page, shown in the following screenshot, make any desired changes to the application **ID**, **Display Name**, or **Path** and click on **Finish**:

4. Click on **Add** to open the **Find User or Group** window, entitle AD users or groups as needed, click on **OK**, and then click on **OK** in the **Add Entitlements** window to complete the process. This is shown in the following screenshot:

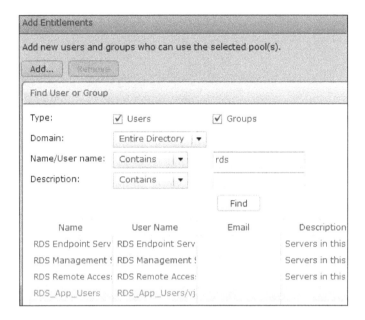

The process used to entitle users and groups in Horizon View is described in greater detail in the VMware document *Entitling Users and Groups* (https://pubs.vmware.com/horizon-view-60/topic/com. vmware.horizon-view.desktops.doc/GUID-B0C436DC-6B18- 4F92-A0BB-8250ECF8859D.html).

The application pool has been created and is now available to stream applications to target users.

Using the Horizon View Client to access RDS-streamed applications

In this recipe, we will explore how RDS application streaming works from a Horizon View Client perspective. Unlike desktop pools, whose names are often created arbitrarily by the Horizon View administrator, RDS applications appear much as they would in a Windows Explorer window.

Getting ready

As mentioned in the introduction to this chapter, in order to access RDS-streamed applications, we must use either the software-based Horizon View Client or a thin or zero client that supports either the PCoIP or RDP protocol. The HTML client is not yet supported with Windows RDS hosts. In this recipe, we are using the standard Windows-based client.

How to do it...

The following steps outline how to use the Horizon View Client to access application pools. In this example, we have already authenticated one of our Connection Servers using a user account that has been entitled to the application pool created in the previous recipe. Perform the following steps:

1. Use the Horizon View Client to authenticate one of the Connection Servers in the pod.

2. Click on one of the applications from the list presented in the Horizon View Client window. This is shown in the following screenshot:

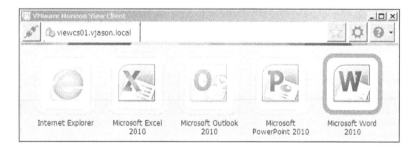

3. The application will appear just as it would if it were launched from the client's device; when finished, simply close it as we normally would.

We have now verified that RDS application streaming is working as intended. While a given user can only have one active session on a given RDS host, Horizon View allows users to stream multiple applications using a single client session.

Monitoring the status of RDS hosts and sessions in Horizon View

VMware Horizon View includes multiple status pages for monitoring the status of Windows RDS hosts and their client sessions. In this recipe, we will review the different status pages and review what each status page is used for.

Getting ready

The status pages reviewed in this section will appear blank unless Windows RDS hosts have registered with the Horizon View pod. These tasks are performed using the **Horizon View Manager Admin** console.

How to do it...

The following steps outline how to use the **Horizon View Manager Admin** console to review the current status of our Windows RDS hosts:

1. Navigate to **Resources | Machines**, as shown in the following screenshot, click on the **RDS Hosts** tab, and review the status of each Windows RDS host, including the agent version, number of active sessions, and whether or not the server is currently available:

2. Navigate to **View Configuration | Registered Machines**, as shown in the following screenshot, and review the status of each Windows RDS host, including the agent version, maximum number of supported sessions, current farm membership, and whether or not the server is currently enabled and available. This is shown in the following screenshot:

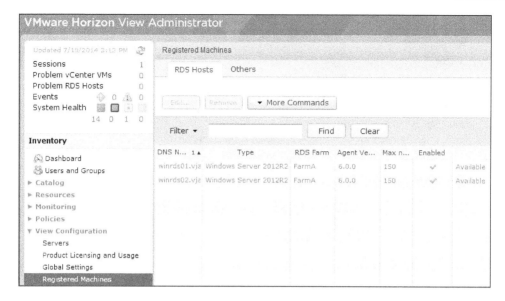

3. Navigate to **Monitoring | Sessions**, as shown in the following screenshot, and review the status of each client session. The **Desktop** and **Application** buttons can be used to control the types of clients that are displayed. Multiple pieces of information about the client connection are displayed, and other options are available, such as disconnecting or logging off the session. This is shown in the following screenshot:

Modifying an RDS application pool in Horizon View

This recipe will discuss the steps that are required to modify the configuration of an existing Horizon View application pool. Limited options exist at the application pool level, as settings that impact the client connections are edited at the farm level, as described in the *Modifying an RDS farm or server in Horizon View* recipe that follows next.

Getting ready

These tasks are performed using the **Horizon View Manager Admin** console, assuming that there are existing application pools that require modification.

How to do it...

The following steps outline the procedure used to modify a RDS application pool. Note that each individual application in Horizon View is considered an application pool and, as is the case with desktop pools, they are managed independently of one another. Perform the following steps:

1. Navigate to **Catalog | Application Pools** and click on the application pool that needs to be updated.

2. To remove an application pool, click on **Delete**.

3. To edit an application pool, click on **Edit...** (highlighted in red), as shown in the following screenshot. Make changes as required to the fields shown, which include setting a new application's **Start Folder**, specifying launch-time parameters, changing the application's **Display name**, **Version**, **Publisher** and **Description**, or even changing the **Path** to the application shortcut that is used to launch the application on the RDS host. Once the required changes have been made, click on **OK**. This is shown in the following screenshot:

4. To add additional AD user and group entitlements or remove existing ones, click on the **Entitlements...** drop-down menu and select either **Add entitlement...** or **Remove entitlement...** as required. This is shown in the following screenshot:

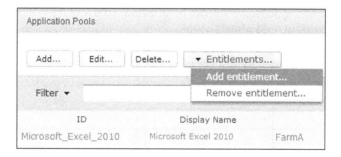

Modifying an RDS farm or server in Horizon View

This recipe will discuss the steps required to modify the configuration of an existing Horizon View RDS farm or server. These include key configuration items that impact the client connection protocol, session handing, and the maximum number of RDS sessions per host.

Getting ready

These tasks are performed using the **Horizon View Manager Admin** console, assuming that there are existing RDS farms or hosts that require modification.

How to do it...

The following steps outline how to edit the settings of an existing RDS farm or individual RDS host. Perform the following steps:

1. Navigate to **Resources | Farms** and click on the RDS farm that needs to be updated.

2. Right-click on the farm and click on **Disable** to prevent additional clients from logging in; existing sessions will not be affected. This feature is typically used prior to performing a farm-wide maintenance.

3. Click on **Delete** to delete the RDS farm. Note that an RDS farm cannot be deleted unless any application pools it contains are deleted first.

4. Click on **Edit...** to open the **Edit Farm** window, as shown in the following screenshot:

5. Make the required changes and click on **OK**. These changes are described earlier in this chapter, in the *Creating an RDS farm in Horizon View* recipe.

6. Navigate to **View Configuration | Registered Machines** and click on the RDS host that needs to be updated.

7. Right-click on the RDS host and click on **Disable** to prevent additional clients from logging in; existing sessions will not be affected. This feature is typically used prior to performing maintenance on specific RDS hosts.

8. Click on **Remove** to remove the highlighted RDS host from the Horizon View pod. Note that an RDS host cannot be deleted if it is currently a member of an RDS farm; if it is a member of an RDS farm, the farm must be deleted before the RDS host can be removed.

9. Click on **Edit** to open the **Edit RDS Host** window, as shown in the following screenshot:

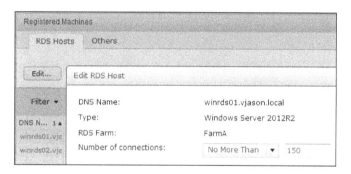

10. The only RDS server option that can be changed is the number of connections it supports. The default and recommended value is 150, although we can configure unlimited connections by changing the value in the **Number of connections** drop-down menu to **Unlimited**.

Index

W

Thank you for buying
VMware Horizon View 6 Desktop
Virtualization Cookbook

About Packt Publishing

Packt, pronounced 'packed', published its first book "*Mastering phpMyAdmin for Effective MySQL Management*" in April 2004 and subsequently continued to specialize in publishing highly focused books on specific technologies and solutions.

Our books and publications share the experiences of your fellow IT professionals in adapting and customizing today's systems, applications, and frameworks. Our solution-based books give you the knowledge and power to customize the software and technologies you're using to get the job done. Packt books are more specific and less general than the IT books you have seen in the past. Our unique business model allows us to bring you more focused information, giving you more of what you need to know, and less of what you don't.

Packt is a modern, yet unique publishing company, which focuses on producing quality, cutting-edge books for communities of developers, administrators, and newbies alike. For more information, please visit our website: www.PacktPub.com.

About Packt Enterprise

In 2010, Packt launched two new brands, Packt Enterprise and Packt Open Source, in order to continue its focus on specialization. This book is part of the Packt Enterprise brand, home to books published on enterprise software – software created by major vendors, including (but not limited to) IBM, Microsoft and Oracle, often for use in other corporations. Its titles will offer information relevant to a range of users of this software, including administrators, developers, architects, and end users.

Writing for Packt

We welcome all inquiries from people who are interested in authoring. Book proposals should be sent to author@packtpub.com. If your book idea is still at an early stage and you would like to discuss it first before writing a formal book proposal, contact us; one of our commissioning editors will get in touch with you.

We're not just looking for published authors; if you have strong technical skills but no writing experience, our experienced editors can help you develop a writing career, or simply get some additional reward for your expertise.

VMware vSphere 5.x Datacenter Design Cookbook

Hersey Cartwright

VMware vSphere 5.x Datacenter Design Cookbook

ISBN: 978-1-78217-700-5   Paperback: 260 pages

Over 70 recipes to design a virtual datacenter for performance, availability, manageability, and recoverability with VMware vSphere 5.x

1. Innovative recipes, offering numerous practical solutions when designing virtualized datacenters.

2. Identify the design factors—requirements, assumptions, constraints, and risks—by conducting stakeholder interviews and performing technical assessments.

3. Increase and guarantee performance, availability, and workload efficiency with practical steps and design considerations.

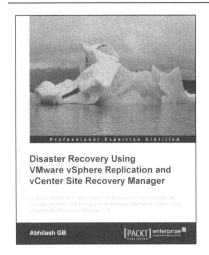

Disaster Recovery Using VMware vSphere Replication and vCenter Site Recovery Manager

Abhilash GB

Disaster Recovery Using VMware vSphere Replication and vCenter Site Recovery Manager

ISBN: 978-1-78217-644-2   Paperback: 162 pages

Learn to deploy and use vSphere Replication 5.5 as a standalone disaster recovery solution and to orchestrate disaster recovery using vCenter Site Recovery Manager 5.5

1. Learn how to deploy and use vSphere Replication as a standalone disaster recovery solution.

2. Configure SRM to leverage array-based or vSphere replication engine.

3. Use SRM to orchestrate the execution of recovery plans.

Please check **www.PacktPub.com** for information on our titles

VMware ESXi Cookbook

ISBN: 978-1-78217-006-8   Paperback: 334 pages

Over 50 recipes to master VMware vSphere administration

1. Understand the concepts of virtualization by deploying vSphere web client to perform vSphere administration.

2. Learn important aspects of vSphere including administration, security, performance, and configuring vSphere Management Assistant (VMA) to run commands and scripts without the need to authenticate every attempt.

3. VMware ESXi 5.1 Cookbook is a recipe-based guide to the administration of VMware vSphere.

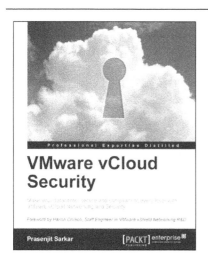

VMware vCloud Security

ISBN: 978-1-78217-096-9   Paperback: 106 pages

Make your datacenter secure and compliant at every level with VMware vCloud Networking and Security

1. Take away an in-depth knowledge of how to secure a private cloud running on vCloud Director.

2. Enable the reader with the knowledge, skills, and abilities to achieve competence at building and running a secured private cloud.

3. Focuses on giving you broader view of the security and compliance while still being manageable and flexible to scale.

Please check **www.PacktPub.com** for information on our titles

www.ingramcontent.com/pod-product-compliance
Lightning Source LLC
Chambersburg PA
CBHW062102050326
40690CB00016B/3172